Global Studies in Social and Cultural Maritime History

Series Editors

Brad Beaven
Historical and Literary Studies
University of Portsmouth
Portsmouth, UK

Joanne Begiato
School of History, Philosophy & Culture
Oxford Brookes University
Oxford, UK

Isaac Land
Department of History
Indiana State University
Terre Haute, IN, USA

This series seeks to reconnect the maritime sphere with broader social and cultural histories across the globe. It looks to an emergent area of historiography: how the maritime was a space of global social and cultural exchange. It offers a platform for the growing community of scholars working in 'new maritime history,' which looks beyond (but by no means ignores) the economic, political, and military history of the seas, to understand its wider connections to social, cultural, geographical, and imperial histories.

The editors welcome proposals on 'the maritime' in its widest sense, including projects framed in terms of coastal history or the paramaritime. Therefore, studies examining the ways that littoral societies or inland communities, spaces, and people connected to the sea are also welcome. So are studies of interstitial watery realms (straits and portages; reticulated systems of lakes, rivers, or inland seas; archipelagos or island clusters). The series considers proposals from across a long chronological period, from antiquity to the twenty-first century.

We are especially keen to publish work that offers insights into the important themes of sailors' gendered sexual identities and sexual activities, including the perspectives of non-normative and proscribed sexual activity, and aiming to incorporate queer approaches and break free of heteronormative frameworks. Similarly, we actively encourage proposals which investigate the global south or incorporate race and ethnicity into their research scope, for example by addressing the experiences of non-European born sailors, or European and American sailors' interactions with non-westerners.

Johnathan Thayer

Citizenship, Subversion, and Surveillance in U.S. Ports

Sailors Ashore

palgrave
macmillan

Johnathan Thayer
Queens College, CUNY
Queens, USA

Global Studies in Social and Cultural Maritime History
ISBN 978-3-031-45617-6 ISBN 978-3-031-45618-3 (eBook)
https://doi.org/10.1007/978-3-031-45618-3

Cover credit: North Wind Picture Archives / Alamy Stock Photo

This Palgrave Macmillan imprint is published by the registered company Springer Nature Switzerland AG.
The registered company address is: Gewerbestrasse 11, 6330 Cham, Switzerland

Paper in this product is recyclable.

Acknowledgments

I have received financial support from the following sources in the making of this book: the Joseph S. Murphy Graduate Fellowship in Labor History, the Early Research Initiative Knickerbocker Award for Archival Research in American Studies, the E. P. Thompson Fellowship in United States History, the Andrew W. Mellon Foundation, the office of the Dean of Social Sciences at Queens College, and my union, the Professional Staff Congress (PSC CUNY).

Thank you to all who supported me during my time at the CUNY Graduate Center, especially Joshua B. Freeman and Kathleen D. McCarthy. Thank you to Rudy Hartmann, Riah Lee Kinsey, and Mackenzie Kristofco for their research assistance. Thank you especially to Rudy for his work with merchant seamen census data, specifically as appears in Chaps. 1 and 6. Thank you Katie Uva for her excellent editorial assistance.

Thank you to the Coastal History Network for providing an intellectual home without borders, especially during the isolating years of the COVID-19 pandemic.

Lastly, thank you to the many archivists, librarians, and public historians who have shaped this book.

Contents

List of Figures

Introduction: Sailors Ashore

Since the founding of the nation, merchant seamen have pushed at the boundaries of the United States, both literally at its coastlines and epistemologically at evolving parameters of citizenship. As the labor source that fueled a maritime "commerce wedded to the concept of liberty"[1] in the Early Republic, merchant seamen challenged notions of individual freedom, mobility, and masculinity, and asked questions of both civil society and the nation's fledgling federal government as to who could claim protections from the state, to what extent workers could define the nature and terms of their own labor, and what sociocultural worlds would be considered acceptable under the moral ideals of a new nation anxious to project certain assertions of its own identity on the world's stage.

Imperial crises of the Early Republic lent urgency to these questions. Beginning in the 1790s until the end of the Napoleonic Wars, merchant seamen encountered a British navy desperate for recruits to man vessels in its long war with France, French privateers attempting to protect their fragile new republic by policing maritime commerce with belligerent nations, and Barbary pirates taking advantage of American targets sailing under the flag of a novice entrant onto the high seas of empire. These encounters forced the United States government to quickly and authoritatively define its own role in protecting its "citizen sailors"[2] against the threat of impressment, capture, or worse at the hands of foreign nations. In response, the federal government produced an elaborate system of identity documentation, setting in motion the development of a modern administrative bureaucracy responsible for defining and regulating a system of citizenship paperwork. Additionally, the federal government adopted a rallying cry of "Free Trade and Sailors' Rights" that pitted revolutionary ideals of liberty and egalitarian rights against the threat that British impressment of American sailors posed to the identity and legitimacy of the young Republic.

With the resolution of the War of 1812 the United States government, and by extension U.S. merchant seamen, had weathered these significant foreign threats. Anxieties and contestations regarding "sailors' rights" turned inwards, to the sailortowns that thrived in every American port town and city along the nation's coastline. Threats to American identity, as defined by an elite and emergent propertied class, came not only from foreign nations but also from internal sources of sociocultural discord. This book proposes to address the inward turn in American urban-maritime history through a study of sailortowns that locates these coastal, urban spaces at the center of a series of prolonged confrontations over the nature of citizenship for merchant seamen in the U.S. from the 1830s through the end of World War II. Each of the chapters that follow reinforces the book's central argument: that merchant seamen have always been inherently alien and have constantly posed subversive challenges to concepts of U.S. citizenship, and that in response, both civil society and the state have consistently attempted to marginalize, surveille, and exclude sailors from the full rights entitled to American citizens.

Chapter 1

Along the piers surrounding the Battery in Manhattan, merchant seamen carved out an enclave of their own far from the fashionable row houses and respectable lives of Victorian-era New York City. Marginalized socially, culturally, economically, legally, and geographically due to the nature of their transient work and lifestyles, merchant seamen confronted the city's bourgeoisie with a shocking front of bluewater masculinity within the narrow and winding cobble-stoned streets of sailortown. In reaction, philanthropists and missionaries launched a protracted campaign to staunch the perceived invasion, planting ministry outposts, sailors' homes, and a series of "floating chapels" amidst the boardinghouses and grog shops that lined the notorious streets and alleyways of New York's sailortown.

Maritime charity in the Port of New York represented a type of inverse colonialism in which bourgeois reformers attempted to eradicate social, cultural, and economic aspects of the city's sailortown that they perceived as subversive to respectable and stable Victorian conceptions of urban life.

Through the lens of charitable organizations founded in New York during the early- to mid-nineteenth century, this chapter interprets encounters between merchant seamen and their would-be reformers as essential contestations over the nature of nineteenth and early-twentieth-century urban life in New York. In place of a relatively weak federal presence in local governance and enforcement, these local encounters set precedent for later contests over seamen's relationship to the state on a national stage.

Chapter 2

With the passage of the Thirteenth Amendment in 1865, Congress officially banned involuntary servitude in addition to slavery. Despite this ban, the federal judiciary and Congress failed to provide a working definition of involuntary servitude that would establish guidelines for deciding court cases involving contracts between wage laborers and their employers. This lapse in definition was partially resolved in 1897 when the Supreme Court ruled on *Robertson v. Baldwin*, in which four U.S. citizen merchant seamen brought their case before the Court, arguing that their imprisonment as punishment for breaking contract through desertion constituted a violation of the Thirteenth Amendment. This chapter presents *Robertson v. Baldwin* as a precedent-setting and culminating point in the history of free labor, and a turning point that sparked a national controversy over the nature of contract labor and the legacy of emancipation and the Thirteenth Amendment. The Supreme Court's ruling against the merchant seamen, which privileged freedom of contract over the sailors' rights to the full protections of the Constitution, exemplified the "Janus-faced"[3] nature of the legal system's treatment of merchant seamen: both as wards of the state subject to extraordinary mechanisms of restriction and control, and simultaneously as a "special class" of workers entitled to extraordinary protections from the state. Sailors' mobility, an essential component of sailor culture ashore, had been abruptly curtailed by the nation's highest court, albeit temporarily.

Chapters 3 and 4

In the wake of the *Titanic* disaster, maritime labor strikes broke out in Southampton, England (*Titanic*'s home port), in New York City, and along the East Coast of the U.S. Sailors walked out in enormous numbers to protest a lack of "safety at sea," and leveraged public opinion to advocate for more sweeping reforms. This turbulent, often violent underbelly of the safety at sea movement has been overwhelmed by the mythic memory of the *Titanic* disaster, overshadowing an essential timeline in the development of merchant seamen's relationship to the state. In the U.S., the fledgling Transport Workers' Federation (TWF) attempted to organize workers from all industrial sectors of waterfront labor along the East Coast but met with resistance from both local law enforcement and the skilled worker-oriented Sailors' Union of the Pacific, led by maritime labor leader Andrew Furuseth. Riding on the crest of popular support for safety at sea reforms following *Titanic*, reformers including Furuseth and Progressive Senator William La Follette eschewed more radical rank-and-file sailors and the TWF in favor of lobbying Congress for sweeping maritime workplace regulations that would benefit their overwhelmingly skilled, white, U.S. citizen membership. Significantly, passage of the 1915 Seamen's Act hinged on a clause that guaranteed a seaman's right to desert his vessel and the entitlement of most merchant seamen to shore leave, effectively nullifying the impacts of the Supreme Court's decision in *Robertson v. Baldwin* and inadvertently creating a backchannel for non-citizen sailors to access and enter U.S. shores that would eventually provoke a national reckoning with what would come to be known as the "alien seamen" problem.

Chapter 5

In addition to establishing increasingly restrictive criteria by which to exclude would-be migrants from entering the U.S., the Immigration Acts of 1917, 1921, and 1924 also built an infrastructure of state mechanisms with the purpose of enforcing those criteria. Border and port control systems contained gaping loopholes that merchant seamen and their impersonators exploited in large numbers throughout the 1920s and into the 1930s. Non-citizen merchant seamen, entitled by the 1915 Seamen's Act to shore leave in U.S. ports regardless of their citizenship status, took full advantage of their legal rights to mobility by smuggling themselves into the U.S. via shore leave by the tens, and possibly hundreds of thousands, strategically subverting and circumventing the mechanisms of U.S. immigration restriction in the process. This chapter engages with the density of primary records dealing with the problem of "alien" or "mala fide" seamen within the context of immigration restriction. Newspaper accounts, transcripts from hearings held by the U.S. House of Representatives

Committee on Immigration and Naturalization on the topic of "Deportation of Alien Seamen," and records regarding the legislation itself reveal a prolonged national obsession with instances of "smuggling" or illegal immigration involving merchant seamen and ships, especially concerning Chinese seamen.

This chapter examines the timeline of the so-called alien seamen problem, concluding with a series of dragnet immigration raids in New York City, New Jersey, and San Francisco in 1931, the spectacle of which provoked widespread public outrage over government overreach and violations of seamen's Constitutional rights. Once again, merchant seamen found themselves at the center of national debates over citizenship, with state actors reacting to anxieties manifested in Congressional hearings and legislation by launching vigilante purges of rogue "aliens" amid the nation's port cities and sailortowns.

Chapter 6

The raid on "alien seamen" at the Seamen's Church Institute in February 1931 was at the center of heightened tensions between merchant seamen, civil society, and the U.S. government, both at the local and federal levels. Leading up to the raid, the 1920s was a decade of crisis for the American shipping industry: increased competition from foreign-flagged merchant ships as well as expanding rail systems meant less American maritime shipping commerce, fewer jobs, and unemployed seamen crowding the slips of downtown Manhattan like never before. Merchant seamen out of work and "on the beach" overcame racial, ethnic, and industrial differences to organize into formidable labor collectives. These groups pressured the gatekeepers of civil society, craft unionism, and the government through grassroots political agitation and direct action. At the Seamen's Church Institute, administrators responded by enlisting public and private authorities in conducting surveillance operations and countering industrial maritime labor's offensive with attempts at coopting sailor culture ashore into the Institute's conservative mission. Despite the Institute's best efforts, the city's merchant seamen largely retained the inherent transience and foreignness that simultaneously preserved their social, cultural, and economic agency, and made them such a persistent threat to acceptable forms of propriety and citizenship as workers on the margins of society during the early 1930s.

These chapters are situated firmly in maritime and urban history and questions of citizenship, representing a narrative that persistently returns to the central argument of the book: merchant seamen, because of their marginal positionality, occupied a vanguard position in the evolution of nineteenth and early-to-mid twentieth century concepts of American citizenship. Each chapter represents a case study in which merchant seamen provoked anxieties and confrontations with the state and civil society over questions regarding their rights, protections, and entitlements as U.S. citizens. These confrontations, in turn, shaped the nature and definition of U.S. citizenship. The multifaceted sources that this work draws on over its long timeline support this claim and make it a contribution to the body of existing scholarship that focuses on merchant seamen as influential actors in U.S. hisory, primarily during the Revolutionary and Early Republic eras.

This book builds on the work of many other maritime historians who focus on the Age of Sail or earlier time periods, including Marcus Rediker, Daniel Vickers, and W. Jeffrey Bolster. Nathan Perl-Rosenthal and Matthew Taylor Rafferty both write about the evolution of American citizenship from a maritime perspective in the Revolutionary and Early Republic eras. Both historians examine the legal shaping of citizenship in courtrooms and Congress, but whereas their narratives project outward onto the high seas, the chapters that follow remain firmly planted on land.[4] I share Paul Gilje's focus on sailor culture ashore, and this book intends to extend that focus beyond the "Age of Revolution" by addressing the sociocultural impact of industrialization, the rise of steam engines and the decline of traditional "skilled" maritime labor on sail ships, and new (but deeply-seated) confrontations between sailors and shoreside institutions, individuals, and the state from the 1830s into the twentieth century.[5]

Graeme Milne presents a global survey of sailortowns with a broad geographic scope that is not exclusive to U.S. port cities.[6] Bruce Nelson's *Workers on the Waterfront* is a seminal work on maritime unionism, but it focuses exclusively on the 1930s whereas this book extends to the origins of maritime unionism during the late nineteenth century.[7] Leon Fink's timeline overlaps with my own, but his focus is on an interpretation of the history of maritime commerce at the vanguard of globalized capitalism,[8] whereas this book focuses on a constellation of historical forces that collectively fit within the concepts of citizenship, subversion, and surveillance, including histories of maritime charity, labor legislation, immigration, and war, in addition to economic contexts.

Finally, this book has been influenced by Isaac Land's call for a "new coastal history." In addition to Land's publications and conference presentations, his contributions to Portsmouth University's Port Town and Urban Cultures "Coastal History Blog," and Brad Beaven, Karl Bell and Robert James's, *Port Towns and Urban Cultures: International Histories of the Waterfront, c. 1700–2000* have led me to focus on the littoral urban shore and sailortowns as essential sites of interaction and conflict from which histories of national and international impact emerge.[9] Additionally, Beaven's *Leisure, Citizenship and Working-Class Men in Britain, 1850–1945* has provided comparative contexts in which civil society and the state have attempted to shape the social and cultural lives of British working-class men in the service of national interests.[10]

The book concludes by addressing the question of how merchant seamen responded to the Great Depression through the lens of the Merchant Marine Act of 1936, passed with the purpose of developing and maintaining a U.S. merchant marine that would be virtually self-sustaining and free from dependency on foreign fleets and labor. The narrative ends with the coming of World War II, in which merchant seamen express through their own words and perspectives as civilians who nonetheless suffered a higher casualty rate than any branch of the armed services during the war, and yet were excluded from postwar benefits despite the extent of their sacrifices. Such a conclusion reinforces yet again the essential argument of this book: that merchant seamen have always been inherently alien and have constantly posed challenges to concepts of U.S. citizenship, and that the response by both civil society and the state to these challenges has consistently been attempted marginalization, subjugation, and exclusion.

These confrontations and challenges begin in the streets, back alleys, boardinghouses, and piers of the nation's port cities and sailortowns, providing a lens through which larger narratives of national legal and political developments are presented. Through this approach, this book argues first: that the forces of industrialization that transformed ship technology simultaneously transformed the working-class lives of merchant seamen, intensifying class conflict and producing collective networks of subversion and resistance within the urban borderland spaces of sailortowns in which sailors fought to maintain control over their mobility, agency, and rights. Second, that given their social, cultural, economic, geographic, and legal marginalization, merchant seamen have occupied essential roles in the parameters of U.S. urban, legal, labor, immigration, and wartime history. Third, that the constellation of these histories, embedded in the encounters and negotiations that merchant seamen provoked along the nation's coastlines and sailortowns, collectively represents a unique and essential perspective on the history of U.S. citizenship.

Notes

1. Paul Gilje, *Liberty on the Waterfront: American Maritime Culture in the Age of Revolution* (Philadelphia. PA: University of Pennsylvania Press, 2007), 98.
2. Nathan Perl-Rosenthal, *Citizen Sailors: Becoming American in the Age of Revolution* (Cambridge, MA: Harvard University Press, 2015).
3. William E. Forbath, *Law and the Shaping of the American Labor Movement* (Cambridge, MA: Harvard University Press, 1991), 7.
4. Perl-Rosenthal, *Citizen Sailors*; Matthew Taylor Rafferty's *The Republic Afloat: Law, Honor, and Citizenship in Maritime America* (University of Chicago Press, 2013).
5. Gilje, *Liberty on the Waterfront.*
6. Graeme Milne, *Sailortowns: People, Power, and Place on the Nineteenth Century Waterfront* (London: Palgrave Macmillan, 2016).
7. Bruce Nelson, *Workers on the Waterfront: Seamen, Longshoremen, and Unionism in the 1930s* (Chicago, IL: University of Illinois Press, 1990).
8. Leon Fink, *Sweatshops at Sea: Merchant Seamen in the First Globalized Industry, from 1812 to the Present* (Chapel Hill, NC: University of North Carolina Press, 2011).
9. Isaac Land, "Tidal Waves: The New Coastal History," *The Journal of Social History*, 40(3), 2007, 731–743 and *The Coastal History Blog*, https://porttowns.port.ac.uk/coastal-history-blog/, accessed November 2, 2023; Brad Beaven, Karl Bell and Robert James, eds., *Port Towns and Urban Cultures: International Histories of the Waterfront, c. 1700–2000* (London: Palgrave Macmillan, 2016).
10. Brad Beaven, *Leisure, Citizenship and Working-Class Men in Britain, 1850–1945* (London: Oxford University Press, 2009).

CHAPTER 1

Saiors' Wardship, Maritime Ministry, and the Contest for New York City's Sailortown, 1843–1915

New York City's sailortown during the mid-nineteenth century was low and marshy and populated by transient waterfront workers, merchant seamen, and newly arrived migrants. Bounded by Dover Street, New Bowery, Division Street, Grand Street, the East River, and Corlears Hook, sailortown's streets contained a dense, yet remote section of the city "being at right angles to the river, laid out on a different axis than those of any other part of the city."[1] Far removed from polite society, sailortown lay at the margins of New York, both geographically and in the imaginations of the majority of the city's rapidly expanding population: "I dare say, not one New Yorker in a thousand knows even where it was, so rapid are the changes of whole populations of the city" recounted the biographer Alfred Knock.[2]

As Knock aptly declared, "[l]ife [in sailortown] was interesting. It was tough, it was rowdy, it was often evil, but it was always interesting."[3] Sailortowns had long drawn the attention of seamen ashore with their "easy-going fellowship," "whole-hearted enjoyment of life," and the pleasures and temptations that just as often resulted in "evil treatment" as it did harmless socialization:

> Wild tales were told of 'knock-out drops,' carried by waiters and female entertainers in the lower-grade saloons to expedite the robbery of a victim. Composed of chloral hydrate, these drops could easily be detected by one

J. Thayer, *Citizenship, Subversion, and Surveillance in U.S. Ports*, Global Studies in Social and Cultural Maritime History,
https://doi.org/10.1007/978-3-031-45618-3_1

> not too far gone in his cups, but once down were deadly in their effect. Whenever the stertorous breathing of the victim indicated that he was in a serious way, he was hastily dragged outside and deposited, if possible, in front of a rival's door … the practice … played considerable part in the shanghaing of sailors.[4]

But, as Knock makes clear, there was another side to sailortown. A certain fellowship amid such suspect and often dangerous conditions prompted "[s]lightly uneasy stirrings of the social conscience towards seamen" among the city's upper classes, and a wave of maritime charity sprung forth in the first half of the nineteenth century.[5] In 1817, the Marine Bible Society of New York was formed, followed in 1818 by the establishment of the Society for Promoting the Gospel Among Seamen in the Port of New York and the founding of the Roosevelt Street Mariners' Church. The American Seamen's Friend Society established its headquarters in New York in 1828 and Sailors' Snug Harbor opened its grounds in 1830. Knock counted seventy Bethel Unions, thirty-nine Marine Bible Societies, fifteen Seamen's Churches and Floating Bethels operating around the world by 1825.[6] In 1844, the Floating Church of Our Saviour held its first service at Pike Street, and the era of maritime charity in the nation's ports was well underway (Fig. 1.1).

Invasion

While the nation would remain predominantly rural through the end of the nineteenth century, the 1820s and 30s saw unprecedented population migration and the dramatic growth of cities. Waterways were at the heart of this national growth.

Manhattan, perhaps more than any other city in the United States, epitomized these trends. The completion of the Erie Canal in 1825 and the consequent opening of inland markets made accessible via the Hudson River and Great Lakes combined with a deep and welcoming harbor to make New York a juggernaut of maritime commerce and an epicenter of international trade. These developments led to the construction of larger, faster ships capable of transporting higher volumes of cargo that transformed maritime labor. Within this rapidly expanding system of international capitalism, seafaring became an increasingly competitive business that alienated merchant seamen from the communities that had formerly nurtured young men into sailors. As profits rose and maritime shipping

Fig. 1.1 The Floating Church of Our Saviour, moored at the foot of Pike Street in Manhattan in February 1844. Seamen's Church Institute Digital Archives

firms consolidated, voyages became longer, conditions on ships became harsher, and turnover through desertion and abandonment became more frequent.[7]

Consequently, seafaring communities in port towns became increasingly contained within ghettoized "sailortowns" at the marginal shorelines of port cities that were dependent on maritime commerce to fuel their development and expansion. As Daniel Vickers argues in his study of the nineteenth-century maritime economy in the port city Salem, Massachusetts, whereas Salem had supported a local maritime economy led by captains and shipowners familiar to the community who employed their extended families and neighbors, new maritime commerce systems relied on decentralized shipping networks that were dependent on a labor force that was increasingly foreign both in nationality and in terms of unfamiliarity with the maritime communities within which they worked and lived. Vickers argues that these changes produced two results:

working conditions on Salem ships harshened considerably, producing more desertions, and seamen became increasingly marginalized within the Salem port community, geographically pushed to the edges of the waterfront and culturally distanced from respectable members of Salem's population.[8]

Merchant seamen, as the human targets of these forces of marginalization, found themselves alienated from shoreside communities, and responded by forming their own dense micro-economies of commercial, cultural, and social exchange that served the needs and desires of a uniquely transient class of maritime laborers. Within these micro-economies developed thriving networks of longshoremen, boat people, cart men, waterfront vendors, merchants, importers/exporters, custom house agents, saloon and grog shop owners, boardinghouse and brothel keepers, sex workers, nautical equipment purveyors, sail makers, cordwainers, coopers, tailors, shellfish hawkers, thieves, shipyard laborers, harbor dredgers, and of course, merchant seamen. The racial and ethnic makeup of these individuals in New York City, including men who spilled out of ships from the far corners of the known world, Black American sailors, and a hodgepodge of Jacksonian-era youths drawn from the rural frontiers of the nation to its most rapidly developing city, made sailortown the epitome of nineteenth-century American metropolitanism.

At the heart of the social, cultural, economic, and geographic boundaries of sailortowns was the sailors' boardinghouse.[9] Thomas Gunn dedicated a chapter to sailors' boardinghouses in his 1857 *Physiology*, describing a scene as typically perceived by outsiders:

> At one end of the room two fiddlers are uniting in the production of harmonic discord sufficient to drive Ole Bull frantic. A third has succumbed, either to professional enthusiasm or to the amount of liquor injudiciously bestowed upon him by his admiring audience, and now lies in a corner, his countenance decorated after the style of a New Zealand chief by an artistic performance in burnt cork. His two friends have, also, sympathizingly relieved him of a pocket of copper coin; it being the custom at the conclusion of each dance to bestow voluntary contributions on the orchestra ... To this accompaniment half a dozen persons of either sex are dancing... Stamping, capering, jigging to and fro, hands across and down the middle –such is the order of the night – till the sanded floor vibrates again, and the glasses on the table tinkle with sympathetic excitement. The male dancers are all sailors, their partners being coarse, fat, vulgar-looking young women, whose bloated features indicate confirmed habits of drunkenness. They have very hoarse

> voices, wear necklaces and large brass ear-rings, call each other sisters, and affect bright red or yellow dresses. Three of them reside constantly in the house, and are important adjuncts to the landlord in the one great object – pillaging his guests.[10]

This sensationalized combination of drunkenness, cultural exoticism, theft, and questionable female companionship proved especially threatening to nineteenth-century guardians of bourgeois moral respectability. In New York, boardinghouses loomed large in the public imagination as supposed dens of wayward unsupervised youths and urban dealers in vice. Merchant seamen became the target of anxieties about urban living by embodying a caricature of subversiveness: inherently transient, diverse in nationality and race, mostly young, unattached men who were awarded "advance notes" upon signing shipping articles or paid off at the end of their voyages and prone to "sprees" within the labyrinth of sailortown's back-alley brothels and grog shops.

Additionally, boardinghouses and their keepers often played a central role in waterfront labor recruitment. "Runners" in need of quick, cheap labor would often appear at the doors of sailors' boardinghouses, and many keepers cooperated in exchange for commissions. In cases in which a seaman had accumulated debt that was beyond his means to pay out-of-pocket, arrangements were made to transfer any advance pay a sailor was entitled to directly to the keeper in order to settle up.[11] Knock places New York's boardinghouses at the very heart of sailortown's illicit economy:

> Scattered among the five-story brick tenements of the waterfront, especially on Cherry Street, were the sailors' boardinghouses, the worst of which operated relentlessly to keep the seaman in a state of drunkenness, during which everything from gross over-charging to downright robbery was possible. Next door to the boardinghouses were 'tailor-shops,' which drove a great trade of moneylending at exorbitant interest-rates, under the guise of selling shoddy clothes on credit. What was not cleaned up by these gentry, the saloons and dance-halls or dives got. The rolling gait and wind-beaten face of the old tar were the most familiar sight on Cherry Street and the side streets running into it, and were a signal for all hands to be on deck with blandishmens, blackjuice, knock-out drops, and confidence games.[12]

Inevitably, given the clash of cultures inherent in the nature of New York's sailortown, evangelical reformers encountered this world with the perception that a new form of urban wilderness had rapidly developed beyond the pale of moral and spiritual propriety. The height of nineteenth-century maritime reform in the United States coincided with rapid national developments in transportation, communication, and mobility. This combination of transformative changes hardened class differences and provoked widespread anxieties over perceived threats to the stability of social, cultural, and economic ideals of the Victorian-era American upper class. From the perspective of reformers, sailortown represented an urban borderland between the civilized geographic space and sociocultural echelons of Manhattan's respectable society, on the one hand, and the dark, boisterous, and morally corrupt cobblestone streets and narrow alleyways of lower Manhattan's waterfront districts on the other. The city's lower wards came to represent an urban frontier that necessitated the same spirit of proselytization that motivated and mobilized the missionaries of the Benevolent Empire's antebellum Protestant reform networks to the fringes of American society, as well as the far reaches of the non-Christian world. Brad Beaven has identified the colonial methodologies of urban reform work in the history of the Salvation Army in Victorian London.[13] Similarly, evangelical maritime reformers in Victorian New York adopted the role of missionaries; rather than projecting their values abroad as with typical colonial projects, waterfront missionaries in New York engaged in a form of inverse colonialism by digging in at home to protect their values and eradicate threats from invasion.

Other major economic and cultural forces in the city were at work in this effort to clean up sailortown. Kathleen D. McCarthy has documented a timeline of American philanthropic growth, beginning in the late eighteenth and early nineteenth centuries during which a nascent network of philanthropic societies developed out of colonial precedents, motivated by revolutionary language of individual rights and religious disestablishment, which placed the church firmly in the realm of private actions. The legacy of disestablishment subsequently produced a ministerial profession dependent on philanthropic fundraising that would structure the nature of American philanthropy through the birth and expansion of the Benevolent Empire. Following these developments, philanthropy came to represent a vibrant "third sector" of American political, social, and economic life, in addition to the lived experience of citizens and the actions of government. Private philanthropic organizations and actions thus formed a mutually beneficial and co-dependent relationship with the American state, each serving to subsidize the other in their respective responsibilities toward citizens and clientele, and in their demands for funding toward stabilizing hierarchies of leadership and control bordered by class, gender, and race.[14]

This chapter examines the early history of missionary work within New York's sailortown, specifically the work of the American Seamen's Friend Society (ASFS, founded 1828), headquartered in New York, and the Seamen's Church Institute (SCI, founded 1834), formerly the Protestant Episcopal Church Missionary Society for Seamen in the Port of New York. The ASFS was a leader in maritime ministry throughout the nineteenth century, establishing ministry outposts in nearly every major port city in the nation. The rhetoric that ASFS administrators projected in public characterized merchant seamen as developmentally and morally inferior, and at risk for exploitation at the hands of unscrupulous agents of sailortown. This description created a self-justifying logic that legitimized the Society's ideology of ministry and pastoral work. SCI's early work focused primarily on infiltrating and coopting an exotic parish of extreme multiculturalism into the folds of temperance and Christian morality. Reform, motivated by the energies of maritime ministry, attempted to surveille and staunch this perceived waterfront invasion, contain the physical, social, and cultural borders of sailortown, and ultimately control and subsume this subversive economy and the threats to the maritime labor market and respectable society that its sailor culture and extreme multiculturalism cultivated.

At stake in these confrontations was the extent to which merchant seamen were able to maintain "liberty" in social, cultural, financial, and even spiritual aspects of their lives.

Waterfront agency and mobility were essential incarnations of liberty and were often a central issue in conflicts between merchant seamen and maritime missionaries. These encounters shaped seamen's relationship to the legal and political systems of the state, and by extension, nascent concepts of citizenship.

Conversion

Beginning in the 1830s, an onslaught of philanthropic initiatives began providing services for merchant seamen in the Port of New York. The American Seamen's Friend Society (ASFS), founded in New York between 1826 and 1828, would by the late nineteenth century establish a network of sailors' homes and seamen's missions in most of the major port towns and cities in North America, as well as certain ports in Europe, Asia, and

Africa. In addition to operating a 300-bed Sailor's Home at 190 Cherry Street along the East River from 1842 to 1903, ASFS also established the Marine Temperance Society of the Port of New York in 1833, as part of a larger endeavor to establish marine temperance societies in every port city.[15] Also in 1833, Sailors' Snug Harbor opened in Staten Island, funded by a major bequest from Captain Robert Richard Randall, a wealthy former privateer and merchant who died in 1801. Sailors' Snug Harbor provided free lodging and the services of a resident chaplain for seamen who had sailed under the American flag for at least five years, with operations peaking in the late nineteenth century when more than a thousand seamen called Snug Harbor home.[16] Meanwhile, in 1843–1844, the Protestant Episcopal Church Missionary Society for Seamen, later the Seamen's Church Institute of New York (SCI), converted a ferry boat into a chapel and moored it permanently along the East River at the foot of Pike Street, where Rev. Benjamin C. C. Parker held church services that targeted merchant seamen and other denizens of sailortown. SCI consecrated two more "floating chapels" between 1844 and 1906, in addition to several reading rooms and coffee houses that competed for the seamen's patronage amid the boardinghouses and saloons of lower Manhattan's sailortown.[17]

Despite having origins in New York, both ASFS and SCI had significant national reach and impact. By the late nineteenth century, ASFS had succeeded in consolidating many of the nation's sailors' homes and seamen's missions. Auxiliary missions from around the country submitted monthly reports to ASFS administrators, which were published in the Society's monthly newsletter, the *Sailor's Magazine*.[18] The cultural construction of merchant seamen as unique, exceptional workers that ASFS projected to this national audience served a specific function for nineteenth-century maritime missionaries: because the merchant seaman's perceived natural moral deficiency and lack of a sense of responsibility made him especially liable to cruel treatment both at sea and ashore, he was in need of special protection from those members of a benevolent society who involved themselves in Christian philanthropic work. This understanding of merchant seamen's character justified the mission of maritime ministry organizations and gave reformers specific targets toward which to direct their philanthropic energies.

The copious literature produced by ASFS, most of which was distributed to Society supporters and potential donors, provides thorough documentation of this rationale. In an 1883 speech titled "Christ's Dominion on the Sea," Rev. A. J. F. Behrends describes the "modern sailor" as "a very different man" who leads "a life peculiarly his own, moulded by the sea."[19] For Behrends, the uniqueness of the seaman's life seeps into the physicality of his being: "He wears a dress that marks him, he speaks the dialect of the ocean, his thoughts are shaped by his peculiar life, and his very features bear the stamp of his occupation."[20] Physically marked by his labor, the seaman is presented as a highly identifiable member of marginalized society, his appearance and odd manners erecting cultural barriers "between him and his brothers on the land."[21] Elsewhere, in other ASFS Annual Reports, the seaman is described as possessing "coarse manners" and "rude intelligence," while he is simultaneously exalted for his "courage and generosity," the product of a shared "simplicity" that is "characteristic of the sailor."[22] The seaman is "trained to obedience," frequently carrying orders out "to a fault," making him an easy target for those who would take advantage of him.[23]

Within the logic of maritime reformers, the seaman's particular character led to his exploitation, which made him an ideal target for ministry. As the authors of ASFS's Annual Report from 1897 ask, "unguarded and alone, or surrounded by evil companionships; mother and wife and children, if he has any, and the blessed restraints of a decent social life far, far away; has the sailor less need than others of the curb of a holy religion?"[24] Behrends, in describing the aspects of the seaman's physical and moral composition that marginalized him from respectable society, drew a direct line between the social marginalization of merchant seamen and the possibility for new ministries: "modern commerce has created a new social class, and opened a new field for Christian philanthropy … We must have new agencies and ministries for the citizens of the sea, because the greatly altered conditions and immensely enlarged scope of modern commerce have created a class unknown in the days of Paul."[25] Behrends identifies the seaman's social marginalization as a product of the forces of industrialization, creating "a new social class" of laborers in need of spiritual guardianship.

ASFS focused on two potential outlets for reforming the condition of merchant seamen at sea and in port. The first was a direct appeal to the forces of public opinion. With an annual distribution total of 55,000 issues, the *Sailor's Magazine*, annual reports, pamphlets, and other printed material were distributed nationally to an interested public of potential donors, ASFS's audience was sizeable and capable of significant action if the Society could successfully convince it of the urgency of the issues at hand. Fully aware of this power, ASFS distributed a barrage of literature aimed at convincing the public of their duty to aid merchant seamen in their struggle for fair treatment through the ASFS. One article from 1895 titled "Our Debt to the Sailor" appeals to its readers' middle-class tastes and consumer habits in identifying the seaman as a "public benefactor":

> If you will think for a minute upon your table daily you will find something there for which you are indebted to the mariner. A part of our food, and clothing also, comes to us from over the sea. In bringing these things to us so cheaply, so speedily, and so abundantly, the sailor… is a public servant, and as such he deserves far more than the slight recompense which is grudgingly offered him.[26]

The sense of individualized debt to merchant seamen that ASFS attempted to impose upon its readers also served as further justification for the seaman's status as a ward, not just of the Admiralty courts or of the U.S. federal government, but as a "ward of the church," and ultimately a ward of the individual readers themselves, whose middle-class consumer lifestyles the labor of merchant seamen made possible. The ASFS President's report as published in the Annual Report from 1880 elaborates:

> Now, if the sailor be a ward, it pre-supposes a guardian. Who then are the sailor's guardians? It will not do for us to cast the matter off, and say that the nation is the guardian of the sailor, or that the law-makers are the guardians of the sailor, or that the church as a body is the guardian of the sailor. In this matter, individual responsibility comes down to you, and to me, and to every one of us, as members of the church of Christ, to feel that we should have his interest at heart; –the interests of the sailor, who does so much for us; without whom we should be debarred many of the luxuries we enjoy, without whom our commerce could not be carried on across the seas.[27]

Appealing to the shared identity of its audience as consumers, ASFS constructed a powerful argument for public support of its operations that simultaneously supported the Society financially while providing resources for services for seamen.

ASFS, with its powerful distributive network and sizeable national audience, placed heavy emphasis on the production of printed material as a tool for enlisting the collective support of their readership for the cause of reforming the conditions under which merchant seamen worked and lived. ASFS offered general appeals to the sympathy of the public based on a shared bourgeois identity, reliance on the labor of merchant seamen, and a broad Christian morality that transcended specific political or legal debates. Following this strategy, ASFS presented a second potential outlet for reforming the condition of merchant seamen based on a belief that religious conversion itself could effectively raise merchant seamen out of their plight. Rev. J. Rowell offers a perspective typical of auxiliary missionaries who populated the nation's sailortowns:

> But, now, what can be done to remedy these dreadful abuses? A great deal remains to be done by law … But I am not a member of Congress, and shall never be, so I am forced to try the next best method, which is yet the best mode of all; viz., to get the men themselves out of reach of this abuse by getting them converted to God. Assign what reason you may for the fact, but it is a fact that genuine Christian seamen seldom suffer gross abuse at sea. They often suffer cruel reviling and slander, but I do not remember a single instance of the kind of abuse that I have been speaking of having been inflicted on a genuine Christian man.[28]

Eschewing legislative politics in favor of religious conversion, Rowell reinforced the self-designation of the ASFS at the center of effective reform for merchant seamen.

Despite Rowell's apolitical approach to reform, mirrored by the strategy of the ASFS more generally, the Society did participate in the Joint Conference for the Protection of Seamen, a consortium of maritime ministry organizations formed to provide legal advocacy for select causes in the name of improving the lives of merchant seamen. The focus of the Joint Conference was almost exclusively on sailortown's network of establishments that depended on the business of merchant seamen between voyages or on shore leave. Middlemen, or "crimps," were the perpetual enemies of waterfront reformers who saw them as purely sinister criminals who coercively duped seamen in port, enticing them with food, drink, and sex on house credit while keeping an inflated tab of their debts until it was time to pay up in the form of forfeited advance notes on their next voyage out of port. According to the Joint Conference, seamen who were caught in this system could sail for years without seeing any of their wages, trapped in a peonage system of contract labor from which crimps and shipowners profited immensely at the seaman's expense. Indeed, crimps and captains often worked in concert with each other: if in port for an extended period of time, the predatory captain would impose harsher treatment upon his crew so as to push them to desert and thereby avoid paying the expenses of keeping an idle crew under contract while laid up. Crimps were more than happy to receive the disaffected seamen in their establishments, and the captain would be free to rehire a new crew when he was ready to sail, often at lower wages. If the captain could not motivate his men to desert, then he might enlist the help of crimps to do the work for him, luring the crew away from the ship with the temptations of the waterfront. In his memoirs, SCI Superintendent and Joint Conference leader Rev. Archibald R. R. Mansfield claims that this system worked for the benefit of all parties involved, except for the seamen: "[f]or this turnover, the crimp often received a bonus from the ship, and always paid himself liberally out of the seamen's pocket; the master saved the forfeited wages, and is known sometimes to have shared in the crimp's profit."[29]

Mansfield's version of the informal side of the waterfront economy is far different from what has been uncovered by maritime historians. Marcus Rediker has demonstrated that merchant seamen used tactics such as desertion to reassert control over their labor, jumping ship to escape abusive conditions or low wages and signing on elsewhere in port where better conditions prevailed.[30] Judith Fingard insists that crimps, rather than acting solely as exploitative forces within sailortowns, served as facilitators to seamen who desired to desert their vessels, sometimes offering outlets to legal recourse against abusive captains, or arranging for work on a different ship in port.[31] According to Fingard, crimps became the main targets of maritime reformers because of the threat they posed to respectable society within port towns, positioned to destabilize the influence of the temperance movement and a strictly regulated sexual culture typical of Victorian society.[32] Crimps and deserting seamen also disrupted the flow of commerce within ports, slowing down shipping schedules and impacting the profit margins of companies and the availability of goods for an increasingly consumer-based society. This commercial element was certainly in the minds of the leaders of the Joint Conference, alongside priority given to seamen's rights. As described in the meeting minutes of the Joint Conference, crimps "sought to deprive seamen of their lawful rights, and to injure the commerce of the port of New York or to delay or prevent the shipping of crews upon vessels desiring the leave this port … [crimps] gave menace to the good order and peace of this community."[33]

With the stability of maritime commerce and waterfront society at risk, the Joint Conference set to work on a list of objectives aimed at weakening the crimps' power in port. To curb the crimps' influence on a seaman's freedom to sign and obligation to fulfill shipping articles, the Joint Conference sought to build on the achievements of the 1872 Shipping Commissioner's Act, which required that a seaman sign shipping articles in the presence of a commissioner who could attest to his sobriety. By proposing to employ the services of a "General Agent" in port who would monitor the legitimacy of all contracts, the Joint Conference could actively intervene by keeping seamen out of the crimps' system of perpetual debt.[34] Similarly, the Joint Conference sought to put heavy restrictions on the practice of granting allotment notes or advance payments to seamen who signed shipping articles, arguing that most of that money would wind up in the hands of the crimps, rather than the seaman himself or his family back home. Finally, the Joint Conference called for the establishment of boardinghouse inspectors who would regulate the keepers of hotels and other establishments that often moonlighted as brothels or grog shops.[35]

These regulations followed in the footsteps of members of maritime ministry who had been at work on the ground in New York's sailortown. Rev. Benjamin C. C. Parker, SCI's first waterfront missionary, preached for months in a drafty room above a grog shop on the corner of Pike and South Streets in the heart of Manhattan's notorious sailortown before his administrators were able to secure funding for an audacious project: the purchase and conversion of a decommissioned ferry boat into a floating chapel that would host services exclusively for the city's seamen. Permanently moored along the East River in February 1844, the Floating Church of Our Saviour represented the most daring countermove by the city's evangelical reformers in the battle for the soul of the waterfront. By embedding themselves directly in the heart of the seaman's social, cultural, and economic world ashore, Parker and his colleagues had officially declared war on their enemies by setting up camp within the inner front of sailortown's informal networks.

Control

On December 2, 1843, a labor dispute was threatening to erupt in New York City's sailortown. In his journals, Parker describes an incident in which an "incendiary" handbill was slid underneath the door of the Sailors' Home early on a Sunday morning, inciting the seamen therein to join an effort to raise wages within the port. Interpreting the handbill as a potential perversion of the Sabbath, the keeper of the Sailors' Home implored upon its residents to forget the handbill and instead respect the holiness of that day, saying, according to Parker, that "they had better put that paper out of the way for that day. It was the Sabbath. No good could come of agitating such a subject on Sunday. They would benefit themselves more, and raise themselves more in the estimation of respectable merchants, by going to public worship on the Sabbath than by talking on or moving in such a subject."[36]

This attempt to coopt nascent energies with the potential to motivate collective waterfront labor organization, embodied in a single handbill slipped beneath the door of a sleepy sailors' reading room, and an attempt to repackage it as a testament to the positive effects of Protestant morality, temperance, and Sabbatarianism, gets to the heart of the objectives of maritime ministry in the nineteenth century and beyond. The invocation of "respectable merchants" is particularly telling as evidence of tamping down efforts at self-organization among waterfront workers in the interests of cultivating a controllable, sober, and productive pool of available maritime labor.

According to Parker, the effect of this speech was that 150 sailors from the Home attended services at the reverend's makeshift church instead of engaging in labor advocacy. As Parker describes it, "Nothing more was seen or heard of the handbill that day. Not a man in the whole house out of 210 men was seen at all intoxicated or the worse for liquor, but [everything] was quiet and orderly as if the whole establishment had been the residence of a family of professors of religion."[37] Parker goes on to summarize his version of the progress made upon the moral condition of seamen in the Port of New York since SCI had set up operations along the waterfront:

> Who could have thought to look upon such a sight 10 years ago, no seamen, many just in from long voyages at sea, where they had been confined to the strict discipline & hard work of the forecastle for many long months, now at liberty on shore, wholly unrestrained in one house, except by moral influences, & not a man loud boisterous talkative or in liquor among them. What had produced this change. More than half of them seven or eight years ago, without such a house & such influences as had been made to bear upon them of late, would probably have been found in brothels or reeling in noise, blasphemy and disgusting bestiality in the streets or sleeping away the effects of a debauch on the [sidewalks] in the parts of the city where they dwell. Here were 210 men all sober, well disposed, with all their faculties bright & all their senses, uninjured; all their moral feelings open to good

> impressions, & this was of that late degraded class whom the community have so long neglected as out of the reach of moral & religious influences.[38]

This pious scene stands in stark contrast to the labor meeting that took place adjacent to Parker's church services, at which some 600 seamen gathered at Burling Slip to establish a meeting place at Croton Hull. Amid a meandering journal entry, Parker describes the true business of this meeting: a vote was taken among attendees to demand a raise in wages from nine dollars a month to fifteen dollars. But even this straightforward agenda is couched in several paragraphs of incessant preaching over the moral improvement and sobriety of the seamen present at the meeting:

> Here were 500 sailors on shore all perfectly sober, entering into conventions against the boardinghouses, which have hitherto been their ruin. Voting not to board any more at any other than a temperance boarding house & to protect their shipmates from the extortionate spirit and the corrupting and tyrannical influence of a class of men by whom they have hitherto been wholly controlled & from whose power they have not had strength before to escape. By one mighty effort they here broke the toils in which they had for the last 100 years been kept in Bondage … It has shown that they can triumph over their own evil habits and the power of their enemies, and that they may hereafter unitedly take a stand in the world & individually in society, as a sober, prudent, and intelligent class of men that they never before have occupied.[39]

This idyllic vision for a spiritually contained version of organized maritime labor would be severely tested over the following decades, but in December of 1843, Parker had his visions set firmly in sight for a new centralized location upon which such a consolidation of waterfront Christian morality could be launched:

> Just at this crisis, there is to be presented to them an object for their benefit more beautiful and agreeable than [anything] they have yet in any port in the world seen. It is a beautiful Gothic Church, floating on their own element, moored at the wharf, in which they may worship God in the beautiful and appropriate services of the prayer book, which is to be put into the hands of every man who enters the building, and where they may join audibly in a worship which is deeply devotional without extravagance, and intellectual and spiritual and edifying without formality.[40]

By the end of Parker's tenure at the Floating Church of Our Saviour in 1868, SCI had succeeded in embedding themselves within the heart of New York's sailortown and had developed a powerful methodology for coopting potentially threatening elements of the waterfront into a ministry project that sought to transform seamen into converts. They were also positioned to bring a wayward, marginal district of the city back into the fold of respectable mainland, bourgeois society. However, SCI's missionary methodology was increasingly tested by the strength of the position that sailors' boardinghouses maintained at the epicenter of sailortown's economic, social, and cultural worlds. In order to truly transform sailortown, SCI and its missionaries could no longer wait for the sailor to come to them; they had to take the fight to the sailor on his own turf.

25 South Street: "The Million-Dollar Home for Sailors"

The era of the Floating Church of Our Saviour (1843–1906) coincided with widespread international adoption of steam engine technology, led by the British, that all but ended American dominance of shipping that had characterized the Age of Sail, ushering in a new industrial age of global shipping. By the 1890s, British steamships dominated the world's maritime shipping economy, creating a pull toward foreign maritime labor, intensifying exploitative conditions on ships, and dispersing a more diverse (and from evangelical reformers' perspective simultaneously more vulnerable and more threatening) class of bluewater men teeming at the edges of Manhattan's waterfront.

Having embedded themselves in the heart of the city's sailortown, SCI, through their agent Rev. Parker, launched a missionary project in which the ebb and flow of the city's waterfront washed ashore potential converts just as it pulled them away to voyages out at sea. Here on the city's margins, the next phase in taming the urban frontier was taken up by a young and ambitious preacher, newly ordained, who would lead SCI into a new era of heightened infiltration into sailortown through consolidation of its operations and monopolization of the Institute's control over every conceivable aspect of the sailor's life ashore.

For SCI's Superintendent Mansfield, it was clear that success in the sailors' boardinghouse market would require a radical reconfiguration of operations. In order to do so, he and SCI would need support from the city's formidable "mercantile community," the Church, and other members of respectable society. The 1902 Board of Commissioners for Licensing Sailors' Hotels and Boarding Houses in the Port of New York included a direct appeal for financial support from the Chamber of Commerce and the public at large:

> All that is needed is a little more interest and financial aid on the part of the community to redeem our City from its former bad reputation in the care and treatment of seamen while forced to remain a little while in our port.[41]

As SCI expanded its footprint of operations in New York's sailortown, the Institute would have the support of the consortium of corporate bodies that made up the Board of Commissioners. Indeed, those with interests in maritime commerce in the Port of New York rallied behind SCI by 1905, when it formed a New Building Committee to raise funds for a thirteen-story headquarters dedicated to the welfare of sailors. The construction of the "million-dollar home for sailors," as it became known, was motivated as much by competition with the crimps for control over of sailortown's boardinghouse economy as it was about providing a safe harbor for seamen ashore. Ultimately, SCI's new headquarters at 25 South Street intensified its objectives in plotting the eradication of sailortown altogether.

Born in 1874, Archibald Romaine Mansfield spent the first thirteen years of his life enjoying a pastoral childhood, given license to bask in his rural upstate New York surroundings by his minister father and indulgent mother. The descendent of a long line of ordained leaders of the Episcopal Church, the young Mansfield initially had no intentions to follow suit. That all changed—likely by design—when Mansfield's father dispatched him at the age of thirteen, without his mother's knowledge or consent, to St. John's Military School at Sing Sing. There, Mansfield came of age under the "clocklike routine" of the school's administration, subject to "thrashings for freshness," and introduced to a long list of habits that he would carry with him for the remainder of his adult life: an obsession with precise and economic management, the careful turning of his bed in the morning, and a particular attention paid to blacking the heels of his shoes when polishing.[42]

From Sing Sing, Mansfield went on to St. Stephen's College (now Bard College) in Hudson Valley, New York, where he was drawn to ministry work with the town's farmers and Scandinavian immigrants. After receiving his degree, he began studies at the General Theological Seminary in Manhattan. In 1894, Mansfield took a position with a "powerful and successful Church leader and organizer" to administer Sunday School with some 1500 boys on the Lower East Side. Working on the Lower East Side, Mansfield gained insight into the complex challenges and problems that immigrant youths faced growing up poor and alienated along the city's margins. Mansfield describes this experience in his memoirs:

> As I visited houses here and there on side streets leading off the then notorious Bowery and through those sections radiating from Chatham Square made famous by Jacob Riis in his book 'How the Other Half Lives,' I did not dream that in another year my lot would be cast there among the 'other half.'[43]

That same year, Mansfield received a summons from Benoni Lockwood, manager of SCI, and took over administration of a very unusual parish: the East River Station, consisting of the Floating Church of Our Saviour, a reading room for seamen and Chaplain's residence at 34 Pike Street, and a boardinghouse for seamen under the Institute's control at 52 Market Street. During his fateful meeting with Lockwood, Mansfield followed him into the depths of sailortown, a section of Manhattan with which the young seminary student had been heretofore entirely unfamiliar. Encountering the spectacle of the Floating Chapel at Pike Street, Mansfield recollected that "having crossed the Atlantic" himself, he had never given much thought at all to seamen, nor had he ever heard that there was such a unique church docked along the East River. Merchant seamen, as Mansfield explains, were "a very special and distinct class of men" who were "completely isolated" and who "did not have a chance in the world." Like most people, he had thought of seamen as "always at sea, never on land," and therefore far from his, and the public's, thoughts.[44]

Within this context, Mansfield's tour of sailortown took on the resonance of a spiritual awakening. His walk with Lockwood took him down to South Street and Coenties Slip, "along the East River under the bowsprits of sailing vessels from far and near which lined the Street," and then to the Floating Church, "not many blocks above the Fulton Fish Market." Strolling side by side, Mansfield and Lockwood reconnoitered the perimeter of sailortown, examining its inhabitants and the cultural geography of their strange, marginalized world:

> So this was Sailortown! I could take in very little in the few minutes we were there, but what I saw in my brief view was appalling. All about me lay horrible filth, broken-down dwellings that had been turned into dirty, squalid boardinghouses; countless doggeries so low and vile that it would be base flattery to call them saloons; rows of 'tailor-shops,' alternating with dives of the most odious and repulsive type. At the merest glance, which was all I had that day, I could see every conceivable organization of vice and crime, ready to exploit the sailor and strip him, in the shortest possible time, of every hard-earned cent he had.[45]

This description of depravity referred to a uniquely laid-out pocket of the city's outskirts. According to Mansfield, sailortown encompassed much of the First, Second, Fourth, and Seventh Wards in lower Manhattan. At its lower end, the river bends to the east; at its upper end, the river swings back around Corlears Hook, epicenter for much of the city's shipbuilding during the nineteenth century. Its streets were laid out perpendicular to the river, on a different axis than any other part of the city; anchored, seemingly, on an entirely separate gravitational plane and giving it the resemblance of a vortex, with its streets, shops, residences, and inhabitants all clinging to an incline that led directly to the waterfront. Its center within a center, the heart of sailortown itself, consisted of the blocks between Cherry and Water Streets, from Cherry Hill (now Franklin Square) to Pike Street.

Mansfield describes the lower blocks of the Bowery, which extended away from the waterfront off Catherine Street, as the "Broadway of Sailortown," containing a mix of high and low culture, famous for its theaters—the Thalia, the People's Windsor, the National, Harry Miner's—and of course, its saloons, where a nickel glass of beer came with a cheap lunch. The Mariner's Temple, a spot particularly popular with seamen, offered coffee, a stale roll, and pea soup for a penny. Boardinghouses lined every block, especially in the Fourth Ward. Word of establishments like the infamous McGurk's, nicknamed "suicide hall," spread internationally through advertising cards carried by seamen across the ocean to other sailors' boardinghouses all over the world.[46]

Within this labyrinth of humanity, Mansfield identified the object of his missionary labor: the sailor, whom he described as "the official victim of the district," a group of men at the mercy of businesspeople and other "land sharks" whose sole entrepreneurial purpose depended on the constant exploitation of seamen, who had "no land status at all, not even if he were by nationality American … no vote … and therefore … quite outside the charmed circle of political protection."[47]

Despite this pessimistic interpretation, Mansfield found an alternative quality within sailortown that was worth preserving:

> For the other side, the strange kaleidoscope of life that thronged the streets, the kindliness and democracy of the [neighborhood]; the decency and self-respect maintained against the greatest odds–for this one must turn to the reminiscences of the district's native sons, many of whom look back almost with regret to the [neighborly], good-hearted, give-and-take existence of the 'slums'.[48]

It was this side of sailortown that Mansfield would seek to bring to the surface through his missionary work. Following his stroll through the district with Benoni Lockwood in 1894, Mansfield agreed to come on as Superintendent and remained in that position until his death in 1934.

Under Mansfield's leadership, SCI adopted a revised approach to monopolizing and centralizing control over sailortown. Wherever the sailor ate, drank, socialized, read a newspaper, sat for a game of checkers, read his mail, or took up employment, SCI sought to step in and provide that service for him. Mansfield oversaw the modernization of the sailor's home at 34 Pike Street, updated a similar home along the North (Hudson) River, installed J.W. Abbott as the Institute's private roving officer to patrol sailortown by foot, and literally knocked down the wall between SCI and the British Shipping Office in the Battery. Moving forward, however, Mansfield had his sights set on a much larger objective: raising money for a million-dollar "home for sailors" at 25 South Street. As he described it, the home would be a monumental testament to the mission of the Institute:

> to do for the sailor's good exactly what the crimps had been doing for his harm. They were the first to greet him in the [harbor]; so should we be. They offered him friendship and advice; so should we. They stood by him at the pay-off and took care of his money; so should we. They arranged for his food, lodging, clothing and amusements; so should we. They provided him a gathering-place for companionship and social life; so should we. Finally, they got work for him when he signed off; so should we. Our whole social [program], in short, should be practically identical with that of the crimps, the only difference being that ours should be disinterested while theirs was not. Merely putting the crimps out of business would leave the sailor high

and dry. The thing was to do for the sailor just what the crimps did, but to do it right.[49]

Beginning in 1905, the Institute's newly formed Building Committee purchased a plot of land at Coenties Slip and began a fundraising campaign to finance the construction of a centralized headquarters for the Institute. The campaign rallied the city's philanthropists to the cause of maritime ministry, soliciting major contributions from industrialists, shipping companies, and the city's powerful and wealthy religious leaders. Combined with support from the Board of Commissioners for the Licensing of Sailors' Boardinghouses, the Institute soon met its goal to raise $1,000,000 and began construction on its new headquarters at 25 South Street. SCI's own Board of Managers was a veritable who's who of monied industrialists and shipping magnates. Andrew Carnegie, Henry C. Frick, Augustus D. Julliard, and three Vanderbilts (Frederick, William, and Alfred) all donated substantial amounts of money towards SCI's maritime ministry project.[50]

On April 15, 1912, a delegation that included Mayor William Jay Gaynor laid the cornerstone of the Seamen's Church Institute's new headquarters at the corner of South Street and Coenties Slip. The Institute was consolidating; Mansfield had been made Superintendent and under his and longtime board member Edmund Baylies' direction, all of SCI's operations were brought together under one roof. The new building would be capable of housing 580 seafaring men in its dormitories, with rates as low as fifteen cents per night.

Inside SCI's headquarters, the new facilities offered more than just beds. Its designers set out to build a center where seamen could come to relax, be entertained, and feel at home. To this end, amenities such as a soda fountain and a luncheonette were established, offering affordable meals and non-alcoholic drinks. Hungry seamen were greeted with a cornucopia of options: a liverwurst, American cheese, bologna or egg sandwich at the cost of ten cents, while Swiss cheese and salami cost fifteen. For the parched seaman, five cents would buy him a coffee, tea, milk, or a glass of Spur Cola, Seven-Up, or Dr. Pepper. SCI's "boozeless bar," as it was referred to in a *New York Daily News* article, was designed as an alternative to the saloons that seafarers typically frequented while in Port. SCI's soda bar was made to look the part, according to the Daily News:

> It is going to be a real bar, all right. None of these imitation marble, be-mirrored and gilded soda water contraptions. Except that it will be cleaner, every detail will suggest to the men that they have their foot on the same old brass rail and are polishing the mahogany of the same old place they frequented before the advent of the 'boozeless bar.'[51]

In addition to food and drink, 25 South Street housed a game room, where seamen could shoot pool or play board games. A post office operated where seamen could send and receive letters and packages. Many seamen made 25 South Street their permanent address and would have mail waiting for them each time they arrived in port after finishing another stint aboard a ship. The Savings Department allowed seamen to deposit money earned from their voyages where it could gain interest and would be safe from the crimps. Almost as soon as SCI opened the doors at 25 South Street, seamen nearing New York harbor could look out into the horizon and see the steady green light beaming from the newly dedicated Titanic Memorial Lighthouse and know that there would be a place for him to get a cheap meal, relax, and spend the night on the other side (Fig. 1.2).

The New York State Census, conducted in 1915 and 1925, and the U.S. Federal Census, conducted once every ten years, provide snapshots of the boarders present at the moment the census takers arrived at SCI's doors. While the 1920 Federal Census seems to have passed by 25 South Street entirely, other census takers meticulously recorded information about a staggering number of seamen who temporarily called SCI home.

In 1915, SCI had only just opened its new headquarters, and had yet to build the "annex," an expansion that was designed to accommodate even more seamen than the 398 who were recorded as boarders in the state census that year. The next set of data comes ten years later in 1925, by which time the number of boarders had increased to 1049.[52] SCI offered 580 single dormitory rooms, meaning that the census recorded nearly twice as many boarders at 25 South Street than the maximum that SCI's dorm rooms could accommodate. There are several potential explanations for this significant disparity. First, it is possible that the census taker took data related to SCI's Post Office and recorded individuals with accounts as boarders. Second, the census taker(s) might have simply recorded information for everyone inside the building on the day(s) during which the census was conducted. Given SCI's extensive network of services, this explanation would account for many—potentially

Fig. 1.2 SCI's thirteen-story headquarters at 25 South Street towered over its neighbors along the East River waterfront when it opened in 1912. Seamen's Church Institute Digital Archives

hundreds—of seamen who were inside the building without renting dormitory rooms. Instead of listing a ship in port or a distant connection as their permanent address, SCI came to stand in as a home for these men not only in the strategy and propaganda of its ministry project but also in the official records of the state and federal census.

Regardless of the explanation, the number of total boarders attests to SCI's success in attracting seamen to 25 South Street. However, these raw numbers should not be taken as proof that SCI's ultimate goal of eradicating the boardinghouses and leisure places of sailortown was successful. On the contrary, sailors' boardinghouses continued to thrive in the district despite sharing the market with 25 South Street, and the services of the Board of Commissioners for Licensed Sailors' Boardinghouses continued to be of use. The 1922 annual report of the Board lists forty-four houses that were issued licenses, just four less than the forty-eight that the Board granted in 1902. In 1927, SCI itself applied for a license, emphasizing in its application that they did not employ runners and did not offer alcohol on their premises. It would appear that the Institute's successes developed alongside sailortown's existing culture, rather than replacing them entirely as Mansfield had hoped.

The census data recording boarders at 25 South Street from 1915 to 1940 reveal characteristics that represent the typical occupant at SCI: moderately young to middle-aged, unmarried, and from SCI's perspective, at risk. The boarders at 25 South Street averaged thirty-one years in 1915, thirty-four years in 1930 (1925 New York State Census did not record age), and forty-two years in 1940. This could be evidence that SCI attracted relatively older seamen, or it could be indicative of changes in the industry, which was logically attracting fewer young men into the maritime professions during times of depression in the shipping industry, such as the 1920s and most of the 1930s. Marital status, only recorded in the 1930 and 1940 censuses, nonetheless lends further insight into the demographics of 25 South Street (Figs. 1.3 and 1.4). In 1930, 684 out of 738 seamen were "Single," and in 1940, 897 out of 1060 were "Single."

Despite SCI's relatively older clientele, boarders from 1930 to 1940 remained bachelors by overwhelming margins. It was this characteristic of

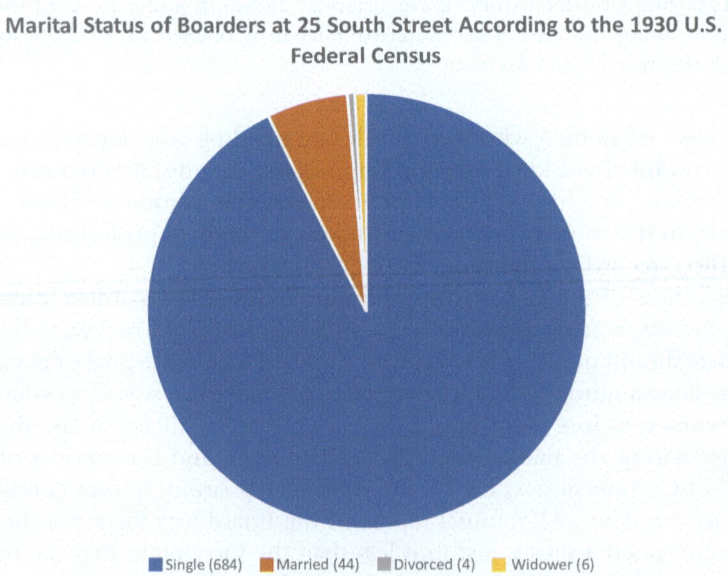

Fig. 1.3 Marital status of Boarders at 25 South Street 1930

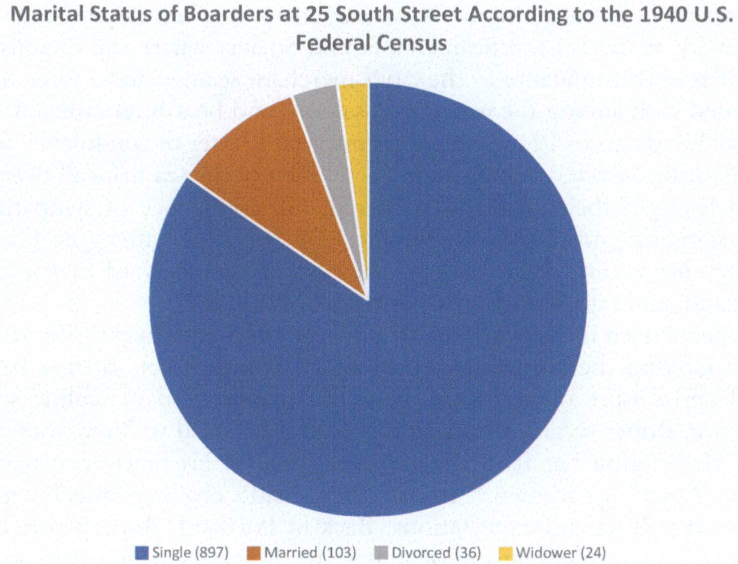

Fig. 1.4 Marital status of Boarders at 25 South Street 1940

bachelorhood, or the deliberate alienation from the institution of marriage and the influence of matrimonial partnership with a woman and the responsibilities of a nuclear family, that represented the greatest threat to the wellbeing of the merchant seamen for reformers at SCI. Even if men were in middle age, their distance from these civilizing influences ostensibly made them vulnerable and at risk of falling into the stereotypical pitfalls of the sailor's life ashore. 25 South Street, and all of its component parts, was constructed to redeem these men through systematic control over every aspect of their financial, social, spiritual, and domestic lives.

Janet Lord Roper, "Mother to 50,000 Seamen"

In 1915, three years after SCI opened the doors at 25 South Street, the Institute's administrators, led by Mansfield, made the unconventional decision to hire Janet Lord Roper, recently widowed by the itinerant seamen's chaplain Rev. Harry Roper. Before coming to New York City, Roper had spent twenty-one years working alongside her husband at seamen's missions in Gloucester, Massachusetts, Portland, Oregon, and New

Brunswick. Before meeting her husband, an 18-year-old Roper began her life's work at the Boston Seamen's Friend Society where she established herself as both confidante to the city's merchant seamen and a force to be reckoned with among the waterfront saloons and boardinghouses. At the time of her death in 1943, her career inspired a letter of condolence from President Roosevelt, which read in part: "men of the sea from all over the world brought their problems to her in full confidence of sympathetic understanding and practical helpfulness."[53] Soon thereafter, the Liberty ship SS *Janet Lord Roper* slid off the rails at the shipyard in Fairfield, Maryland, and into service at sea during World War II.

Roper arrived in New York City alone in 1915 and quickly found herself wandering the labyrinthine halls of 25 South Street. At first bewildered and unsure of her place in such a massive and masculine social structure, Roper received instructions from Mansfield to "find your own job," challenging her to figure out her place in his newly constructed "dream hotel" for seamen.[54] In part, Mansfield's challenge was based on gendered politics and expectations. Back in Portland, Roper's role consisted of a mixture of conventional maternal hostess and substitute leader in place of her ailing husband. Roper found herself hosting "biscuit parties" at her home one day and leading sermons and meetings at the waterfront mission the next. In New York, Mansfield recruited Roper to give his formidable sailors' home a touch of "woman's influence." In the language of her biographer Jonathan Finn, it was expected that Roper would act as "mother, confidante, and confessor, strong enough to relieve human tragedies and sympathetic toward weaknesses that produced them; she would have to be religious but with an all-encompassing faith; she would have to be worldly, yet basically spiritual."[55]

Roper's unpublished biography, based on interviews conducted shortly before her death, describes the front lines of the reform effort directed at individual seamen, whose primary sins and weaknesses, according to the reformers, were their distance from home and domestic stability. SCI, through Roper and other mechanisms, attempted not only to control the sailor at leisure and in the maritime labor market but also his masculinity, imposing regimes of domestic training through financial responsibility, a purity of diet, and a connection to distant mothers, sisters, wives, and girlfriends whom he had left behind for a life at sea. Roper's memoirs and her correspondence with seamen and their estranged family members and loved ones lend insight into the architecture of gendered ministry work along the city's waterfront, designed primarily to facilitate and encourage a type of conversion narrative in which the estranged sailor was reunited with female partners that represented the stable, domestic life that he abandoned when he chose to go to sea.

During and after World War I, family members inundated Roper's office with mail searching for missing seamen, lost amidst the chaos of global conflict. In response, Roper established the Missing Seamen's Bureau, a department of SCI that dispatched bulletins listing missing men to every major port in the world. The work of the Bureau continued well after the end of the war, with Roper managing a permanent department dedicated to reuniting seamen with estranged family members. The literature of nineteenth-century seamen's missions commonly featured conversion narratives involving merchant seamen. The publication of the American Seamen's Friend Society, *The Seamen's Friend*, is filled with "testimonials" from seamen who had found the Christian religion and reformed their ways, usually manifested in the signing of a temperance pledge and a resolution to stay clean in avoiding the moral pitfalls of the world's sailortowns. "Mother" Roper defined her job at SCI in terms of facilitating conversion narratives of a different sort; by presenting herself as a reasonably secular "listener" for transient men who were either single or estranged from their families, Roper mediated conversions by reconnecting men with stable, domestic lives, often in the figure of a mother, wife, or daughter. Instead of finding religion, seamen "found" their roles within the domestic familial spheres they had missed or avoided by going to sea and resolved to "come clean" in conforming to the expectations placed upon them by the middle-class reformer mentality that Roper embodied.

Conclusion

At 25 South Street, SCI operated under a dual mission: it took Mansfield's vision of 25 South Street as an institutional home for transient seamen and a competitive alternative to the exploitative underworld of crimps who operated in the boardinghouses and surrounding economy of sailortown, and combined it with Roper's perspective. For Roper, 25 South Street served as headquarters for a project of reforming and repairing domestic and familial relationships that took on a global scale. 25 South Street was thus both a proxy home for seamen and a site in which the "true" homes of seamen were actively reshaped and managed.[56]

The contested urban space of New York's sailortown served as a venue for a series of confrontations between merchant seamen and shoreside individuals, communities, and institutions. The origins and acceleration of maritime ministry work in the Port of New York beginning in the 1830s and continuing throughout the nineteenth century, was, in part, a reaction to a perceived invasion of merchant seamen who arrived from the wilderness of the high seas to form the teeming settlement of sailortown at the margins of the city's lower wards. At the heart of these confrontations was the existential threat that merchant seamen's projected bluewater masculinity and multiculturalism posed to Victorian sensibilities of moral and spiritual propriety. In response to seamen's inherent transience and mobility, enshrined in their right to shore leave and embodied in the institution of sailors' boardinghouses, maritime reformers launched projects that involved tactics of maritime ministry work and legislative advocacy. These projects followed a trajectory enacted in three stages: first, a stage of initial infiltration, characterized by SCI's model of inverse colonialism as embodied in the plantation of the Floating Church of Our Saviour in the heart of sailortown in 1843; second, cooptation and conversion, in which agents of maritime ministry such as Rev. Benjamin Parker worked to recruit merchant seamen to their services and convert them by delivering sermons, distributing religious tracts, and soliciting temperance pledges; and third, regulation and control manifested in the opening of SCI's headquarters at 25 South Street, in which the mission of institutionalized leisure, commerce, and reformed domesticity was carried out.

Despite the substantial energies and funding that backed these projects to control them in port, merchant seamen did not submit passively to would-be reformers and regulators. Instead, merchant seamen consistently found alternative means of maintaining "liberty" in port. Specifically, the practice of desertion, long a common means for seamen to break contract and retain agency in abandoning unfavorable employment conditions, continued to be commonly practiced in sailortowns on both coasts of the United States, despite its official illegality and the looming punishment of imprisonment if caught and prosecuted. By the end of the nineteenth century, after decades of informal practice and inconsistent enforcement of such penalties, merchant seamen's assertions of liberty through desertion came into direct conflict with the state through formal legal attention to the practice. The case of the *Arago* seamen from 1895 to 1897, in which four merchant seamen argued that their imprisonment as punishment for breaking contract through desertion constituted a violation of the Thirteenth Amendment, is a case study in confrontations between merchant seamen and the state over the parameters of their rights to Constitutional protections and, by extension, U.S. citizenship. Further, it is evidence that the trajectory of staunching invasion, converting, and controlling merchant seamen adopted by nineteenth-century maritime reformers had direct applications for the U.S. government in dealing with similar confrontations over the nature of citizenship.

Notes

1. Alfred J. Nock, *Mansfield Biography*, unpublished manuscript, Records of the Seamen's Church Institute of New York and New Jersey, 20.
2. Ibid., 26.
3. Ibid., 27–30.
4. Ibid., 33.
5. Ibid., 37–38.
6. Ibid., 38.
7. Daniel Vickers, *Young Men and the Sea: Yankee Seafarers in the Age of Sail* (New Haven, CT: Yale University Press, 2005). For a perspective on similar developments in Canadian sailortowns, see Judith Fingard, *Jack in Port: Sailortowns of Eastern Canada* (University of Toronto Press, 1982).
8. Vickers, *Young Men and the Sea*, 204.
9. Johnathan Thayer, "Sailors' Homes': Sailors' Boardinghouses, Maritime Reform, and Contested Domestic Space in New York's Sailortown," in Downing, Thayer, Begiato, eds., *Negotiating Masculinities and Modernity in the Maritime World, 1815–1940*, 205–224.
10. Thomas Butler Gunn, *The Physiology of New York Boarding-Houses*, (New York: Mason Brothers, 1857), 162.
11. Paul Gilje, *Liberty on the Waterfront: American Maritime Culture in the Age of* Revolution, (Philadelphia: University of Pennsylvania Press, 2004), 16 and Graeme Milne, *People. Place, and Power on the Nineteenth Century Waterfront: Sailortowns*, (London: Palgrave Macmillan, 2016), 123.
12. Knock, *Mansfield*, 33.
13. Brad Beaven, *Leisure, Citizenship and Working-Class Men in Britain, 1850–1945* (Manchester University Press, 2005), 36.
14. Kathleen D. McCarthy, *American Creed: Philanthropy and the Rise of Civil Society, 1700–1865* (Chicago: University of Chicago Press, 2003), 2, 24, and 60.
15. Roald Kverndal's *Seamen's Missions: Their Origins and Early Growth* (Pasadena, CA: William Carey Library, 1986), 514.
16. Ibid., 518–519.
17. Records of the Seamen's Church Institute of New York and New Jersey.

18. *Sailor's Magazine*, June 1898, Records of the American Seamen's Friend Society.
19. Rev. A. J. F. Behrends, "Christ's Dominion on the Sea," 1883 Annual Report, Records of the American Seamen's Friend Society.
20. Ibid.
21. Ibid.
22. Rev. Edward R. Coe, "The Gospel and the Sailor," 1882 Annual Report, Records of the American Seamen's Friend Society.
23. *Sailor's Magazine*, July 1898, Records of the American Seamen's Friend Society.
24. 1897 Annual Report, Records of the American Seamen's Friend Society.
25. Behrends, "Christ's Dominion on the Sea."
26. *Sailors' Magazine*, September 1895, Records of the American Seamen's Friend Society.
27. 1880 Annual Report, Records of the American Seamen's Friend Society.
28. Rev. J. Rowell, "Report," 1897 Annual Report, Records of the American Seamen's Friend Society.
29. Nock, *Mansfield*, Chapter Thirteen.
30. Marcus Rediker, *Between the Devil and the Deep Blue Sea: Merchant Seamen, Pirates and the Anglo-American Maritime World, 1700–1750*, (Cambridge University Press, 1987).
31. Judith Fingard, *Jack in Port: Sailortowns of Eastern Canada*, (University of Toronto Press, 1982), 190.
32. Ibid., 219.
33. Fingard, *Jack in Port*, 213 and Joint Conference for the Protection of Seamen, Minutes Book, May 12, 1899, Records of the Seamen's Church Institute of New York and New Jersey.
34. Joint Conference for the Protection of Seamen, Minutes Book, May 12, 1899.
35. Ibid.
36. Rev. Benjamin C. C. Parker, "Journal of the Floating Church of Our Saviour 1843 July 17–1844 June 30," Records of the Seamen's Church Institute of New York and New Jersey.
37. Ibid.
38. Ibid.
39. Ibid.
40. Ibid.
41. Board of Commissioners for Licensing Sailors' Hotels and Boarding Houses in the Port of New York, "1902 Annual Report," Records of the Seamen's Church Institute of New York and New Jersey.
42. Nock, *Mansfield*, Chapter One.
43. Ibid., 7.

44. Ibid., Chapter One.
45. Ibid.
46. Ibid., 30.
47. Ibid., 36.
48. Ibid., 27.
49. Ibid., 362.
50. Johnathan Thayer, "Merchant Seamen, Sailortowns, and the Philanthropic Encounter in New York, 1843–1945," in David Worthington, ed., *The New Coastal History: Perspectives from Scotland and Beyond*, (London: Palgrave Macmillan, 2021), 79.
51. Unknown, *New York Daily News*, 1911. Seamen's Church Institute of New York Scrapbook 1911–1912, Records of the Seamen's Church Institute of New York and New Jersey.
52. Census data was compiled as part of a Maritime Heritage Program grant awarded to the Seamen's Church Institute by the National Park Service in 2015.
53. Letter from Franklin D. Roosevelt to Seamen's Church Institute, 1944, Records of the Seamen's Church Institute of New York and New Jersey.
54. Jonathan Finn, *Janet Roper: Mother to 50,000 Seamen* (unpublished manuscript), Records of the Seamen's Church Institute, 296.
55. Ibid., 278.
56. Thayer, "Merchant Seamen, Sailortowns, and the Philanthropic Encounter in New York, 1843–1945," 81.

CHAPTER 2

Merchant Seamen and the Parameters of Involuntary Servitude: The *Arago* Deserters and the United States Supreme Court, 1895–1897

On July 7, 1895, the merchant barque *Arago* arrived in port at San Francisco with four of its crewmembers in irons. Having been sighted by the afternoon crowds gathered along the shore, the vessel's erratic path into the harbor attracted unusual attention. Gazing out on the channel, onlookers observed with increasing concern as the *Arago* abruptly lowered her sails and veered dangerously along the rocks. A tug was quickly dispatched and the ship brought safely to shore, having narrowly avoided running aground. At shortly after five o'clock, a police flag was raised in the *Arago*'s rigging, the harbor police descended upon the wharf, and the four crewmembers, now prisoners, were extracted from the ship.[1]

The case of the *Arago* would prove to be a landmark in the legal history of contract labor in the United States. The arrested seamen—John Bradley, Philip Helzen, Morris Hansen, and Robert Robertson—had signed shipping articles with the *Arago* for a voyage scheduled to take them along the Pacific Coast of the U.S. to Valparaiso, Chile, and back. However, once they reached port in Astoria, Oregon, the seamen jumped ship and deserted. Holding the men in violation of their shipping articles, Capt. Perry hastily issued warrants and saw that the men were arrested and held in a local jail for sixteen days before being forcibly returned to the ship and

J. Thayer, *Citizenship, Subversion, and Surveillance in U.S. Ports*, Global Studies in Social and Cultural Maritime History,
https://doi.org/10.1007/978-3-031-45618-3_2

ordered back to work. Once at sea, the men refused and were placed back in shackles until the ship reached San Francisco.

Having arrived at San Francisco in chains, the story of the *Arago*'s imprisoned seamen spread quickly. The seamen could hardly have expected to find themselves in a city more sympathetic to their plight than San Francisco in 1895. Seamen and labor activists had founded the Coast Seamen's Union there in 1885, an organization out of which Andrew Furuseth had emerged as the undisputed leader of the movement for seamen's rights, a cause enthusiastically supported by then Mayor of San Francisco James D. Phelan as well as local congressman James G. Maguire. Operating in 1895 as the Sailors' Union of the Pacific (SUP), the union and Furuseth put their considerable influence and energies into helping the *Arago* seamen, all four of whom were rank-and-file SUP members, to make their case out of writ of habeas corpus before the District Court of Northern California. Despite the SUP's assistance, the District Court unceremoniously rejected the *Arago* seamen's suit. The case was then carried on to the heights of the United States Supreme Court, where it was argued as *Robertson v. Baldwin* on grounds that the arrest of the four seamen and forcible prevention from breaking their contract constituted involuntary servitude, and decided in January 1897.

Ultimately, the majority opinion of the Supreme Court also ruled against the *Arago* seamen, siding with U.S. Marshal Barry Baldwin, who had taken the seamen into custody in Astoria. Specifically, the Court rejected the claim that the seamen's arrest constituted a violation of the clause of the Thirteenth Amendment abolishing involuntary servitude, arguing instead that merchant seamen constituted a type of worker that "from time immemorial been treated as exceptional," and that therefore "shall not be regarded as within [the Thirteenth Amendment's] purview."[2] Where did this exceptional status originate? Why were merchant seamen considered to be outside the purview of the protections of the Thirteenth Amendment thirty-two years after its passage? What did the *Arago* decision mean for larger claims of merchant seamen to the rights and privileges of U.S. citizenship, and by extension, the claims of other workers who labored on the margins of American society in 1897?

The ruling of the *Arago* seamen's case was based on an assumption of merchant seamen as having a status that was exceptional; the Court viewed them as alien social, cultural, and economic interlopers who paradoxically performed essential work in manning merchant ships and providing the lifeblood of U.S. maritime economic infrastructure. Further, the rhetorical classification of merchant seamen as inherently deficient or irresponsible members of society that philanthropic groups employed to justify their own projects throughout the nineteenth century also proved useful for U.S. officials ranging from local marshals to the U.S. Supreme Court in justifying the extreme legal marginalization and exclusion imposed upon this special class of workers.

Merchant seamen's assertion of liberty in the form of desertion was at the core of these confrontations. Seamen's effort to assert control over their labor through desertion posed a threat to prevailing ideologies of U.S. political economy and the stability of maritime commerce. In response, the judicial system adopted a strategy of infiltration, cooptation, and control, paralleling the methods of nineteenth-century maritime reformers described in Chap. 1. The initial arrest and prolonged imprisonment of the *Arago* seamen represented a direct attack on the seamen's use of desertion. The Court then rhetorically subsumed merchant seamen as wards of the state in order to justify their exclusion from the Thirteenth Amendment. Finally, the decision rendered by the Supreme Court in 1897 against the *Arago* seamen set a legal precedent for the absolute power of masters and mates over their crews, thereby empowering a rash of employers in industries dependent on other classes of marginalized workers to exert similar control and to test the limits of their newly won powers.

Legal History, Labor History, and Merchant Seamen

Robertson v. Baldwin was a key Supreme Court ruling regarding U.S. citizenship at the turn of the twentieth century. The *Arago* case served as a testing ground for the Supreme Court to determine the very nature of contract labor under the protections of the Thirteenth Amendment, the significance of which was reflected by the case's nickname as the "Second Dred Scott Decision" among the SUP and others sympathetic to the case's plaintiffs.[3] In delivering its decision against the *Arago* seamen, the Court bestowed a belated definition on the parameters of the Thirteenth Amendment, thereby shaping the increasingly restrictive nature of American contract labor that developed during the so-called Lochner Era. During this era, the Court delivered a string of rulings against workers and in favor of business based on an interpretation of substantive due process, a concept guaranteed by the Fifth and Fourteenth Amendments that entitles people (a category to which corporations officially belonged) freedom from governmental deprivation of "life, liberty, or property" without due process of the law. Cases during the Lochner Era were likely to be judged based on an interpretation of regulatory laws as interfering with individual economic liberty and freedom of contract. While the Lochner Era is considered to have begun with *Lochner v. New York* in 1905, in which the Supreme Court invalidated a New York state law that set a maximum number of hours bakers were allowed to work on the basis of freedom of contract, it could logically be extended backward to January 1897 to include *Robertson v. Baldwin* as a precedent-setting case that allowed for later decisions ruling against laborers working under contracts.[4]

This chapter has three primary objectives. First, it seeks to resurface *Robertson v. Baldwin* as a landmark case in the history of American labor and citizenship. Where the case has been covered by historians, it is given cursory attention as one example among many used to support a larger thesis external to the specifics of the *Arago* case itself.[5] Oddly, the case appears most frequently in legal history as a useful precedent for modern interpretations of the Second Amendment related to the right to carry a concealed weapon.[6] This tangential treatment of the case misses the essential fact that in *Robertson v. Baldwin*, the Supreme Court for the first time offered a concrete definition of involuntary servitude following the Thirteenth Amendment. The following pages take this fact as the case's primary significance and seek to center the maritime context and maritime implications of the case.

Second, in surveying the existing historiography relevant to the *Arago* case, this chapter seeks to bridge the scholarship of maritime historians with that of legal and labor scholars who study transitions in ideology regarding American contract labor from emancipation into the early twentieth century. In so doing, it becomes evident that there is substantial territory shared across seemingly disparate fields, the end product of which will be a more comprehensive view of what may appear at first an isolated incident.

Third, this chapter breaks with maritime historians who have ignored or dismissed the archives of maritime ministry organizations, such as the American Seamen's Friend Society and the Seamen's Church Institute of New York, based on a misguided view that their patronizing rhetoric and ideological biases render them useless for reconstructing the experiences of merchant seamen.[7] On the contrary, the analysis of this patronizing rhetoric provides essential insights into how the state and the philanthropic sector both curtailed freedom while constructing that curtailment as protection.

Materially, the *Arago* case centered on a deceptively simple legal question: do the masters of ships have the right to enforce shipping articles by use of penal sanctions? Put another way: can a seaman be arrested for breaking his contract? Despite such a plainly stated premise, by the time the Supreme Court finally issued an opinion on January 25, 1897, it was clear that the case had implications far beyond the immediate fate of the four seamen who had deserted the *Arago* in Oregon in 1895. *Robertson v. Baldwin* represented a culminating point for a free labor ideology that by 1897 had been reduced to a simple but increasingly absolute adherence to freedom of contract. It ushered in a period of American labor law history in which an increasingly laissez-faire economic ideology reduced the concept of freedom to an adamant insistence on individual property rights, either to be upheld absolutely in the case of corporations and employers, or, enforced individually through the protection of the right to contract out one's labor without limit.[8]

Where exactly the individual laborer fit within this system had been partially resolved by the Thirteenth Amendment, which outlawed slavery and involuntary servitude, but left the definition of the latter concept unstated. After thirty-two years of labor structured by coercive contracts enacted on Southern plantations and pockets of Northern industry, the *Arago* decision ultimately served as the vehicle through which the Supreme Court finally put forth a working definition of involuntary servitude that could be used to evaluate the legality of certain contracts that tested the limits of the Thirteenth Amendment's protections. The *Arago* case marked a transition from Reconstruction-era conceptions of free labor shaped by government intervention to an increasingly draconian system that insisted on absolute freedom of contract up to the point of self-enslavement. At the end of the nineteenth century, this transition produced a dominant economic ideology that had become adamantly anti-paternalistic, viewing "wards" with increasingly hostile suspicion, whether they be freedmen, American Indians, or merchant seamen, as "unnatural" hindrances to the "natural" machinations of free trade dependent on absolute adherence to freedom of contract.[9] The *Arago* decision would go on to shape the nature of contract labor in the rural South, industrial North, and as far away as Hawaii, where debates over annexation hinged on the central question of whether the *Arago* decision validated Hawaii's existing system of indentured labor. Situating the *Arago* decision within the legal and labor historiography of the nation's transition into a postbellum economy based on abstracted conceptions of free labor demonstrates its transformative effect on maritime labor specifically, but also American labor more broadly.

Merchant seamen were a logical sector of the nineteenth-century labor force through which to bring these issues to high-profile attention and debate. Having long been considered wards, whether of the British admiralty courts or the United States federal government, merchant seamen were consistently subjected to extraordinary forms of restriction and control under U.S. law, ostensibly with the justification that seamen represented morally underdeveloped, irresponsible citizens who required the guardianship of the government.[10] In addition to affording seamen special protections under U.S. law, this justification also provided a convenient means of protection for the commercial interests of shipowners and the growing network of investors, businessmen, and consumers who depended on a consistent merchant shipping industry in order to keep the emerging national system of capital flowing.[11]

Since the nation's founding, the merchant marine had held a central importance in relation to the health of American capital, and by extension, the United States' position on the global political stage. As a result of its significance, the merchant marine represented an early testing ground for the young federal judiciary to determine the boundaries and definition of labor rights and citizenship in the Early Republic. As Matthew Raffety argues, merchant seamen during the Early Republic were a particularly litigious group of laborers, frequently bringing grievances against their employers to local courts in port towns.[12] In addition, Marcus Rediker has documented the extralegal tactics such as work stoppages, slow-downs, desertion, mutiny, and piracy that seamen used to reassert control over their labor.[13] Seamen were at the vanguard of the negotiation of the power dynamics of an emerging wage labor system; they put pressure on the nation's inchoate conceptions of citizenship, forcing the federal judiciary to take a definitive stance in response to British impressment of American merchant seamen into the British Navy during the years leading up to the War of 1812.[14]

Within the decision of the federal judiciary, as well as the reactions of the reformers, labor activists, and newspaper reporters who responded to the *Arago* decision, there existed a shared central irony that hinged on the merchant seaman's longstanding classification as a "ward" of both benevolent society and the federal government: within the rhetoric of reform, activists seeking to repeal the *Arago* decision perpetuated this ward status as they simultaneously attempted to change the legal system that that same status had created. Similarly, the federal judiciary attempted to justify extraordinary restriction and control of merchant mariners as a form of freedom of contract, while simultaneously arguing that seamen were naturally inferior citizens who therefore required the government's oversight.

Exploring the origins and manifestations of this central irony explains why merchant seamen found themselves excluded from the protections of the U.S. Constitution as late as 1897, where that exclusion originated within the historical context of U.S. labor during the second half of the nineteenth century, and what effect that exclusion had on merchant seamen's status as U.S. citizens at the turn of the twentieth century.

Desertion and Mobility in "Pirate City"

When the *Arago* seamen deserted their vessel in Astoria, Oregon, they were participating in a long tradition of illegal mobility practiced by seamen to maintain relative control over the terms and conditions of their employment. As Marcus Rediker argues, seamen were among the world's first wage laborers. Across the Atlantic Ocean, which served as a primary zone of exchange within a mercantilist, and later, industrial capitalist global economy, merchant seamen embodied an essential component of free trade. Contractual agreements in the form of shipping articles served to guarantee exchanges of labor, a formal system that replaced earlier, more informal, localized, and social forms of labor exchange. The formality of contracts became necessary due to the extreme conditions of seafaring labor in combination with the singular importance of maritime commerce within the global economy. This transition into the "contested negotiation of wage work" necessitated a strategy of "creative survival" among seamen, who were frequently subjected to oppressive conditions and violence on ships.[15] The authority of mates and captains was countered by seamen with extralegal tactics of resistance, including mutiny, piracy, and desertion.[16]

Desertion, in particular, became a manifestation of the contested power dynamics that the contractual labor system introduced to merchant shipping. While seamen deserted their vessels for many reasons, it was always an action that subverted the power of captains and mates who held authority over them, and it often functioned as a means for a seaman to reclaim control over his own mobility within an increasingly restrictive labor system. In studying the port city of Salem, Massachusetts, Daniel Vickers documents a corollary between rising desertion rates alongside the development of an increasingly industrialized maritime shipping industry. Vickers found that a total of just three percent of seamen deserted on voyages in which Salem was the port of origin between 1726 and 1800, while that number increased to twenty-two percent between 1801 and 1825 and thirty-three percent between 1826 and 1850. As Vickers concludes, "It is hard to imagine that this rising incidence of desertion did not reflect something real that was changing in the quality of working life on board Salem vessels during the first half of the nineteenth century."[17] As the advent of steam engines in the early nineteenth century enabled larger cargoes and longer voyages, Salem transformed from localized port of origin to port of call within a globalized market, with maritime labor increasingly de-centered within urban social and cultural geographies, experienced by seamen and perceived by city dwellers as a "marginal activity, even within the seaports it supported."[18]

When the *Arago* seamen opted to desert in Astoria, they were first and foremost electing to end their contractual relationship with the ship, and by extension, its captain, whom the sailors claimed had been abusive towards the crew. Astoria's sailortown, despite its notorious reputation as a den of vice and danger, also represented a safe haven for the *Arago* deserters. Had Capt. Perry not reacted with such vigor to the seamen's actions, the *Arago* deserters would have been free to navigate the intricacies of Astoria's maritime labor market from within a network of recruitment was centered in sailors' boardinghouses and negotiated through word-of-mouth and other informal channels of information exchange. If the *Arago* deserters had followed a typical pattern, they would have most likely spent some time and money ashore, and after several days or even weeks, decided to sign on with one of many ships waiting in the busy port city eager to hire seamen, preferably under conditions more favorable than their last ship.

It was this contrast between a sailortown's reputation for bad behavior and corruption on the one hand, and its inherent usefulness for merchant seamen attempting to maintain control over the terms of their own labor on the other that reformers, politicians, and the courts found so baffling. Astoria, indeed, was a town with no shortage of nefarious characters and tales of criminality. Described by one memoirist as "the pirate city by the sea,"[19] Astoria had gained worldwide attention by the 1890s for its elaborate systems of shanghaiing. Many anecdotes survive of visitors from out-of-town being approached by friendly ship "owners" and being offered a "tour" of a ship docked in port, only to discover the phony owner gone, and anchors being raised as the ship left port for a months-long voyage with the helpless tourists now enlisted as members of the crew. As long as the captain had procured signed ship's articles for each of his "crew," whether forged or otherwise coerced through the tactics of crimping, he was legally entitled to command their labor for the duration of the scheduled voyage. Often, this process involved crimps getting their victims drunk and tricking them into signing articles or accumulating debt that could only be paid off by going to sea and forfeiting wages. Waterfront saloons with trap doors and tunnel systems used to transport drunk or drugged seamen to ships-in-waiting feature prominently in the lore of crimping, especially in Astoria and nearby Portland. Sailors' boardinghouses were also often central sites for the crimping enterprise. James Turk ran boardinghouses in both cities and was rumored to have shanghaied his own son once for "blood money," usually a portion of the victim's advance, or a fee collected from the ship's recruiter. Bridget Grant, notorious boardinghouse keeper and crimp, was the matriarch of a family that made its entire business in Astoria's sailortown through a conglomerate of boardinghouses, saloons, and enterprises that were all dependent upon the seaman's patronage, whether voluntary or coerced.

Reformers and politicians seized upon spectacular accounts and characters engaged in the crimping economy to advance an agenda intended to "clean up" sailortowns and thereby stabilize the labor pool for maritime commerce. These reformers claimed to be helping seamen help themselves while ashore, but by targeting the economies of sailortown, they were also cutting off networks that frequently provided safe havens for merchant seamen on the move, constricting their ability to end bad contracts and negotiate new ones, and restricting their individual liberties as wage laborers in a maritime economy that was becoming increasingly exploitative of its labor pool. Desertion was an essential component in this system, and it is no coincidence that it was at the heart of the case of the *Arago*.

The Right to Desert

In most instances, ship captains would have shown little hesitation in replacing wayward crewmembers with idle seamen "on the beach," transiently inhabiting the world's sailortowns. In jumping ship, seamen forfeited any wages due to them, which benefited Captains and ship owners and made replacing deserters with new crewmembers far more economical than pursuing legal recourse. What made the *Arago* case exceptional was the vigor and persistence with which Capt. Perry pursued the four seamen who deserted his ship; not only originally in Astoria but subsequently en route to San Francisco, but again upon reaching port there, Capt. Perry had his men incarcerated and chose to pursue legal action to the fullest extent of the law. Yet the *Arago* seamen proved more than up to the Captain's challenge to their freedom.

Essential to the seamen's case was the support of the SUP, led by then-Secretary Andrew Furuseth. In a letter written to Furuseth from jail, Robert Robertson, who served as spokesperson for his fellow *Arago* seamen, complained that the ship's crew had been subjected to poor conditions while at sea and that their right to jump ship in search of alternatives had been violated by Captain Perry and the local officials at Astoria:

> The captain felt sure that he had us ... and on the trip he fed us on salt horse and bulldozed us. We went to him and told him that since we did not suit him, he had better pay us what was coming to us. This he refused to do, so we left him and our money at the first opportunity, and we are in prison as a result. What are we going to do about it?[20]

Desertion was an essential tool that seamen employed to counter poor conditions and treatment such as the "salt horse" diet and "bulldozing" physical abuse that Robertson accused Capt. Perry of imposing on his crew. While an effective defensive tactic for seamen, desertion was also illegal, and deserters had long been subject to arrest if they were caught and prosecuted, a fact dating back to the passage of the 1790 U.S. Merchant Marine Act. The act contained a clause that sanctioned the use of arrest to enforce shipping articles. The Merchant Marine Act was one of the first pieces of legislation passed by the First Congress of the United States, a testament to the priority Early Republican leaders placed on establishing a stable and secure merchant fleet. With the young nation desperate to assert itself within Atlantic trade markets and eager to assume a place on the global geopolitical stage, a robust and regulated merchant marine was essential.

The details of the Merchant Marine Act included a combination of clauses alternately aimed at protecting and coercing the labor of merchant seamen. This approach to regulating the merchant marine followed almost exactly the British model, which had long regarded mariners as "wards of the admiralty," entitled to certain protections from the government while simultaneously subjected to extraordinary regulatory measures based on a perception of their deficient character and considered appropriate based on the extraordinary conditions under which they worked.[21] Following this approach, the 1790 American legislation included protective stipulations that guaranteed a mate's right to request inspections of vessels, placed limits on the amount of debt that could be collected from a seaman on a given voyage, and established requirements for medical supplies to be carried on board, as well as setting a minimum number of seamen employed per a ship's given tonnage. Simultaneously, the 1790 Act established an equally formidable list of coercive measures, including mandated penalties for seamen who failed to report to a ship at the appointed time, penalties for harboring "fugitive seamen," and a 300 percent wage penalty for each day that a contracted seaman went missing from his ship. If a seaman was absent from his vessel for more than forty-eight hours, he forfeited his wages and any possessions that remained on board, in addition to being charged a fee meant to compensate the master of the ship for the expense of finding a replacement. Most significant in the case of the *Arago*, seamen could be arrested for refusing to sail on a ship deemed seaworthy after inspection, or if he deserted his vessel entirely. The master of a vessel had simply to demonstrate that a seaman had signed a contract in order to legally have him detained, at which point he would be held in prison until his vessel was ready to leave port when he would be forcibly escorted to the vessel and commanded to resume labor under threat of re-imprisonment.[22] This is exactly what happened to the four deserters in Astoria in 1895.

Both in concept and in language, the coercive clauses of the 1790 Merchant Marine Act that established penalties for desertion served as a direct model for the phrasing of the 1793 Fugitive Slave Act, a fact seized upon by Furuseth and the SUP in referring to the 1790 Act as the "Fugitive Sailor Law."[23] The text from the 1790 Act that addresses desertion is worth quoting here in its entirety:

> If any seaman who shall have signed a contract to perform a voyage shall, at any port or place, desert, or shall absent himself from such vessel, without leave of the master, or officer commanding in the absence of the master, it shall be lawful for any Justice of the Peace within the United States, upon the complaint of the master, to issue his warrant to apprehend such deserter, and bring him before such Justice; and if it then appears that he has signed a contract within the intent and meaning of this title, and that the voyage agreed for is not finished, or altered, or the contract otherwise dissolved,

> and that such seaman has deserted the vessel, or absented himself without leave, the Justice shall commit him to the House of Correction or common jail of the city, town or place, to remain there until the vessel shall be ready to proceed on her voyage, or till the master shall require his discharge, and then to be delivered to the master, he paying all the costs of such commitment, and deducting the same out of the wages due to such seaman.[24]

Although desertion was technically illegal throughout the nineteenth century, seamen encountered varying levels of enforcement depending on the time and place of their actions. As Richard B. Morris has demonstrated using the port of Baltimore as a case study, the use of penal sanctions to enforce shipping articles was a fairly common practice there throughout the mid-nineteenth century, but decidedly less common during the years leading up to the *Arago* case.[25] In mining the Baltimore municipal archives, Morris found 708 cases of seamen detained for desertion in that city alone between 1861 and 1893, when the city stopped keeping such records. Only seventy-six of those cases occurred between the years 1880 and 1893, with no cases at all occurring in 1885, 1888, 1890, and 1891. Morris attributes this reduction to the general decline of the American merchant marine over the course of the nineteenth century. The statistics support Morris' interpretation. During the 1830s, U.S. merchant ships carried ninety percent of international cargo out of American ports. By 1860, that number had fallen to fifty percent; by 1890 it was nine percent, with the British making inverse gains in the percentage of the world's maritime commerce they carried during those same years.[26] Due to such a drastic reduction in the American merchant fleet, instances of the use of penal sanctions to enforce shipping articles had become increasingly rare by 1895, especially in relatively new ports outside of the Northeastern U.S. Furuseth's biographer Hyman G. Weintraub corroborates this trend: writing about the arrest of the *Arago* deserters in Astoria, Weintraub observed that "seamen had long realized that … owners had the legal right to take such action, but in practice it had not happened within the memory of any of the coasting sailors … The actual arrest of a deserter shocked the [SUP]."[27] By combining Morris' data from Baltimore jails with Weintraub's anecdotal evidence, it is reasonable to assume that the use of penal sanctions against merchant seamen who broke shipping articles was rare in the port towns of the Pacific Coast by 1895.

The declining number of deserting seamen who found themselves imprisoned was due not least to the Maguire Act of 1895.[28] Sponsored by Rep. James G. Maguire of San Francisco, and long a priority of the SUP, the bill abolished the use of penal sanctions to enforce shipping articles on coastwise journeys. Shipowners and others with a financial stake in the administration of maritime commerce overwhelmingly protested the bill, denouncing it as "arbitrary and unjust," "communistic and subversive of discipline," and bemoaning the "premium" that it placed on desertion, language typical of the laissez-faire absolutism that privileged an abstracted and "natural" free market system devoid of "unnatural" interferences.[29] In the face of such opposition, the bill's passage in February 1895 was a testament to the growing strength of the SUP and its political supporters. Despite the significant victory for seamen's rights advocates, the Maguire Act contained substantial loopholes that left seamen vulnerable to disciplinary action that the Act intended to eliminate. First, the bill's protections were worded vaguely enough to allow for creative interpretations by certain masters and shipowners. Second, the lack of any central body capable or willing to enforce the law left such enforcement to the seamen themselves and their representatives.[30]

Largely a product of the malleability of the Maguire Act, the initial historical significance of the *Arago* case was in the challenge it posed to the recently passed law. In his letter to Furuseth, seaman Robertson claimed that when he and his fellow deserters were brought before the local shipping commissioner in Astoria, Robertson cited the Maguire Act as the reason for the legitimacy of their actions. According to Robertson, the shipping commissioner claimed that he had never heard of the Maguire Act. Upon having its contents explained to him, the commissioner declared that it did not apply to the *Arago* case because the seamen had signed articles for a trip that included a stop in Valparaiso, Chile, thus rendering it exempt from the protections that the Act afforded seamen on coastwise journeys.[31] The shipping commissioner's on-the-spot response to Robertson's invocation of the Maguire Act proved durable, as his opinion was repeated in the District Court of Northern California's rejection of the seamen's suit.

Having deserted in June 1895, the *Arago* seamen were forcibly escorted back to their ship after spending sixteen days in an Astoria prison, and arrested again on July 7 at San Francisco. On the evening before their trial before U.S. Commissioner Heacock, officers of the SUP convened to come up with a strategy of defense to present the following day on behalf of the seamen, who were being held at the Alameda jail. An article in the *San Francisco Call* quotes Furuseth as saying that "it was a question whether seamen could be forced into involuntary servitude in the coast trade or be permitted to choose their own ships and masters."[32] Such a statement suggests that Furuseth and the SUP were already formulating an argument challenging the parameters of involuntary servitude that would take the case to the Supreme Court.

The significance of the *Arago* case was apparent to both parties and onlookers from the beginning of the trial process. One account published in the *San Francisco Call* a week after the trial referred to it as "[o]ne of the most far-reaching legal battles ever instituted in the United States circuit court."[33] A different article in the *Call* described the large public crowd that had gathered in the San Francisco courtroom to hear the *Arago* seamen's defense, including "both ship-owners and sailors, and quite a number of skippers ... as the question to be decided is almost of as vital importance to them as to the owners and sailors."[34] The author of the same article, which appeared the day after the trial, had a keen sense of what exactly was at stake in the ruling: "Should it be decided that sailors have a right to [quit] work after having signed for a voyage it will take from the ship-owners their most effective weapon in fighting the Sailors' Union, and also in its engaging deep-water sailors."[35] Harkening back to shipowners' objections to the proposed Maguire Act, the *Arago* seamen's case put before the District Court of Northern California posed the same challenge to shipowners' control over a seaman's labor that the 1895 law did. If a seaman was allowed to break his contract without facing imprisonment, he would retain a new entitlement to legal mobility that could be used against his employers. This process of negotiating control between shipowners, captains and mates, and the seamen under their command had been taking place since the advent of wage labor on ships, albeit under informal and explicitly illegal circumstances.[36] Should the *Arago* seamen's challenge to the legality of penal sanctions have proven successful, they and their fellow seamen would be granted new legitimacy and legal rights in pursuing control over the terms and nature of their own labor.

The seamen's central argument focused on the nature of their exceptional status under U.S. labor law. As argued in court, a ruling in favor of the seamen would grant them the same right to quit work without facing penalties other than a loss of wages that other free laborers had long possessed.[37] As the Los Angeles *Herald* described it, the seamen were challenging their imprisonment based on the fact "that it is an unlawful discrimination against one class of the population–since men in other gainful occupations cannot be imprisoned, fined, impressed and coerced into service for failure to comply with their contracts."[38] The same article describes the argument put forward by the side of the shipowners: essentially, without such extraordinary measures of regulation and control over a seaman's labor, the entire enterprise of merchant shipping would quickly descend into a spiral of terrifying ineffectiveness resembling "Byron's Dream of Darkness, wherein ships, sailorless, rotting on the seas, would soon be realized; that the American flag would soon be driven from the sea in the era of chaos and pandemonium that would ensue."[39] Such fantastic rhetoric is indicative of the seriousness of the threat that the *Arago* deserters posed to the established order of a disciplined, profitable U.S. merchant marine.

With little judicial fanfare, the shipowners won the first battle at the District Court level. The *Arago* seamen quickly appealed and honed their argument to focus on the assertion that a violation of habeas corpus had occurred, claiming that they were put on board the *Arago* in Astoria against their will and had a right to refuse to work on the way to San Francisco. With attorney H.W. Hutton representing the seamen before Judge Morrow, the seamen called upon the Judge's sense of American freedom, arguing that a law allowing for the arrest of seamen who deserted their ship was "an arbitrary one, and deprives men of their liberty. In that respect it is not an American law and should not be recognized in American courts." Identifying themselves with other free laborers who populated the postbellum industrial labor system, the seamen contested that "Congress had no more right to make laws to punish sailors for violating their civil contracts than it has to punish tradesmen who refuse to carry out their agreements." In the end, Judge Morrow was not persuaded. While he allowed that the seamen were American citizens, and therefore entitled to certain rights, he concluded, "[t]he fact remains ... that there is a vast difference between land laws and sea laws. The latter have never been properly defined, and they may never be." With that, he ruled against the *Arago* seamen and proceeded to launch into "a classical dissertation about the days of ancient Greece and Rome to carry out his points."[40]

The *Arago* seamen were far from finished, however. In the days following the trial, it had become clear that their case had outgrown the limitations of the District Court of Northern California. Before Judge Morrow had even delivered his decision, the Los Angeles *Herald* predicted that "[t]he contest will be speedily carried to the Supreme Court of the United

States."[41] The case of the *Arago* deserters touched on essential questions with potentially broad implications for all marginalized American laborers in 1895: what exactly did the Thirteenth Amendment protect against, and who exactly did it protect? And what did involuntary servitude mean as invoked in the Thirteenth Amendment? The Supreme Court was in a position to deliver answers to these questions when the *Arago* decision was brought before it as *Robertson v. Baldwin*.

Robertson v. Baldwin

The *Arago* seamen and their legal counsel waited the better part of 1896 before receiving an opportunity to argue their case before the highest court in the nation. During that time, the seamen's case had been expanded beyond the particularities of the Maguire Act to focus primarily on the claim that their imprisonment for breach of contract constituted a violation of the Thirteenth Amendment's abolition of involuntary servitude. On January 25, 1897, the Court delivered its opinion, ruling against the seamen and upholding the decision of the District Court of Northern California. Justice Brown wrote the majority opinion, taking the issue at hand as an opportunity to express the majority's interpretation of the Thirteenth Amendment, which he argued "depends upon the construction to be given to the term 'involuntary servitude'... [d]oes the epithet 'involuntary' attach to the word 'servitude' continuously, and make illegal any service which becomes involuntary at any time during its existence; or does it attach only at the inception of the servitude, and characterize it as unlawful because unlawfully entered into?"

Brown ultimately sided with the latter interpretation, arguing that a contract lawfully entered into can never be considered unlawful and insisting that such an interpretation ensured the viability of forms of essential servitude that would otherwise be undermined by an unrestricted right to abandon contractual obligations. Brown identified such essential labor as that of a soldier at war or a merchant seaman aboard a vessel, who Brown worried might be inclined to "abandon his ship at any intermediate port or landing, or even in a storm at sea." Putting aside how useful an option of voluntarily abandoning ship during a storm at sea would be, Brown made clear that he and the majority sided with freedom of contract over freedom of person, but seemingly only as applied to some classes of laborers. But while freedom of contract served to override the seamen's claim to have been subjected to involuntary servitude, the use of penal sanctions to enforce their contracts was another matter:

> The breach of a contract for a personal service has not, however, been recognized in this country as involving a liability to criminal punishment, except in the cases of soldiers, sailors, and possibly some others, nor would public opinion tolerate a statute to that effect.

Brown's statement suggests that while "public opinion" would not tolerate the use of penal sanctions in enforcing the contracts of ordinary workers, their use in holding soldiers, sailors, "and possibly some others" to the terms of their labor agreements would indeed be appropriate. In approving the use of penal sanctions to enforce contracts on certain classes of laborers, Brown and the Court majority were in step with the devolution of nineteenth-century free labor ideology, the strength of which had propelled the nation into the Civil War, through the pangs of Reconstruction, and into the Gilded Age of capitalism in which the *Arago* decision was delivered. The dramatic devolution of Reconstruction was indicative of a more widespread constriction of free labor ideology that retreated into a narrowly conceived adherence to freedom of property on which the legitimacy of labor systems would be evaluated through the first decade of the twentieth century. Within this system, an individual's labor was considered to be his own property, and said individual had the exclusive right to contract out that property under his own terms, free from external interventions.[42] With this trajectory in mind, *Robertson v. Baldwin* was a harbinger of the so-called Lochner Era of the Court. Given this timeline, the *Arago* case proved to be a testing ground for the Court to outline principles regarding freedom of contract that would guide their decisions well into the 1930s.

Brown and the Court majority's next task was to justify the classification of merchant seamen as an exceptional class of laborers to which penal sanctions could be appropriately applied. Whereas the majority claimed that "public opinion would not tolerate" similar methods of contract enforcement as applied to other laborers, seamen were exempt from such considerations. To support his claim, Brown offered the following:

> From the earliest historical period the contract of the sailor has been treated as an exceptional one, and involving, to a certain extent, the surrender of his personal liberty during the life of the contract. Indeed, the business of

> navigation could scarcely be carried on without some [guarantee], beyond the ordinary civil remedies upon contract, that the sailor will not desert the ship at a critical moment, or leave her at some place where seamen are impossible to be obtained—as Molloy forcibly expresses it, 'to rot in her neglected brine.' Such desertion might involve a long delay of the vessel while the master is seeking another crew, an abandonment of the voyage, and, in some cases, the safety of the ship itself. Hence, the laws of nearly all maritime nations have made provision for securing the personal attendance of the crew on board, and for their criminal punishment for desertion, or absence without leave during the life of the shipping articles.

As precedent, Brown reached far back in time, offering the Ancient Rhodians, the fifteenth-century Catalonian Consulate of the Sea, the twelfth-century Rules of Oléron, the Horseatic League of 1597, and the Maritime Ordinance of Louis XIV as examples of laws put in place to keep seamen from deserting their vessels. But was it always as simple a motivating factor as maintaining the safety of vessels at sea that was behind this lineage of coercive laws? Brown's concluding paragraph suggests otherwise:

> Indeed, seamen are treated by Congress, as well as by the Parliament of Great Britain, as deficient in that full and intelligent responsibility for their acts which is accredited to ordinary adults, and as needing the protection of their parents and guardians ... The ancient characterization of seamen as "wards of admiralty" is even more accurate now than it was formerly.

In addition to his inventory of ancient precedents, Brown could have produced an equally impressive list in which the consensus opinion among men of both the state and the public reflected a shared perception that seamen were indeed deficient in character, and therefore entitled to unique status as wards under U.S. law.[43] Merchant seamen had long been considered unique citizens under the law of various countries, the United States being no exception. Amplifying this perception, merchant seamen had grown increasingly foreign over the course of the nineteenth century, both in a national and a cultural sense, as the industrialization of the American maritime shipping industry changed the nature and character of its labor systems.

Surveying the work of maritime historians regarding these issues gives additional weight to Brown's concluding passage and suggests that this other-ness of American merchant seamen, who by 1897 had been pushed to the extreme margins of respectable society and acceptable forms of contract labor, may have accounted more for their exceptional status under U.S. law than any other factor. Other appeals made by the Court to the imperatives of maintaining stability and safety on merchant ships were tertiary to larger, more potent realities of the threat that merchant seamen, empowered with the right to desert their vessels, would pose to maritime commerce, and by extension national economic prosperity and the projection of naval power internationally.

The Court's decision in *Robertson v. Baldwin* had immediate and far-reaching consequences for other workers at the margins of American society in 1897. Returning to Richard B. Morris' study, the 708 cases that he unearthed from Baltimore city jail records in which merchant seamen were arrested for desertion between 1861 and 1893 indicate that the use of penal sanctions to enforce seamen's contracts not only persisted, but at least in the instance of Baltimore, thrived in the years following the ratification of the Thirteenth Amendment, leading Morris to conclude that "emancipation and the Thirteenth Amendment did not end legal pressure for the specific performance of labor contracts," in fact, "the Baltimore jail records are proof of the fact that the last 'slaves' to be emancipated were the seamen of all races and nationalities."[44] While Morris clearly overstates his point in comparing merchant seamen to chattel slaves, he presciently gestures toward a more useful interrogation of the effectiveness in using emancipation as the point at which truly "free" labor replaced various forms of "unfree" labor systems that thrived prior to the Civil War.

Robert J. Steinfeld seeks to complicate this understanding of the creation of modern free labor, arguing that all exceptions within the so-called free labor market following emancipation and the Thirteenth Amendment—such as black peonage, "coolie" labor, and merchant seamen—were products of a failure to resolve a fundamental contradiction that existed within contemporary liberalism's commitment to "freedom," consisting of competing adherences to liberty of person and liberty of contract. *Robertson v. Baldwin* clarified the legal parameters of the labor market for marginal workers by coming down definitively on the side of liberty of contract. As Steinfeld concludes, "[f]or more than a decade Southerners had passed legislation to penally enforce labor contracts, but rarely had this legislation punished contract breaches directly. More often, subtle subterfuges were used ... Under the logic of *Robertson v. Baldwin*, such subtlety would be unnecessary."[45]

Within the new rules established by *Robertson v. Baldwin*, the Supreme Court entered a prelude to the Lochner Era, demonstrating a sustained anti-paternalist approach to the judiciary that adhered to an increasingly laissez-faire political economy that privileged freedom of contract as a remedy to the supposedly corrosive social impact of wardship. During this period, the Supreme Court expanded its powers by placing itself in the position of "paternalistic patriarchs," enacting a paradox that embraced extraordinary regulation, control, and restriction enforced in the name of anti-paternalist freedom of contract while the Court simultaneously took it upon itself to provide special protections to those designated as wards, such as women and children laborers, American Indians, and merchant seamen, who in Justice Brown's phrasing, were in need of protection "against the consequences of their own ignorance and improvidence."[46]

This fundamental paradox was prevalent not just in the courts of the United States in 1897 but also among the general public from whom opinion was generated and distributed. Examining the rhetoric of the press, labor unions, and maritime ministry organizations in the wake of the Supreme Court's decision illuminates the process described by Steinfeld as the "moral resolution of fundamental conflicts within liberalism" by attempting to document the "political events and moral standards" involved in the *Arago* case and its aftermath. It becomes evident that the paradox of paternalism did not exist solely at the state or federal level but also included actors from all sections of society. Only through the resolution of said paradox in the public arena would the status of merchant seamen under U.S. law come to be reformed.

Reaction

Looking back on the *Arago* decision in his memoirs, Rev. Archibald R. R. Mansfield, first Superintendent of the Seamen's Church Institute of New York (SCI), recalled his bafflement upon hearing the decision of the Supreme Court: "[the] judicial logic made it clear to the public that there existed a class of men who had to work no matter how they were treated, that their contract carried no implication of decent treatment, but that arbitrary bad treatment was merely a sort of occupational risk which their contract obliged them to assume."[47] Mansfield was not alone in his reaction to the decision. Newspapers from every corner of the nation ran articles detailing the case, many with strong editorial commentary condemning the Court's decision and speculating as to its potential implications. As Mansfield wrote, the *Arago* decision "focused public attention on the matter at issue and precipitated all the humanitarian sentiment in the country in behalf of fair dealing with the sailor."

Surveying the nation's newspapers in the aftermath of *Robertson v. Baldwin* confirms that the interest and energies of the press had indeed been aroused. An article titled "An Important Decision" from the *Cook County Herald* of the Lake Superior port town Grand Marais, Minnesota, provides a typical example. Beginning with a detailed description of Justice Brown's majority opinion, the article then compares the case to the Dred Scott decision and the 1842 *Prigg v. the Commonwealth of Pennsylvania* decision, which interpreted the Fugitive Slave Law as overriding a Pennsylvania state law protecting Black individuals from being taken out of the state into slavery, claiming that the latter decision represented such a close model for *Robertson v. Baldwin* that if "the words 'fugitive sailor' be substituted for 'fugitive slave' ... it would exactly cover the present case." Evaluating the potential impact of the *Arago* decision, the article claimed that the Court's ruling could mean "that the [T]hirteenth [A]mendment of the constitution is wiped out completely."[48] An almost identical article ran in *The Broad Ax* of Salt Lake City, Utah, echoing comparisons to Dred Scott and *Prigg*, and lamenting the Court's apparent disregard for the Thirteenth Amendment, "savior and champion of personal rights and personal liberty, [which] declared to every citizen of the United States, I will make you free indeed. Surely the liberty of a citizen is more precious and sacred in the eyes of the law, than a private contract."[49] Similar articles summarizing the case ran in newspapers from Wichita, Kansas[50] and Omaha, Nebraska,[51] as well as Washington, D.C., San Francisco, Astoria, Seattle, and New York City.

Many reporters, as well as reformers and labor leaders, employed a version of antislavery rhetoric that focused on the opposition between freedom of contract and freedom of person central to the questions posed in the Salt Lake City *Broad Ax* article. Steinfeld identifies this opposition as the "fundamental conflict within liberalism" during the second half of the nineteenth century. By comparing the status of merchant seamen with that of slaves, these reactors to the *Arago* decision drew on a long tradition of antislavery sentiment, repurposing that tradition in order to inspire reform. Significantly, such comparisons were also explicitly situated within the context of Southern peonage labor, which took hold during Reconstruction and proliferated when the North restored "home rule" to former-Confederate states in 1877, abandoning prior direct interventions intended to restructure the labor systems of Southern plantations. An article in the *San Francisco Call* from May 1897 articulates this context in relation to the *Arago* decision, declaring that:

> [I]t is alarming to contemplate the extent to which contract slavery may be forced upon the landless laborers of the country, white as well as black … prompted by the plainest inducements of self-interest on the part of employers, to exclude such landless and therefore helpless and dependent laborers from employment until they shall be compelled by their privations to sign such contracts for personal servitude as will bind them for life or for long terms to the contract and dominion of individual masters.[52]

The persistence of such a racially defined framework of contract labor, informed directly by the nation's traumatic timeline of slave labor and emancipation, is indicative of the challenges that the *Arago* case posed to the viability of postbellum conceptualizations of freedom following the Thirteenth Amendment. The rhetoric of antislavery, a long and well-established tradition of dissent within nineteenth-century America, provided a framework within which opponents of the Supreme Court's decision could frame their criticism, revealing a consensus of expectations and an arsenal of rhetorical pressures that those critics forced on the state regarding the regulation of contract labor. In addition to editorializing news reporters, labor unions added their voices to the swelling opposition that spoke out against the *Robertson v. Baldwin* decision. Through pamphlets, letters, and convention speeches, labor leaders adopted an antislavery rhetoric similar to that found in the press that articulated the uniquely oppressed status of merchant seamen under U.S. law. Marchers at a parade in San Francisco to celebrate the twelfth anniversary of the SUP in December 1897 carried signs that made clear how seamen themselves interpreted the *Arago* decision. A sign displayed prominently at the front of the march plainly declared that "[t]he people are with us," and was followed by dozens more, including:

> The United States Supreme Court construes the laws;
> the people make them.
> We carry our case up
>
> In 1862 Lincoln proclaimed all persons free.
> In 1897 the United States Supreme Court declared the seaman a serf

In 1856 Dred Scott decision reversed by the people 1861-1865 In 1897
Arago decision
will be reversed by the people

and:

In 1790 fugitive sailor law passed In 1793 fugitive slave law passed.[53]

The reportage on these signs gives a rare archival glimpse into how *Robertson v. Baldwin* was processed by merchant seamen with boots on the ground in the early years of their labor organization. The similarities between the rhetoric they employed in the parade and the editorial musings of the nation's press suggest a pervasiveness of opposition that transcended class or social identity.

In addition to opposition on the street, the administrative bodies of the San Francisco Labor Council and the Central Labor Unions of New York, Brooklyn, and Washington, D.C., all held meetings in the months following the *Arago* decision, which was covered by the local press. Samuel Gompers himself attended meetings of the American Federation of Labor in Nashville and Kansas City, where the *Arago* decision was denounced, as did Eugene Debs at the Labor Leaders' Convention in St. Louis. Transcripts of speeches capture the heightened rhetoric used to rally solidarity among those in attendance and recall fiery condemnations of slavery that were common in the antebellum North. H. E. Highton addressed a raucous mass meeting at the Metropolitan Temple in San Francisco on February 2, 1897, amidst a band playing "inspiring airs" between speeches and a packed crowd that included Mayor Phelan. "The thought that an American sailor," Highton began, "should ever be called upon to carry in his mind the thought that at some time or some place his back was laid open by the lash of some petty tyrant rouses my blood almost to the point of revolution."[54] Highton was followed by several speakers who repeatedly impressed upon the crowd the need to "abolish [the] slavery of American sailors," with one speaker reflecting that "this country had fought out the question of slavery of the black man and had set him free. That white men should be held in bondage in this same fair land [is] a circumstance not to be longer tolerated." James H. Barry concluded the meeting by lamenting the persistence of "chattel slavery" in the United States, insisting that "[slavery] does exist, but, by the great Jehovah, it shall be abolished," before launching into an extended critique of the Supreme Court.[55]

Andrew Furuseth made a trip to Washington, D.C. in January 1898 to lobby before Congress on behalf of the *Arago* seamen. In an article in the *San Francisco Call* documenting the trip, Furuseth is quoted as saying that "the imprisonment of a sailor for violation of a civil contract is a species of slave labor and is a relic of barbarism," a sentiment that was echoed in an elaborate pamphlet printed by the SUP that credited Furuseth as its author. The cover of the pamphlet is divided into two halves, its left side titled "THIS IS THE FUGITIVE SAILOR LAW ENACTED 1790," with an excerpt from the 1790 U.S. Merchant Marine Act pertaining to the use of imprisonment to enforce desertion printed below. The right side is titled "THIS WAS THE FUGITIVE SLAVE LAW ENACTED 1793," followed by an excerpt from that law pertaining to the return of fugitive slaves. Below the excerpt, Furuseth interjects: "[the Fugitive Slave Law] is supposed to have been made void by the Thirteenth Amendment to the Constitution of the United States. In view of the Supreme Court decision in 'Robert Robertson et al. vs. Barry Baldwin,' January 25, 1897, IS IT VOID?"[56]

Furuseth's provocative question gets to the essence of what motivated the overwhelming outrage and apprehensiveness with which *Robertson v. Baldwin* was met among news reporters and union leaders. In excluding certain citizens from the protections of the Thirteenth Amendment, the Supreme Court opened old wounds left by moral debates over slavery leading up to the Civil War. That war had seemingly resolved the issue once and for all. But in the wake of *Robertson v. Baldwin*, those with a particular interest in the case, as well as the public at large, were left to question how much had, in fact, been left open to interpretation.

Maritime reformers played an essential role in the interpretation of the *Arago* decision and the mobilization of moral capital and legislative negotiation required to temper the scope of its impact. On December 30, 1896, the Joint Conference for the Protection of Seamen, a consortium of seamen's missions and maritime law practitioners that included representatives from the American Seamen's Friend Society (ASFS) and the Seamen's Church Institute of New York (SCI), was founded under the leadership of SCI administrators J. Augustus Johnson and Rev. Archibald R. R. Mansfield. The first issue facing the Joint Conference was the fate of the *Arago* seamen.

In studying the records of ASFS and SCI, the motivations and logic behind missionaries' efforts at reforming the legal status of seamen provide crucial insights into the popular perception of American merchant seamen in the late nineteenth century. Maritime reformers approached the "problem" of seamen's marginal status in ways that reaffirmed powerful stereotypes classifying seamen as morally deficient citizens who were consequently at the mercy of abusive captains and mates at sea and unscrupulous middlemen ashore. This process of othering marginalized seamen socially, culturally, and geographically on land made possible and reinforced abusive cycles of labor at sea and exploitation during time spent ashore that maritime missionaries bemoaned and were dedicated to reforming. Maritime missionaries offered strategies of reform that focused on a mixture of evangelical Christian conversion and legal advocacy, targeting the laws that empowered and protected those who made their business exploiting seamen. The paradoxical rhetoric employed by reformers on behalf of seamen was often naïve in its approach to solving the problems that merchant seamen faced at the close of the nineteenth century, but just as often those same reformers evinced a deep understanding of the legal system they were attempting to reform, and a shrewd ability to manipulate legislatures to accomplish certain goals. Studying the implementation of this rhetoric leading up to and immediately following *Robertson v. Baldwin* provides insight into the contradictions that subjected merchant seamen to extraordinary treatment under U.S. law and produced motivations for reform of that same treatment in legislative victories of 1898 and 1915.

With the *Arago* decision fresh in the minds of both the members of the Joint Conference and the public at large, the Joint Conference chose to put forward an agenda that prioritized neutralizing the waterfront's crimps at the expense of pursuing a full achievement of seamen's rights. Tellingly, the Conference made two crucial compromises during the legislative process of a bill that would eventually become the White Act of 1898, revealing the limitations of their own powers in regard to reforming the status of merchant seamen under U.S. law. Furuseth and the SUP had pushed legislation aggressively in the months following *Robertson v. Baldwin*, enlisting the support of Senator Stephen White of California in drafting a bill that would extend the provisions of the Maguire Act of 1895 by establishing legal protections for seamen who deserted their vessels on coastwise journeys, among several other provisions. In reviewing the proposed bill, the Joint Conference decided to submit their recommendations to the New York City Marine Association, an organization of businessmen involved in the city's maritime commerce industry. The Association advised the Joint Conference to back down on the bill's strict abolishment of wage allotments, the common practice of strategic withholding of wages earned by seamen to be distributed at strictly defined stages in the course of a given voyage, arguing that such a clause could prove damaging to the city's shipping industry. As Mansfield explains, "They remembered the experience of owners and captains in 1884, when allotments were abolished, except to relatives, and the crimps struck back by tying up the whole port. With this in mind, the Association was naturally not in favor of any measure that was in any way likely to jeopardize shipping, even temporarily, and it was convinced that regulation of allotments would not work any better in 1897 than it did in 1884."[57] The abolition of allotments was a key issue for the SUP, and the Joint Conference's acquiescence to the Marine Association's recommendation widened a rift between the union and maritime ministry organizations that would persist well into the twentieth century. Looking back on the decision years later, Mansfield expressed regret for giving the union reason to distrust the Joint Conference:

> It was just the kind of thing to confirm Furuseth and the seamen's union in their suspicions. For their own part, they were not interested in any compromise, but they were not as yet strong enough to carry both measures through. The first bill passed, but the more important second bill, with its provisions about shipping agents and allotments, was held over to the next session. We lost a chance there, for with the support of the Joint Conference it would no doubt have passed.[58]

The rift with Furuseth's union was compounded by the Conference's decision to leave language regarding the legality of imprisoning seamen as punishment for desertion vague enough so as to be left to the inclinations of local courts. Mansfield attributed this decision to the necessity of compromising on some points in order to get the larger bill, with its many other provisions, passed.[59] Regardless, the fact that the Joint Conference was willing to let the issue of desertion recede into the background reveals that their priorities in reforming the waterfront lay elsewhere, specifically in those issues that applied to the functional regulation of maritime commerce and the restoration of respectable society to waterfront districts rather than issues related directly to seamen's rights. Even given the relatively conservative agenda of the Joint Conference, their platform proved too radical for some members. ASFS representatives who attended early meetings quickly dropped out, refusing to offer financial support to fund a General Agent in port, and expressing a reluctance to join in any collaborative advocacy work at the expense of the independent operation of their own Society. The Marine Association too, after making its recommendations regarding allotment notes, dropped out of the Conference in the wake of the White Act's passage in 1898, having become "convinced that the Conference was merely a group of impractical visionaries."[60] SCI was left to take over primary responsibility for the operation of the Joint Conference, with Mansfield and lawyer J. Augustus Johnson continuing their leadership roles during the years leading up to the 1915 LaFollete Seamen's Act, which finally banned the use of imprisonment to punish desertion once and for all.

Conclusion

The Supreme Court's decision in *Robertson v. Baldwin* placed an emphatic restriction on the mobility and individual liberty of merchant seamen engaged in the waged labor of an industrializing economy of maritime commerce. The outcome of the case ultimately proved that the mechanism of desertion, which merchant seamen had harnessed for centuries as a tactic to maintain control over their own labor, was an essential threat both ideologically to a U.S. political economy that increasingly privileged freedom of contract over freedom of person and practically to the agents of maritime commerce and its financiers. So great was the threat of desertion that the Supreme Court was willing to put forward a distorted interpretation of the Thirteenth Amendment in order to put a stop to it. By the end of 1897, the *Arago* deserters and all merchant seamen found themselves excluded from the protections of the U.S. Constitution and, by extension, the full rights and protections entitled by citizenship.

Other workers at the margins of the U.S. economy were similarly impacted by the precedent that the Court's decision had established. After *Robertson v. Baldwin*, a series of decisions at the state and federal level involving potentially coercive contracts explicitly drew on the *Arago* decision, including cases involving the long-term contracts of Black sharecroppers in the South and the contracts of Northern lumber workers who were arrested on the charge of "false pretense," or a failure to fulfill the terms of signed contracts. Perhaps the most widely debated legal implication stemming from *Robertson v. Baldwin* involved the annexation of Hawaii in July 1898; many politicians, labor leaders, and members of the press feared that the *Arago* decision provided sufficient precedent for Hawaii's existing system of indentured servitude to be legally absorbed into the U.S., sparking an explosive political controversy that recalled the "popular sovereignty" debates over the expansion of slavery into U.S. territories during the 1850s.[61] In addition to Hawaii, a rash of state and federal cases broke out centered on the imprisonment of laborers for not fulfilling contracts under a false pretense clause that derived from the Supreme Court's handling of the *Arago* seamen.[62] Such coercive contracts were not exclusive to the South. During the first decade of the twentieth century, three Northern states—Minnesota in 1901, Michigan in 1903, and Maine in 1907—enacted false pretense statutes that were designed to keep workers who had received transportation to remote lumber or mining sites under work schedules as specified in contracts signed in advance under threat of imprisonment.[63] By 1911, the tide had started to turn. In *Bailey v. Alabama*, the Supreme Court struck down false pretense statutes as violating the Peonage Act of 1867.

Merchant seamen, who were protected from imprisonment if they deserted within a U.S. port by the White Act of 1898, were still subject to such punishment in foreign ports until the Seamen's Act of 1915, which brought seamen into a system of labor that was gradually modernizing as it emerged out of the spirit of reform that defined the Progressive Era. The Seamen's Act of 1915 marked the legislative realization of a turn in public opinion against the exceptional status of merchant seamen under U.S. law that began with the *Arago* seamen and their encounter with the Supreme Court. This exceptional status, one that had been imposed upon seamen since the earliest years of the Republic, pushed the *Arago* deserters to the margins of the U.S. Constitution and citizenship. The resolution of their case, and the awakening of sentiment that it induced within the sphere of public opinion, gave belated shape to the parameters of contract labor in the wake of the Thirteenth Amendment and set fundamental precedent as the nation entered the twentieth century. The sinking of *Titanic* would initiate another wave of public attention and sympathy paid to the issue of seamen's rights. The safety at sea movement, which prompted international inquiries, created a voracious public appetite for reform and provoked an awakening of radical maritime labor activism in British and

U.S. ports, leading to a political reckoning that resulted in the 1915 Seamen's Act. This reckoning, and the confrontations between a matrix of competing interests and agendas that it involved, is the subject of Chap. 3.

Notes

1. "Into Port In Irons: Four of the Crew of *Arago* Arrested for Mutiny on the High Seas," *San Francisco Call*, July 8, 1895, 10.
2. *Robertson v. Baldwin*, 165 U.S. 275 (1897).
3. Andrew Furuseth, "Fugitive Sailor Law / Fugitive Slave Law" (pamphlet), Records of the Seamen's Church Institute of New York and New Jersey.
4. The "Lochner Era" gets its name from the case *Lochner v. New York*, 198 U.S. 45 (1905), but the era is commonly dated earlier than the *Lochner* case to *Allgeyer v. Louisiana*, 165 U.S. 578 (1897) decided on March 1897, more than two months after *Robertson v. Baldwin*. See: Aviam Soifer, "The Paradox of Paternalism and Laissez-Faire Constitutionalism: United States Supreme Court, 1888–1921," *Law and History Review* 5, no. 1 (Spring 1987), 249–279.
5. The legal historian Robert J. Steinfeld covers Robertson v. Baldwin most extensively in *Coercion, Contract, and Free Labor in the Nineteenth Century* (New York: Cambridge University Press, 2001), 270–278. Steinfeld situates Robertson v. Baldwin on a timeline of state court interpretations of the Thirteenth Amendment, arguing that the primary significance of the case is in the precedent it set for future cases involving coerced contracts that were argued at the state level. The case is briefly covered elsewhere by Leon Fink, *Sweatshops at Sea: Merchant Seamen in the World's First Globalized Industry* (Chapel Hill: The University of North Carolina Press, 2011), 61 62, and by Andrew Furuseth's biographer Andrew Weintraub, *Andrew Furuseth: Emancipator of the Seamen* (Berkeley: University of California Press, 1958), 34–36.
6. Such interpretations seize on a passage from the Court's majority ruling written by Justice Brown: "The law is perfectly well settled that the first ten Amendments to the constitution … [are] subject to certain well-recognized exceptions arising from the necessities of the case. Thus, the right of the people to keep and bear arms (article 2) is not infringed by law prohibiting the carrying of concealed weapons…"
7. Typical of maritime historians' treatment of maritime ministry organizations is Matthew Taylor Rafferty, who in *The Republic Afloat: Law, Honor, and Citizenship in Maritime America* (University of Chicago Press, 2013) portrays organizations like the ASFS as capitalizing on public sympathies

following the War of 1812 to fund a ministry that infantilized seamen and was met with hostile resistance from seamen themselves, who objected to the paternalism of charities. Judith Fingard, in *Jack In Port: Sailortowns of Eastern Canada* (Toronto: University of Toronto Press. 1982), argues that the combined efforts of the state, maritime business, and maritime reformers in Canadian sailortowns served primarily to regulate merchant seamen's mobility within waterfront labor markets, guided primarily by impulses to keep seamen disciplined in order to "serve the needs of capital" (30).

8. Eric Foner, *Reconstruction: America's Unfinished Revolution, 1863–1877* (New York: Harper & Row, 1988) has demonstrated that this contract-based manifestation of free labor ideology has its roots in the devolution of Reconstruction. With the South defeated, Northern Republicans perceived in the New South an opportunity to spread free labor ideology based on the Northern industrial wage system into virgin territory that had been held back by the slavery system. Out of the transition from slavery to free labor, Southern planters who had formerly depended on slave labor faced the problem of how to entice labor out of an emancipated workforce. In order to regain control over freedmen's labor, planters countered newly acquired black mobility with restrictive laws and contracts. As Foner describes this transition, the former master–slave relationship was replaced with contractual agreements, the freedom of which was compromised by various coercive tactics, including denied access to land ownership, the use of fines or imprisonment to punish non-compliance, and the threat of violent enforcement from local white supremacist organizations such as the Klu Klux Klan. With the passage of the Fourteenth Amendment ostensibly ensuring black civil rights, Northern Republicans increasingly insisted that blacks were unequivocally equal citizens under U.S. law, and any special ties to the protections of the federal government should therefore be severed so that blacks could compete fairly in the free market. As Heather Cox Richardson in *The Death of Reconstruction: Race, Labor, and Politics in the Post-Civil War North, 1865–1901* (Cambridge: Harvard University Press, 2001) argues, Northern Republicans increasingly came to perceive blacks' inability to successfully integrate into an abstracted "free" labor market following emancipation as evidence of their intentional rejection of free labor ideals, a transgression for which blacks were "willingly read … out of American society" by their former Northern Republican allies. Thus, the Supreme Court declared the Civil Rights Acts unconstitutional in 1875 and federal troops withdrew from the South in 1877, leaving Southern state governments to revoke black suffrage and perpetuate a system of labor based on coercive contracts and privileged access to resources and representation.

9. Soifer, "Paternalism and Laissez-Faire Constitutionalism," 251–252.
10. See: Martin J. Norris, "The Seaman as Ward of the Admiralty," *Michigan Law Review* 52, no. 4 (1954), 479–504. The legal precedent most frequently cited for this classification of seamen is the Supreme Court case *Harden v. Gordon* (1823), in which Justice Story declared: "Seamen are by the peculiarity of their lives liable to sudden sickness from change of climate, exposure to perils, and exhausting labour. They are generally poor and friendless and acquire habits of gross indulgence, carelessness and improvidence. Every court should watch with jealousy an encroachment upon the rights of seamen, because they are unprotected and need counsel; because they are thoughtless and require indulgence; because they are credulous and complying; and are easily overreached."
11. See: Fingard, *Jack in Port*, 30.
12. Raffety, *The Republic Afloat*, Chapter One.
13. Marcus Rediker, *Between the Devil and the Deep Blue Sea: Merchant Seamen, Pirates and the Anglo-American Maritime World, 1700–1750* (New York: Cambridge University Press, 1987) and with Peter Linebaugh, *The Many-Headed Hydra: Sailors, Slaves, Commoners, and the Hidden History of the Revolutionary Atlantic* (Boston: Beacon Press, 2000).
14. Paul Gilje, *Free Trade and Sailors' Rights in the War of 1812* (New York: Cambridge University Press, 2013).
15. Rediker, *Between the Devil and the Deep-Blue Sea*, Introduction.
16. Rediker, *Between the Devil and the Deep-Blue Sea* and Rediker and Linebaugh, *The Many-Headed Hydra.*
17. Daniel Vickers, *Young Men and the Sea: Yankee Seafarers in the Age of Sail* (New Haven, CT: Yale University Press, 2005), 197.
18. Ibid., 204.
19. *The Oregonian*, March 13, 1979, as cited in Denise Alborn, "Shanghai Days in Astoria," *Cumtux* (Clatsop County. Historical Society) 9, no. 1: 9–15.
20. "In an Astoria Prison: Deserters From the *Arago* Who Will Have to Finish Their Trip," *The San Francisco Call*, June 22, 1895, 9.
21. Norris, "The Seaman as Ward of the Admiralty," 491 and 493.
22. The Merchant Marine Act of July 20, 1790, Ch. 29, 1 Stat. 131.
23. See J. M. Gutoff, "Fugitive Slaves and Ship-Jumping Sailors: The Enforcement and Survival of Coerced Labor," *Journal of Labor and Employment Law* 9, no. 1 (2006), 87–116, and Furuseth, "Fugitive Sailor Law / Fugitive Slave Law" (pamphlet), Records of the Seamen's Church Institute of New York and New Jersey. Gutoff demonstrates that the 1790 U.S. Merchant Marine Act was indeed a model for the 1793 Fugitive Slave Act, but does not seem aware that this fact was well known among mer-

chant seamen themselves, and was used rhetorically by seamen's rights reformers in the decades following emancipation to appeal to Congress that the use of penal sanctions to enforce shipping articles be outlawed.

24. Furuseth, "Fugitive Sailor Law / Fugitive Slave Law" (pamphlet).
25. Richard B. Morris, "Labor Controls in Maryland in the Nineteenth Century," *The Journal of Southern History* 14, no. 3 (1948), 394–395.
26. Fink, *Sweatshops at Sea*, 32.
27. Weintraub, *Andrew Furuseth*, 35.
28. The Maguire Act of February 28, 1895, ch. 28, Stat. 667.
29. Weintraub, *Andrew Furuseth*, 33, citing reports published in the *Coast Seamen's Journal* in 1894.
30. Ibid., 34, quoting the *Coast Seamen's Journal*, February 3, 1895: "The enforcement of its provisions rests with the seamen themselves through their unions."
31. "In an Astoria Prison: Deserters From the *Arago* Who Will Have to Finish Their Trip," *The San Francisco Call*, June 22, 1895, 9.
32. "Among the Unions," *The San Francisco Call*, July 9, 1895, 4.
33. "Four Mutinous Sailors Will Contest Their Legality," *The Herald* (Los Angeles), July 19, 1895, 2.
34. "The Arago's Mutineers," *The San Francisco Call*, July 11, 1895, 11.
35. Ibid.
36. Rediker, *Between the Devil and the Deep-Blue Sea*.
37. David Montgomery documents the rise of worker turnover in the Northern industrial economy, arguing that "annual turnover rates ranging from 100 percent to 250 percent of the original labor force were found to be common place." By 1913, the Ford plants had to replace 54,000 workers over the course of a year to maintain a labor force of 13,000. *Workers' Control in America: Studies in the History of Work, Technology, and Labor Struggles* (New York: Cambridge University Press, 1979), 41.
38. "Four Mutinous Sailors Will Contest Their Legality," 2.
39. Ibid.
40. "The Rights of Seamen," *San Francisco Call*, July 26, 1895, 8.
41. "Four Mutinous Sailors Will Contest Their Legality," 2.
42. See Leon Fink, "From Autonomy to Abundance: Changing Beliefs about the Free Labor System in Nineteenth-Century America," in Stanley L. Engerman, ed., *Terms of Labor: Slavery, Serfdom, and Free Labor*, (Palo Alto, CA: Stanford University Press, 1999), and Steinfeld, *Contract, Coercion and Free Labor.*
43. See: Norris, "The Seaman as Ward of the Admiralty."
44. Morris, "Labor Controls in Maryland in the Nineteenth Century," 399.
45. Steinfeld, *Contract, Coercion, and Free Labor*, 273.
46. Soifer, "The Paradox of Paternalism and Laissez-Faire Constitutionalism."

47. Alfred J. Nock, *Mansfield Biography*, (unpublished, [1932?]), Records of the Seamen's Church Institute of New York and New Jersey.
48. "An Important Decision," *The Cook County Herald* (Grand Marais, MN), February 20, 1897, 3.
49. "An Important Decision," *The Broad Ax* (Salt Lake City, UT), February 20, 1897, 1.
50. "Rigor Not Relaxed. Important Case Involving Seamen's Rights Decided," *The Wichita Daily Eagle*, January 26, 1897, 2.
51. "Goes Against The Seamen. United States Supreme Court Hands Down Important Decision," *Omaha Daily Bee* (Nebraska), January 26, 1897, 5.
52. "Famous Arago Case on Appeal," *San Francisco Call*, May 2, 1897, 2.
53. "Contracts to Labor: Should Not be Enforceable by the Law. Labor Federationalists Object to the Supreme Court Ruling Which Makes Slaves of Workmen," *Los Angeles Herald*, December 17, 1897.
54. "Senator Frye Gets a Roast: A Mass-Meeting that Spoke Out Loud for 'Poor Jack,'" *San Francisco Call*, February 3, 1897, 7.
55. Ibid.
56. Andrew Furuseth, "Fugitive Sailor Law / Fugitive Slave Law" (pamphlet).
57. Nock, *Mansfield*, Chapter Fifteen.
58. Ibid.
59. Ibid., Chapter Sixteen.
60. Ibid.
61. See: "Labor Opposed to Annexation: Involuntary Servitude May, in Consequence, Be Extended to This Country," *San Francisco Call* June 20, 1897, 7; "Coolie Labor and Annexation," *The Record-Union* (Sacramento, CA), October 25, 1897, 2; "Sanctions Contract Slavery. With Annexation Would Come This Serfdom of White Laborers," *San Francisco Call* December 15, 1897, 2.
62. For example, in *State v. Murray* (1906) the Louisiana state court upheld the validity of a false pretense statute based on the Supreme Court's ruling in *Clyatt v. United States* 197 U.S. 207 (1905), in which the Court ruled that peonage constituted involuntary servitude except in special cases, specifically citing merchant seamen and *Robertson v. Baldwin* as an example of such an exception.
63. General laws Minnesota, ch. 165, 212–213; Michigan Comp. Laws, 408.582–408.583; Maine Rev. Stat., ch. 128. 12. See Steinfeld, *Coercion, Contract, and Free Labor*, chapter 8. Steinfeld writes, citing John Clifton Elder's report "Peonage in Maine" that "rural justices of the peace committed numerous men to jail or sent them back to the woods to work out their contracts in the years following passage of the act. One rural justice said that he alone had heard of 50 or 60 cases since the act was passed."

CHAPTER 3

"Pandemonium on the Quay": The *Titanic* Disaster, the *Olympic* Mutiny, and the 1912 Transport Workers' Federation Strike

The decision of the Supreme Court in *Robertson v. Baldwin* went a step beyond reinforcing the long-established legal status of merchant seamen as wards of the state. In denying the *Arago* deserters protections under the Thirteenth Amendment, the Court proved that it was willing to deny seamen their full entitlements as citizens of the United States in order to uphold freedom of contract and protect the absolute power of masters and mates in maintaining an orderly, productive maritime labor pool. In doing so, the Court continued a long tradition of paradoxical regulation of the merchant marine; as wards of the state, seamen were both entitled to extraordinary protections from the state and subject to extraordinary measures of control.

Robertson v. Baldwin aroused public sentiment and proved useful for maritime labor unions in advocating for the abolition of imprisonment as the penalty for desertion. The 1898 White Act ostensibly did just that in U.S. and foreign ports near the nation's coastlines, but its language was vague enough to allow for interpretation, and, more problematic for seamen, the law neglected to protect them in foreign ports, where they were often coerced into leaving their ships so that a new crew could be hired at cheaper rates determined by local market conditions.

J. Thayer, *Citizenship, Subversion, and Surveillance in U.S. Ports*, Global Studies in Social and Cultural Maritime History,
https://doi.org/10.1007/978-3-031-45618-3_3

The sinking of the White Star Line's "unsinkable" liner *Titanic* in April 1912 prompted another wave of public sympathy for those who worked on merchant ships, this time on an unprecedented scale. Between April 15 and June 26, 1912, a period that began on the day of the sinking and ended with the declaration of a massive seamen's strike along the East Coast, the *New York Times* alone ran 1192 articles that mentioned *Titanic*.[1] A combination of the press, reformers, labor unionists, and politicians turned the public's insatiable appetite for news and content related to the disaster into a powerful sympathy that was put to use in a number of ways.

The International Seamen's Union (ISU), which had been active since 1898 in lobbying Congress for a revised version of the White Act, found themselves in a position to push for even more aggressive legislation than even they had previously thought possible. Certain Progressive politicians, caught up in the interventionist fervor of the era, were eager to ally themselves with maritime labor union leaders and acted on prevailing public sentiment to introduce said legislation. Meanwhile, reformers in New York City, the port to which *Titanic* was bound and where its survivors arrived on board *Carpathia*, launched the next phase of their maritime ministry project surreptitiously on the very morning that word about the sinking reached shore.

Industrial maritime labor unions in Britain and the East Coast U.S. initiated waves of direct action. Marine firemen on both sides of the Atlantic led walk-offs and an intersectional strike that united workers along the waterfront and placed demands on shipping companies to provide more provisions to ensure safety at sea, better food and quarters on ships, and most important of all in the U.S., recognition of the unions that collectively formed the Transport Workers Federation, a fledgling syndicalist collective with a mission to organize all of the industrial trades along the waterfront in port towns on the East Coast.

Shipowners, on the other hand, were put on the defensive in publicly justifying their business practices. J.P. Morgan, acting as both head of the recently formed shipping combination the International Mercantile Marine Company and Board member and lead donor to the Seamen's Church Institute's new headquarters at 25 South Street, found himself the target of enraged and emboldened industrial maritime unionists in New York. Pacific Coast shipowners, such as magnate Robert Dollar, were called before a series of Congressional committee hearings considering maritime labor reform following the *Titanic*'s sinking and offered testimony that opposed reforms, while facing harsh questioning from committee members about the rights afforded to seamen on their vessels, the methods by which they were compensated, and the measures in place to ensure their safety. These three issues—seamen's emancipation, equalization of wages, and safety at sea—came to form the essence of the 1915 Seamen's Act, introduced in Congress by Republican Senator Robert La Follette of Wisconsin.

Less than two weeks after the sinking, the firemen of *Titanic*'s sister ship, *Olympic* walked off their jobs in Southampton in protest over unseaworthy lifeboats. Their protest, occurring just minutes before a scheduled departure, prompted the authorities to charge the men with mutiny. The resulting court decision protected the supposedly mutinous firemen on the grounds of the legitimacy of their protests regarding safety at sea. Industrial unionism had taken hold in Britain under the leadership of J. Havelock Wilson and the British Seamen and Firemen's Union just one year prior, and it took little time for its impact to be felt in British ports and eventually across the Atlantic. In late June of 1912, tens of thousands of waterfront workers struck up and down the East Coast of the U.S., called to a general transport workers' strike by industrial maritime unionists in New York. Inspired by their counterparts in Britain, the fledgling TWF attempted to unite all of the disparate units of waterfront labor that rapid industrialization had divided along the lines of trade, skill, and race.

Ultimately, a constellation of conservative forces tamped down the spirit of industrial unionism in New York in 1912. Shipping companies fought back with strike breakers. Local police launched attacks on sailortown. The Seamen's Church Institute, having declared war on the district's nefarious elements, began construction on a million-dollar headquarters dedicated to saving the seaman from himself, backed by the funding of J.P. Morgan and a long list of industrialists. Finally, the ISU, an affiliate of the American Federation of Labor (AFL), which had persistently refused to support the transport workers' strike, focused instead on its partnerships with Congress to push ahead with a legislative agenda that coopted the energies of industrial maritime unionists to secure passage of a signature legislative accomplishment in the 1915 Seamen's Act.

Whereas seamen's emancipation and safety at sea were issues that provided the bill's advocates with powerful rhetorical weapons, an essential component of the 1915 Seamen's Act was the range of mobility that it afforded merchant seamen in port. *Robertson v. Baldwin* had shed light on the exceptional limitations on freedom of person that limited merchant seamen's entitlements as citizens. The reforms to seamen's mobility in port that began in 1898 with the White Act were radically reshaped in 1915. The fundamental right to shore leave for all seamen, long established and honored, combined with the newly won right to quit without fear of imprisonment that the 1915 Act guaranteed, created a maelstrom of confrontations between seamen, masters and mates, and shoreside agents that would take decades to resolve.

Specifically, the Act unwittingly created a means to circumvent immigration laws, which would steadily develop into a full-fledged political crisis known as the "alien seamen" problem. Asian seamen, especially Chinese, who had provided a cheap labor source for steamships operating in the Pacific, most explicitly posed a challenge to the mechanisms of racial control put in place by the Chinese Exclusion Act of 1882 and the Immigration Act of 1907.

The 1915 Seamen's Act was, in part, the product of the ISU's rejection of the TWF's syndicalism, and the Union's determination to pursue practical gains through political means that would ultimately sustain protections for white, U.S. citizen, skilled maritime workers and, by extension, bolster membership to their own organization. The central irony at the heart of the 1915 Seamen's Act was that in successfully redirecting the momentum of industrial unionism in favor of the AFL's brand of voluntarism, the legislation that the ISU and their Progressive allies in Congress steered into law would eventually lead to a crisis of U.S. citizenship in which merchant seamen were again at the center. Ultimately, Progressive reforms to seamen's emancipation, equalization, and safety at sea once again asked questions and challenged the boundaries of U.S. citizenship as codified in immigration law.

The Cornerstone-Laying Ceremony at 25 South Street

April 16, 1912, was supposed to be a day of celebration for supporters of the Seamen's Church Institute of New York (SCI). After years of planning and fundraising, the Institute was finally ready to start construction on its new "million-dollar home for sailors" at 25 South Street in lower Manhattan. The finished building would have thirteen stories of dormitory-style rooms and offer banking, employment, postal, and medical services for the half-million seamen who annually passed through New York's busy downtown port.[2] The Institute's benefactors, including some of the city's wealthiest philanthropists, could rejoice in the fact that unscrupulous boardinghouse keepers and saloon owners of New York's sailortown now had formidable competition.

To mark the day, SCI officials joined members of local government and prominent clergy in the auditorium of the unfinished building to lay the cornerstone. Mayor William Jay Gaynor and Episcopal Bishop of New York Rev. David H. Greer led the ceremony, offering speeches praising the work of the Institute and the humanity of the seaman.[3] But the intended atmosphere of the gathering was dramatically affected by news of a tragic coincidence: the unsinkable *Titanic* had been lost in the early hours of April 15. The newspaper boys on the sidewalks outside the building shouted out headlines reporting that 1500 people had perished along with the ship. The pride of the White Star Line, whose owner, J. Pierpont Morgan, had personally donated $100,000 toward the construction of SCI's new building, would never reach the American home port of New York.[4]

The news hit hard among the shipping magnates and distinguished guests gathered inside 25 South Street. With so many of them directly affected by the tragedy, the cornerstone-laying ceremony transformed into an improvised service of mourning. Forced to address the unthinkable loss, speakers made last-minute edits to their speeches. SCI became a central site for the collective commemoration of *Titanic*'s sinking in the immediate aftermath of the disaster. The newly dedicated building at 25 South Street became a point of cultural intersection between the upper-class benefactors of the Institute and the working-class seamen of the Port of New York from the moment news about the sinking of the ship first hit New York and continued over a period of time that spans the "safety at sea" reform movement and the violent waterfront protests that took place in the weeks after the disaster.

The editors of *The Lookout*, SCI's institutional publication issued monthly since 1910, devoted most of the April 1912 issue to an article titled "The Cornerstone Laid," which detailed the ceremony at 25 South Street. Noting the "peculiar significance" of the day, the writer describes the coincidental circumstances surrounding the ceremony:

> And yet it seemed particularly appropriate that on this day, when heart and mind were turned toward the sea and the sailors who had gone down beneath the deep waters, there should be gathered a notable company of

> men and women to join in a service marking one of the final steps in the completion of a tremendous project solely for the benefit of seamen and their families.[5]

Considering its origins and the list of donors who contributed to the New Building Fund, the cornerstone-laying ceremony represented a major event in the history of lower Manhattan. The mayor himself was on hand to personally lay and seal the stone along with a Bible, annual reports of the Institute, and copies of the New York daily papers with headlines of *Titanic*'s sinking. The mayor then delivered a brief speech, remarking, "[t]he fact that so many people came here to this remote part of the city to participate in this ceremony shows more interest in it than I had anticipated, and shows that it is certain to be a success."[6]

The following day, *The World* ran a story about the institute's new building with the headline: "Deep Grief Told at Stone Laying of a Sea Home: *Titanic* Disaster Gives Tragic Tone to the Formal Ceremony at the Church Institute, South Street."[7] The new SCI headquarters was off to a solemn start.

On April 18, 220 survivors of the *Titanic*'s crew arrived at Pier 54 in New York on board RMS *Carpathia*.[8] While some of the surviving passengers returned to their homes or to the homes of friends or relatives, crewmembers were afforded no such comfort. Still under the employment of the White Star Line, the crew was ordered to remain secluded aboard a moored ship in New York Harbor until the company was prepared to ship them back to Southampton on the ocean liner *Lapland*.[9]

The surviving crew managed to escape their seclusion on April 19, hours before *Lapland*'s departure, to attend a service in their honor at the American Seamen's Friend Society. Working in collaboration with agents from SCI, the Society distributed new sets of clothing to male crew members, including underwear, shirts, socks, boots, a cap, suspenders, a safety razor, and a comb. Additionally, twenty stewardesses were given complete outfits.[10] Of equal value to the survivors was an opportunity to escape from the captivity of their employers. The *New York Herald* wrote on April 20 that the crew had decided to defy the men charged with keeping them confined to *Lapland* to attend the service.[11]

In addition to charity, the crew's escape also gained them access to the New York press, to whom they were eager to express their discontent about how things had been handled after the ship sank. The public sympathy that the sinking had sparked granted the *Titanic* seamen a political power that they were quick to wield against their employers.

For some of the surviving crew, grievances began while they were still in the icy water. Speaking to reporters, crewmembers complained of the "millionaire's boat," a name given to one lifeboat containing some of the ship's wealthier passengers. The sailors who manned that particular lifeboat were supposedly given handsome bonuses after *Carpathia* picked them up.[12] The *New York Herald* identified the gracious donor as Mrs. John Jacob Astor and claimed that the crewmembers who rowed her to safety were each given twenty dollars in gold.[13] One of the ship's surviving firemen who was on a different lifeboat expressed his frustration to the *New York Times*: "And we … we who saved immigrant women and their children, we get nothing. It ain't fair…"[14] An editorial to the *New York Times* from an "ex-purser" echoed the fireman's indignation, suggesting that some of the thousands of dollars donated toward relief of the ship's third-class passengers should go to the crew, "many if not all of whom manned the lifeboats."[15]

A major issue for the crew was that their pay schedules stopped mid-ocean with the sinking of the ship, despite having signed articles for a full voyage.[16] Able seaman Ralph White, of Southampton, was quoted in the *New York Evening Journal* as a spokesman for the crew:

> We signed up for the entire voyage, but the White Star officials claim that our wages ceased when the *Titanic* went under. In the face of these circumstances it would have been better had we all gone down with the ship as in that case our families would have been provided for by the workingmen's compensation law, and we would not have faced actual starvation as now seems to be our lot.[17]

The same *New York Evening Journal* article claimed that in addition to denying the crew full compensation for the voyage, the White Star Line denied the crew money to wire home to their families to tell them that they were safe and that the crew would have to work during their return voyage to Southampton to pay for their passage aboard *Lapland*.[18]

While the surviving crew's three days in New York were not without controversy, the day after their departure on *Lapland* was dedicated to mourning and commemoration. A service was held at SCI's Church of the Holy Comforter on 341 West Street on Sunday, April 21. It was attended by 400 people, three-fourths of whom were sailors who:

> sat together in the pews on one side of the church. Their faces were sad, for many of them had friends among the *Titanic* crew, and to those who had no intimate associations with any of the victims there was brought with renewed force the realization of the terrors and dangers of their lives at sea.[19]

The sea had consumed *Titanic*, and in the months following the tragedy, forces of an entirely different nature would consume the New York City waterfront. Safety at sea, or lack thereof, was in the public conversation, and the waterfront unions saw their opportunity for much-needed reform.

Mutiny on the RMS *Olympic*

As *Lapland* made its way back across the Atlantic, RMS *Olympic* was making final preparations for its April 24 departure for New York. *Olympic* was a White Star Line sister ship of *Titanic* and had received the doomed vessel's distress call at sea the night of April 15. Capt. Haddock of the *Olympic* ordered his ship full speed ahead for a reported eighteen hours before receiving a wireless message from *Carpathia* reporting that all lifeboats had been picked up and there was no more that could be done. *Olympic*'s crew changed direction and headed back to Southampton dejected and "amazed at the magnitude of the disaster," according to the local press.[20] Capable of taking on 1400 passengers for transatlantic voyages, *Olympic* was selected to replace *Titanic* on the sailing list and continue the operation of the White Star Line's fleet of giant luxury liners.[21]

By Monday the 22, workmen were busy installing collapsible lifeboats on *Olympic*, which was due to sail for New York on the 25. "With the boats already swinging from the great liner's davits," the Southampton paper *Southern Daily Echo* optimistically reported, "there will be now ample accommodation for every soul on board her in the boats in case of emergency."[22] The crew, however, was not quite ready to get back to business as usual. *Titanic*'s sinking had raised legitimate questions about how capable passenger ships were of handling disasters at sea. The issue of lifeboats, both their quantity and quality, was emerging as a particularly urgent problem. Further, as would become evident, the crew of *Olympic* were emboldened by the wave of public sympathy that had developed in reaction to the sinking of their sister ship. Like the surviving crew in New York before them, *Olympic*'s crew took full advantage of the moment to take action against the White Star Line, inciting an audacious walk-off and strike that would bring many of them before the bench of the Portsmouth courts under charges of mutiny. Whereas the *Olympic* mutiny was isolated to Southern England, similar confrontations between seamen and the state would quickly spread to the U.S. For the firemen of *Olympic*, the collapsible lifeboats provided on board were simply not good enough. With the vessel in its final preparations for departure from port, a contingent of firemen, greasers, and trimmers walked down the only gangway still in position at the stern of the ship and "trooped ashore in Indian file with their kit bags over their shoulders." A crowd that had gathered to see the liner off was left to gawk at "the faces of tier upon tier of passengers" looking down on a "strange and unrehearsed scene in puzzled wonder."[23] The *New York Times* reported that the striking crew justified their actions by claiming that the collapsible canvas lifeboats, which had been transferred to *Olympic* from a troopship, were "rotten and unseaworthy and would not open." Just twenty minutes before *Olympic* was scheduled to leave port, a significant number of the crew had "collected their kits, and left the ship, singing, 'We're All Going the Same Way Home,'" a popular contemporary folk song.[24]

The striking crew stalled *Olympic* in port, and the incident received international attention, riding on the wave of public interest generated by the sinking of *Titanic* just nine days prior. With the noontime scheduled departure passed by, *Olympic*'s passengers found themselves stranded on board, now witnesses to what the *New York Times* described as "pandemonium on the quay."[25] A crowd of firemen led by an improvised "tin-whistle band under the direction of a self-appointed conductor" gathered about the ship and prevented anyone from getting on board. A hurried meeting convened by the British Seafarer's Union was held in a nearby outbuilding. Arthur Cannon, Secretary of the Union, led the crew in a vote, and "with complete unanimity" the men voted against returning to the ship.[26]

The following day, with *Olympic* still in port, the striking firemen were allowed to test the collapsible lifeboats themselves. Four boats were launched, and, while three appeared seaworthy, the fourth had been badly damaged and leaked profusely. Local press reported that the striking crew remained unsatisfied with the collapsible lifeboats, and that during the inspection "one of their number had pushed his thumb through the canvas hull" of a boat that was clearly unseaworthy.[27] The White Star Line agreed to replace any of the lifeboats judged to be unsatisfactory, but the strikers had a new demand: dismiss all of the firemen who had remained on board the ship the previous day when the decision was made to strike.[28]

Members of the British Seafarers' Union rallied in support of the strike, gathering along the quay and blocking all entrances to the docks. The spectacle of the previous day's events continued, with the Union "stokers' band" dispatched to the scene, "led by a man dressed as a Redskin" who "directed the spirits of the men into a harmless channel."[29] Meanwhile, the White Star Line had recruited a replacement crew in an attempt to salvage the voyage. In addition to dismissing the firemen who refused to walk off, the strikers now demanded that the replacement crew, who were non-union, be dismissed as well. An official of the White Star Line sent a telegram to the local press, affirming that any willingness to compromise with the striking crew had reached a breaking point:

> We are asked to dismiss non-Union substitutes obtained and those firemen regularly signed on who refused to desert with majority. We have replied agreement to provide non-Union men with special employment, but we will abandon *Olympic* sailing rather than dismiss men who remained loyal.[30]

The White Star Line's hard line stance provoked an unexpected response from their remaining "loyal" crew. Deck hands, learning of the arrival of non-union replacement crew, with spirits aroused by the company's treatment of their fellow sailors, promptly dropped everything, "scrambled on board the tug which had brought the new firemen, and refused to any further duty." At this point, the Shipping Commissioner involved himself by pulling alongside the tug in a harbor vessel and accusing the deck crew assembled there of mutiny and ordering them to return to their ship. The crew refused, and soon thereafter the police had fifty-three deck hands in custody, leaving *Olympic* still in limbo. The seamen, for their part, reportedly "offered no resistance to the police and were quite cheerful in their demeanor, smoking their pipes, and chatting together, as they were marched off."[31]

The fifty-three prisoners were brought before the court in Portsmouth and charged under section 225 of the British Merchant Shipping Act, which stated that "if any seaman was guilty of willful disobedience to lawful command he should be liable to be imprisoned for a period not exceeding four months." The defense claimed that the deck hands walked off not because the replacements were non-union men but because they were a "scratch" crew with little or no experience, and that they "refused to risk their lives with such men," instead electing to jump ship and join the firemen in striking.[32]

Upon hearing arguments from both sides, the Bench reached the decision that the men had indeed willfully disobeyed the lawful commands of the *Olympic*'s captain, finding the defendants guilty of mutiny. The court's sentencing of the mutineers, however, proved almost as sensational as the men's actions themselves and provided evidence of the prevailing mood of the public and the rule of law regarding issues related to safety at sea in the immediate wake of the *Titanic* disaster. "Now comes our difficulty," began Chairman Thomas, in delivering the court's decision:

> We are all human, and these men are human and the question is what are we to do with them? What punishment to inflict? We have been passing through a very, very serious time and everybody is obsessed with the frightful calamity which took place in the Atlantic Ocean. We can't drive it out of our minds, and it is apparent to us that it is in the minds of these men, and they did on this occasion what, under other circumstances, they would not have done.[33]

Thomas continued, praising the behavior of the men in court, recounting the kind words that Capt. Haddock had testified regarding the character of his crew, and stated that the court "would like to see confidence restored among them." He maintained that the court simply could not sentence the men to terms of imprisonment, nor could it fine them. Rather, "having regard to all the circumstances under which the offense was committed," the court dismissed the case outright and ordered the men back to work. The headlines that followed summarized the remarkable proceedings: "Charge Proved but Men Dismissed: Don't Do it Again!"

The sinking of *Titanic* directly informed the mutiny on *Olympic*, meaning that just nine days after the ship went down, the conversation about safety at sea had taken on a decidedly radical tone. Furthermore, public sentiment regarding the crisis of safety at sea had directly affected the decision of the Portsmouth court in their exceptionally lenient sentencing of *Olympic*'s mutinous crew. The resolution of the case, in which the mutinous seamen were found guilty of all charges but released without any punishment, speaks volumes about not only prevailing public sentiment but also the gradual tilt of the court system in support of a class of workers whose labor the *Titanic* disaster had revealed to be worthy of public support and the protection of the state. Both of these impacts stemming from the *Titanic* disaster would endure in scale and duration, reaching New

York City and the sailortowns of the eastern seaports of the U.S. in the months that followed.

The Transport Workers General Strike in New York

On May 25, one month after the *Olympic* mutiny, the industry-oriented *Marine Journal* printed an article titled "Seamen's Unions and the *Titanic* Disaster," criticizing maritime unions for the "ridiculous and unbearable demands" made in the wake of *Titanic*'s sinking and accusing the labor groups of "using this catastrophe as a club ... to hold over the heads of vessel owners." In addition to stricter safety requirements, union leaders in London drew on longstanding grievances (with xenophobic and racist overtones) regarding the lack of English-language competencies among crewmembers to insist that at least two white seamen in addition to a white coxswain be employed for every lifeboat on board, a response to an influx of Asian seamen working for American and British companies. Citing the *Olympic* mutiny as an example of the lengths to which unions would go to get their way, the writer then praised the safety record of the maritime industry: "There will always be risk in travel on sea or land, and what the genius of man has done to conquer the former in making it safer ... commands the admiration of all right-thinking men and women."[34]

By late June, the American unions were making demands for comprehensive reform. The White Act of 1898 had been a significant win for seamen and maritime labor activists in ending the imprisonment of seamen who quit their vessels in U.S. ports, abolishing corporal punishment, and establishing minimum requirements for living conditions on board. Andrew Furuseth and the International Seamen's Union (ISU) prepared to build on this legislative victory by cooperating with Progressive Democrats in Congress to introduce the first iteration of the 1915 Seamen's Act. Meanwhile, rank-and-file maritime workers in New York faced an expiring contract that they had negotiated with shipping company representation in June 1911. That contract had been signed by members of the Waterfront Federation, formed through an alliance of three previously distinct unions of cooks, seamen, and firemen that collectively struck for nine days during negotiations. The alliance formed during the winter convention of the ISU in Baltimore, when the prospect of establishing an industrial department of maritime workers in the American Federation of Labor (AFL), to which the ISU belonged, was rejected, prompting many cooks, seamen, and firemen along the Atlantic and Gulf Coasts to federate. On April 15, 1912, the same day that news of *Titanic*'s sinking reached shore and the Seamen's Church Institute laid its cornerstone at 25 South Street, the new Federation moved to reorganize as the National Transport Workers' Federation of America (TWF), with the express objective to unionize all of the industrial trades associated with waterfront labor, including the firemen, oilers, engineers, cooks, stewards, coalpassers, watertenders, teamsters, seamen, hoist engineers, and longshoremen.[35]

The TWF's founding was an attempt to counteract transformations of the U.S. merchant shipping industry from sail to steam engine technology that had profound impacts on maritime and waterfront workers. Industrialization divided seamen on their own ships, separating engineers and other skilled occupations from the firemen, oilmen, stewards, and other so-called unskilled trades. Industrialization also intensified craft divisions between seamen and waterfront workers such as longshoremen and hoist engineers who were responsible for loading and unloading cargo. In addition to craft, seamen persistently struggled to overcome other divisions that were inherent to the industry, such as nationality, type of carrier, race, and ethnicity. These trade differences produced divisions within organized labor, with each trade forming its own union and typically resisting intersectional alliances. As one Federation leader put it during the strike, "[t]he trouble seems to be that we have too many unions and not enough unionism."[36]

Maritime labor in Britain, which had adopted steam technology at a pace that was several decades ahead of the U.S., had reckoned with these divisions in 1911 when the National Sailors' and Firemen's Union led a national seamen's strike against the British Shipping Federation and its interests, uniting many disparate maritime and waterfront workers and winning recognition from many shipping companies in the process. Back in the U.S. in 1912, workers from around the country followed the International Workers of the World-led textile strikes in Lawrence, Massachusetts, in which unprecedented solidarity across race, ethnicity, and craft demonstrated the potential that industrial unionism had in fighting against American business combinations. The membership of the TWF was directly inspired by these concurrent developments in international organized labor, printing articles in both English and Spanish translation about the textile strikes as they developed in their newsletter *Labor Culture*, and inviting J. Havelock Wilson, head of the British National Sailors' and Firemen's Union (NSFU), to come to New York to speak to striking firemen two weeks into the strike. The formation of the Federation itself was an act of solidarity, uniting the Marine Firemen, Oilers and Watertenders' Union of the Atlantic and Gulf, the Atlantic Coast Semaen's Union, the Harbor Boatmen's Union of New York and Vicinity, and the General Longshoremen of the Port of New York under one masthead. The NSFU itself was listed as an "affiliated union" on the eve of the strike in 1912.[37]

In attempting to build solidarity along the waterfront and maritime trades, the Federation positioned itself in direct opposition to the ISU and, by extension, the AFL. For members of the Federation, the ISU had become "influenced by the conservation tactics" of the AFL, whose leaders they accused of having "been allowed year after year to slip by without accomplishing anything."[38] Denouncing "parliamentarism" and craft unionism, they openly criticized the AFL in print for its "reactionary politics," for "compromising with capitalists," and for "merely seeking, at best, to patch up the increasing holes made by [the current] system."[39] Under the masthead of *Labor Culture*, the Federation boldly proclaimed its motto: "SYNDICALISM, GENERAL STRIKE, DIRECT ACTION." In response, Andrew Furuseth and the ISU largely remained on the sidelines for the duration of the transport workers' strike, not only withholding direct support, but deliberately subverting the Federation's efforts by exacerbating divisions between trades.

On June 28, Federation leaders met with officials from various steamship lines at the offices of the Old Dominion Steamship Company at 81 Beach Street.[40] The meeting did not go well. On the following day, the *Evening Mail* reported, "Thousands Go Out in Coast Line Strike."[41] 33,000 men along the coast had reportedly joined the strike by July 1.[42] Their list of demands included more sanitary sleeping quarters, better-quality food, and a work schedule of four hours on and eight hours off. Most important of all was their demand for recognition of the union, which would guarantee that seamen would be in control of hiring, circumventing shipping offices and their agents.[43]

Whereas the shipping companies might have been receptive to the seamen's demands for changes to working conditions and hours, they were far less willing to relinquish control of the manning process to the union and its agents. In the local papers, officials from the shipping companies depicted the seamen's demand for recognition of the union as unreasonably invasive, suggesting that such recognition would mean that the companies could only employ men supplied by the union, that all men in the engine room would be under review by the union and subject to immediate discharge if they refused to join the union, and that a union delegate would need to be employed on every ship to ensure that no violations of the terms of contract were committed by the officers and engineers.[44] As one shipping company representative put it, "maritime laws from time immemorial have provided that the captain is the supreme authority on board ship. Proper discipline cannot be obtained if the captain divides his authority with the union."[45]

For the union men, without control over hiring, the shipping companies would continue to require men to ship out from their offices, continuing a practice that had plagued the waterfront with corruption since the days of the notorious crimps of nineteenth-century sailortowns. Writing in *Labor Culture*, the TWF's editors predicted dire consequences for relinquishing control to the shipping companies: "[w]ere the Union not recognized, were men not shipping through its offices there would spring up again like mushrooms those men who, by an organized system of graft, would see that those only whom they wish are shipped or discharged."[46]

Sailors' boardinghouses once again lay at the heart of the conflict over hiring between the shipping companies and the seamen. Nefarious boardinghouse keepers were at the center of the crimping scheme, designed to bilk the seaman out of his money while ashore and force him into a sort of peonage from which all involved profited except the seaman himself. Chief engineers involved in these schemes would take payments from boardinghouse keepers, who made sure that only seamen who stayed at their houses and accumulated debts would ship out on outgoing vessels. Indebted seamen would have their wages turned over by the shipping companies directly to the boardinghouse masters to whom they owed money from their last time in port. The editors of *Labor Culture* compared the agent of this system to a "White Slaver" who "commerces in the bodies of the poor" through prostitution trafficking. "Why, if we wanted a job," an article describes, "we had to eat at their place [boardinghouse] and spend our earnings there. Then we were sold to a chief engineer for a box of cigars or a dollar or two."[47]

With the strike on and the boardinghouses full of striking seamen, speculation arose along the waterfront as to which side these "landlords" would take.[48] Prevalent opinion seemed to suggest that the chief engineers, siding with the shipping companies to end the strike so as to return to the old system of hiring, would enlist the boardinghouse keepers to aid them in undermining the striking Federation. However, not all keepers came out against the strikers. "For a time the boarding masters wavered," *Labor Culture* reported, "[n]ow they have sided with the striking firemen, which gives evidence of our power." The Federation followed their claim of support with a series of letters sent to the Marine Firemen's Union from Spanish boardinghouse keepers in Manhattan, expressing their solidarity and offering material support for the strikers. Among the authors of these letters were José Boasoa García of 362 West 11th Street, Juan Barreiro Lopez of 167 Perry Street, Pedro Rodríguez of 174 Perry Street, Juan López of 168 South Street, Juan Bareia of 313 Water Street, Juan Lavalle of 171 Perry Street, and more than a dozen more, all offering free lodging and food to striking firemen. Some of the keepers reported that they were currently providing free lodging for fifty men, with resources to provide for another hundred. Smaller houses offered what they could, such as free haircuts, or the offer of open lines of credit.[49]

It is likely that such offers were exaggerated in print by the Federation to project a reassuring sense of solidarity to its readers, or in an attempt to intimidate the shipping companies by publishing evidence that the striking firemen had such material support, "even if it be for more than a year," as one keeper's letter proclaimed. Two things, however, are indisputable.

First is the fact that ethnic solidarity among Spanish waterfront workers played a major role in initiating and maintaining the strike. James Vidal, a Spanish immigrant, leader of the Marine Firemen's Union, and editor of *Labor Culture*, estimated that in 1912 sixty percent of firemen, oilers, and water tenders in New York were of Spanish descent. The ISU had previously attempted to organize these Spanish maritime workers but had been unsuccessful. Vidal and the Marine Firemen's Union had more success, communicating in the workers' native language through mass meetings, lectures, and *Labor Culture*, which was printed in both Spanish and English translations, with the message of solidarity against not only the shipping companies but also nefarious boardinghouse keepers and engineers who were forming combinations to exploit them. In addition to the Spaniards, the union succeeded in recruiting Portuguese, Greeks, and maritime workers "of other Latin races" to join.[50]

Second, the boardinghouses that served as temporary homes and decentralized headquarters for strike operations posed a formidable threat to local authorities tasked with restoring order to the city's shipping industries. In addition to the Federation's headquarters at 225 West Street, strikers used boardinghouses scattered throughout lower Manhattan as hubs for the exchange of information, planning, and comradery. For example, strikers established a subsidiary headquarters at the boardinghouse at 17 Hamilton Avenue, where police reported there was a consistent crowd "of fifty or sixty men always hanging about the place."[51] These congregations often provoked open conflict with the police and coordinated violence from both sides of the strike. July 8 was a day of particularly pitched violence, in which one rioter and two policemen were shot, and Spanish and Greek oilers were at the center of a "wild throng" following a fight at a boardinghouse and bar at the intersection of Cherry and Roosevelt Streets that pitted strikers against strike breakers. When police arrived on the scene, they were met with pistol fire; two policemen were shot, and one striking Spanish fireman, Jose Palmiera, was killed. The melee continued as "roving strikers moved up and down South Street defying the police and assaulting men that they supposed were strike breakers." The night concluded with a police raid on a sailors' boardinghouse at 21 James Slip, and the arrest of thirty-seven strikers.[52,53] Other events over the course of the strike's timeline suggest an intersectional solidarity within Manhattan's lower wards that extended beyond the boardinghouses and even the maritime trades. On July 10, after police had shot and killed striking fireman Andreas Rodriguez, the TWF led a massive demonstration, carrying his coffin down the length of West Street, around the Battery to Whitehall and South Streets, and into the heart of sailortown down Roosevelt and Cherry Streets. A hearse led a procession of some eighty carriages until the strikers stopped and removed the coffin, lifting it overhead and marching to a Spanish funeral chant, accompanied by encouragements to onlookers, longshoremen, and other waterfront workers to walk off their jobs and join the strike.[54] Such a demonstration was meant to foment intersectional solidarity among the strikers and working-class residents of lower Manhattan. This tactic was repeated a few days later on July 12, when striking firemen, oilmen, and water tenders gathered along the Hudson River to harass strike-breaking cooks and firemen leaving the Morgan Line piers. At the sight of an arriving police squad, "the tenements about emptied themselves, and soon the streets were filled with fighting men and women." In the middle of this riotous scene, "from roofs and windows there came a storm of bricks and stones" that struck and injured several policemen. Order was restored when the police successfully beat back the men, women, and children who had poured out of their apartments into the streets and back into the tenement buildings.[55,56]

Local police reacted to such demonstrations of strength in numbers by revoking licenses for parades, raiding and arresting strikers en masse, and locking down entire neighborhoods of lower Manhattan in as attempt to stifle dissent. Strikers, for their part, focused their ire on J.P. Morgan, the "archmillionaire" and shipping magnate. The owner of the International Mercantile Marine Company prevented all eight of his subsidiary companies that operated out of Atlantic Coast ports from acquiescing to any of the strikers' demands.[57] In turn, the TWF attacked Morgan and the "gigantic beast of capital" in his control. Additionally, the Federation capitalized on public sentiment regarding "safety at sea" and the recent memory of *Titanic*'s sinking to sway public opinion against scabs and in support of the more skilled, competent, and experienced strikers. When the passenger liner SS *St. Louis* attempted to leave port with an inexperienced scab crew, strikers flooded the pier holding signs that read "Passengers, S.S. *St. Louis* is manned with an incompetent crew. Remember the *Titanic*."[58] The strikers dispatched wagons displaying similar messages on banners in large font and littered the waterfront with handbills in an attempt to prevent the liner's departure.[59] Ultimately, the strikers' efforts were futile, and the *St. Louis* got underway with its ragtag crew and bewildered passengers. The rhetoric of safety at sea, however, proved a potent weapon in critiquing the shipping companies for endangering their passengers, cargo, and crew, as well as undermining solidarity among the strikebreakers. Early in the strike, companies operating passenger liners ordered their ships to leave port and weigh anchor away from the waterfront in New York Harbor to allow time to recruit replacement crews. Eventually, many of these ships successfully left port, according to *Labor Culture*, "under the guidance of tailors and shoemakers" and "mere apprentices seeking a sea voyage at the Companies' expense."[60]

While the number of striking seamen in New York was strong, the group ultimately relied on the longshoremen to join them in order to truly disrupt waterfront commerce.[61] The shipping companies had anticipated the strike by training replacement workers three weeks prior to the strike's first day, and ships generally were able to continue operating with minimal delays as a result.[62] By July 1, several papers reported that thousands of longshoremen had joined the strike, but just a day later, the *New York Times* ran an article reporting that too few longshoremen had come out to cause the shipping companies any significant disruption.[63] *Labor Culture* ran several articles after the strike had been officially called off, analyzing the reasons why it had ultimately been a failure. Reportedly, as early as June 30, divisions within the union along lines of trade and ethnicity undermined the TWF's efforts to encourage intersectional solidarity and provoke a general transport strike in New York. First, the marine cooks' union abandoned the Federation to initiate their own negotiations with the shipping companies. Then, the longshoremen and hoisting engineers bowed out, leaving only the firemen and the seamen. The ISU, for its part, was highly selective in what tepid support they offered the strike, losing vigor as time passed. The TWF openly accused the ISU of neglecting to aid in recruiting the longshoremen, offering a limited presence at mass meetings and parades, and failing to show up altogether at the funeral procession of Andreas Rodriguez, fomenting deep resentment between the trades.[64] While some of the unorganized longshoremen joined the strike, the majority of the AFL-affiliated International Longshoremen's Union remained on the sidelines. According to James Vidal, this division was drawn along ethnic lines, with the English-speaking longshoremen refusing to join the Spanish-led strike.[65]

Conclusion

The ISU turned its back on industrial unionism and intersectional solidarity that spanned craft, race, and ethnicity in favor of political reform through an alliance with Progressive politicians. Whereas the Union's determination to pursue practical gains through political means resulted in the passage of the landmark 1915 Seamen's Act, the Act's core objectives of seamen's emancipation, wage equalization, and safety at sea would have unintended consequences. Rather than protecting white, U.S. citizen, skilled merchant seamen labor as intended, the 1915 Act would lead to a crisis of U.S. citizenship of which merchant seamen were at the center.

Notes

1. Library of Congress, *Chronicle of America: Historical Newspapers* database.
2. Edmund L. Baylies, "Address at the Ceremony of Laying of the Corner Stone of the Seamen's Institute," 25 South Street—Ceremony of Laying of the Cornerstone—April 16, 1912, Records of the Seamen's Church Institute of New York and New Jersey.
3. "The Cornerstone Laid," *The Lookout*, April 1912, *The Lookout*, Records of the Seamen's Church Institute of New York and New Jersey, 1.

4. "List of Founders," *The Lookout*, April 1913, *The Lookout*, Records of the Seamen's Church Institute of New York and New Jersey, 9.
5. "The Cornerstone Laid," 1.
6. Ibid., 3.
7. "Deep Grief Told at Stone Laying of a Sea Home: *Titanic* Disaster Gives Tragic Tone to the Formal Ceremony at the Church Institute, South Street," *World* (New York), April 17, 1912. Seamen's Church Institute of New York Scrapbook 1911–1912, Records of the Seamen's Church Institute of New York and New Jersey.
8. "*Carpathia* Here To-Night with *Titanic*'s Survivors," *New York Times*, April 18, 1912.
9. "…as Generous Rush to Aid," *New York Herald*, April 20, 1912.
10. Herbert L. Satterlee, "Report on Clothing, Etc., Given Survivors…", 5 July 1912, Mansfield, Rev. Archibald R.—RMS *Titanic*, Correspondence—1912, Records of the Seamen's Church Institute of New York and New Jersey Records.
11. "…as Generous Rush to Aid."
12. "*Titanic*'s Seamen at Prayer Service," unknown. Seamen's Church Institute of New York Scrapbook 1911–1912, Records of the Seamen's Church Institute of New York and New Jersey.
13. "…as Generous Rush to Aid," unknown. Seamen's Church Institute of New York Scrapbook 1911–1912, Records of the Seamen's Church Institute of New York and New Jersey.
14. "*Titanic*'s Seamen at Prayer Service," unknown. Seamen's Church Institute of New York Scrapbook 1911–1912, Records of the Seamen's Church Institute of New York and New Jersey.
15. *New York Times*, April 22, 1912.
16. "Seamen Neglected," unknown. Seamen's Church Institute of New York Scrapbook 1911–1912, Records of the Seamen's Church Institute of New York and New Jersey.
17. "*Titanic*'s Crew Sails, Ragged and Penniless," unknown. Seamen's Church Institute of New York Scrapbook 1911–1912, Records of the Seamen's Church Institute of New York and New Jersey.
18. Ibid.
19. "Bishop Burch Speaks at *Titanic* Memorial Service," *The Lookout*, May 1912, *The Lookout*, Records of the Seamen's Church Institute of New York and New Jersey, 2.
20. "Arrival of the *Olympic* at Southampton," *Southern Daily Echo* (Southampton, U.K.), April 22, 1912.
21. "Duke Offered Help to Sail *Olympic*," *New York Times*, April 27, 1912, 1.
22. "The *Olympic's* Boats," *Southern Daily Echo* (Southampton, U.K.), April 22, 1912.

23. "Firemen Leave the Olympic: Amazing Incident Delays Liner's Sailing," *Southern Daily Echo* (Southampton, U.K.), April 24, 1912.
24. "Firemen Strike, *Olympic* Held," *New York Times*, April 25, 1912, 1.
25. Ibid.
26. "Firemen Desert Ship and Deck Hands Mutiny: Over Fifty Men in Custody: Vessel's Sailing Abandoned," *Hampshire Independent* (Southampton, U.K.), April 25, 1912.
27. Ibid.
28. "*Olympic* Strikers Make New Demand." *New York Times*, April 26, 1912, 1.
29. "The Olympic Sensation," *Southern Daily Echo* (Southampton, U.K.), April 25, 1912.
30. "Sailing of the *Olympic* Abandoned: Men Refuse to Work: 53 in Custody on a Charge of Mutiny," *Hampshire Advertiser* (Southampton, U.K.), April 25, 1912.
31. "Latest Olympic Sensation," *Southern Daily Echo* (Southampton, U.K.), April 26, 1912.
32. "The Police Court Proceedings at Portsmouth: Remand on Bail Till Tuesday Next," *Southern Daily Echo* (Southampton, U.K.), April 25, 1912.
33. "The *Olympic* and Her Crew: Charge Proved but Men Dismissed: Don't Do it Again!," *Hampshire Independent*, April 26, 1912.
34. "Seamen's Unions and Trade Demands," *Marine Journal*, May 25, 1912. Seamen's Church Institute of New York Scrapbook 1911–1912, Records of the Seamen's Church Institute of New York and New Jersey.
35. "Strike Ended, War Begun!" *Labor Culture*, August 3, 1912, and James Vidal, "Facts About the Strike," *Labor Culture*, August 3, 1912.
36. "12,000 Longshoremen Reported on Strike: Seamen Give Out That They Have Swelled the Number Quitting to 30,000," *Sun* (New York), July 2, 1912, 6.
37. National Transport Workers' Federation of America, *Labor Culture*, International Institute for Social History, Amsterdam, Netherlands.
38. James Vidal, "Facts About the Strike," *Labor Culture*, August 3, 1912.
39. Tom Mann, "Prepare for Action," *Labor Culture*, July 27, 1912, reprinted from *The Toiler*, July 1910.
40. "Dock Strike to Hang On Today's Conference," *Evening Mail* (New York), June 28, 1912. Seamen's Church Institute of New York Scrapbook 1911–1912, Records of the Seamen's Church Institute of New York and New Jersey.
41. "Thousands Go Out in Coast Line Strike," *Evening Mail* (New York), June 29, 1912. Seamen's Church Institute of New York Scrapbook 1911–1912, Records of the Seamen's Church Institute of New York and New Jersey.

42. "33,000 Men Now Out in Big Marine Strike," *Evening Mail* (New York), July 1, 1912. Seamen's Church Institute of New York Scrapbook 1911–1912, Records of the Seamen's Church Institute of New York and New Jersey.
43. "On Duty," *Labor Culture*, July 13, 1912.
44. "Demands Refused, Vote to Strike on Coastwise Lines," *Herald* (New York), June 29, 1912. Seamen's Church Institute of New York Scrapbook 1911–1912, Records of the Seamen's Church Institute of New York and New Jersey.
45. *Sun* (New York), June 26, 1912. Seamen's Church Institute of New York Scrapbook 1911–1912, Records of the Seamen's Church Institute of New York and New Jersey.
46. "On Duty," *Labor Culture*, July 13, 1912.
47. "On Guard!" *Labor Culture*, June 29, 1912.
48. "Our Power Evident," *Labor Culture*, July 13, 1912.
49. Ibid.
50. "Spanish Strike Head Businesslike Figure," *Sun* (New York), July 6, 1912. Seamen's Church Institute of New York Scrapbook 1911–1912, Records of the Seamen's Church Institute of New York and New Jersey.
51. "Bullets Fly in Seamen's Strike," *New York Tribune*, July 9, 1912. Seamen's Church Institute of New York Scrapbook 1911–1912, Records of the Seamen's Church Institute of New York and New Jersey.
52. Ibid.
53. "Shot Dead in Street as Sea Strikers Riot," *Sun* (New York), July 9, 1912. Seamen's Church Institute of New York Scrapbook 1911–1912, Records of the Seamen's Church Institute of New York and New Jersey.
54. "Carry Coffin on Soldiers, Urging Workers to Quit," *World* (New York), July 10, 1912. Seamen's Church Institute of New York Scrapbook 1911–1912, Records of the Seamen's Church Institute of New York and New Jersey.
55. "Women Aid Rioters When Police Charge," *New York Times*, July 13, 1912. Seamen's Church Institute of New York Scrapbook 1911–1912, Records of the Seamen's Church Institute of New York and New Jersey.
56. "Bullets and Brocks Fly in Ship Strike: Police Fire at Roofs When Attacked by Missiles Thrown from Above," *New York Times*, July 16, 1912. Seamen's Church Institute of New York Scrapbook 1911–1912, Records of the Seamen's Church Institute of New York and New Jersey.
57. "Transport Workers' General Strike," *Labor Culture*, July 6, 1912.
58. "*St. Louis* Sails with Strike Breaking Crew," *Sun* (New York), July 14, 1912. Seamen's Church Institute of New York Scrapbook 1911–1912, Records of the Seamen's Church Institute of New York and New Jersey.

59. "'Remember *Titanic*' is Strikers' Warning to Ship's Passengers," *Evening World* (New York), July 13, 1912. Seamen's Church Institute of New York Scrapbook 1911–1912, Records of the Seamen's Church Institute of New York and New Jersey.
60. "Transport Workers' General Strike," *Labor Culture*, July 6, 1912.
61. "Call Longshoremen Out in Ship Strike," *New York Times*, July 1, 1912. Seamen's Church Institute of New York.
62. "Crews of Coastwise Steamships Go On Strike At Eleven Ports," *New York Herald*, June 30, 1912 and "Seamen's Strike Fails to Hold Up Steamships," *Evening Telegram* (New York), June 29, 1912. Seamen's Church Institute of New York Scrapbook 1911–1912, Records of the Seamen's Church Institute of New York and New Jersey.
63. "4,000 Join Sea Strike, Expect 110,000 More," *Evening Journal* (New York), July 1, 1912 and "Few Longshoremen Answer Strike Call," *New York Times*, July 2, 1912. Seamen's Church Institute of New York Scrapbook 1911–1912, Records of the Seamen's Church Institute of New York and New Jersey.
64. "Strike Ended, War Begun! Betrayed!" *Labor Culture*, August 3, 1912.
65. "Facts About the Strike," *Labor Culture*, August 3, 1912.

CHAPTER 4

The 1915 Seamen's Act: Maritime Labor and Progressive Era Maritime Reform

The public interest in safety at sea reform that the tragedy of *Titanic* elicited, combined with the clamor of ensuing waterfront conflicts in both Britain and New York City, brought the issue of maritime safety regulations and workers' rights into the public conversation. As Andrew Furuseth described the public mood between 1912 and 1915, "[t]he great sacrifice of life resulting from the loss of the British steamship *Titanic* aroused the public mind of the civilized world to a realization of the great and manifestly growing dangers of travel by sea."[1] Responding in part to this public appetite for reform, Progressive politicians took up the mantle of safety at sea and made it a core component of their legislative efforts. The Democratic Party platform for 1912 included a section on the U.S. merchant marine that called for the "speedy enactment of laws for the greater security of life and property at sea."[2] In addition to addressing safety at sea, Democratic politicians detailed plans for rebuilding an American citizen merchant marine that would simultaneously bolster U.S. trade overseas and provide the auxiliary support necessary for national defense and increasingly urgent military ventures.

Woodrow Wilson, the Democratic nominee for President in 1912, delivered an acceptance speech in New Jersey in which he commented at length on the centrality of a robust merchant marine in supporting an increasingly internationalist country. "Without a great merchant marine,"

J. Thayer, *Citizenship, Subversion, and Surveillance in U.S. Ports*, Global Studies in Social and Cultural Maritime History,
https://doi.org/10.1007/978-3-031-45618-3_4

Wilson proclaimed, "we can not take our rightful place in the commerce of the world." Advocating for reform of registry laws and tariffs on imports, Wilson continued:

> Merchants who must depend upon the carriers of rival mercantile nations to carry their goods to market are at a disadvantage in international trade too manifest to need to be pointed out ... Our industries have expanded to such a point that they will burst their jackets if they can not find a free outlet to the markets of the world; and they can not find routes they want them to go—and prefer the interest of America in their sailing orders and their equipment.[3]

Finally, the Democratic party expressed support for the abolition of imprisonment of seamen charged with desertion, deemed essential to the leveling of American competition with foreign-flagged ships and the equalization of wages, stating that "[s]uch laws and treaties are un-American, and violate the spirit, if not the letter, of the Constitution of the United States."[4]

Three issues—seamen's emancipation, the leveling of competition between U.S.-flagged vessels and foreign operators, and safety at sea—came to form the essence of what would become the 1915 Seamen's Act. Whereas safety at sea dominated the public's attention and was the focus of more than half of the text of the twenty-two-page bill, the most radical components of the 1915 Seamen's Act can be found in its sections detailing an architecture for seamen's emancipation and equalization of wages between U.S.-flagged ships and merchant vessels of other nations by finally providing resolution to debates and contestations over merchant seamen's legal entitlement to mobility in port.

The architects of the 1915 Seamen's Act, designed principally by Furuseth and navigated politically by La Follette, skillfully turned a range of rhetorical principles that had been used in the past to impose restrictions on seamen's mobility, liberty, and masculinity into a powerful argument for unprecedented rights and entitlements for white American seamen that were intended to equalize wages and bolster union membership. Free labor, the paradoxical status of merchant seamen as wards of the state, and safety at sea all provided rhetorical fodder for the bill's advocates. As Justin Jackson has convincingly argued, white supremacy and flexible capacity, in which an American citizen merchant marine would theoretically provide a reserve fleet capable of independently supporting military operations during times of war, were at the heart of advocates' argument for the bill's passage.[5] This combination of principles represented a well of bipartisan interests from which advocates could draw to construct speeches and detailed defense strategies in the press and at Congressional hearings.

Historical Context

Foreign control of American maritime shipping increased fivefold during the years between the end of the Civil War and the turn of the twentieth century.[6] During that time, the U.S. experienced a period of broad and rapid industrialization. American shipbuilding was an exception to these transformations, lagging behind Britain and other European nations that had been early adopters of steam engine technology, leaving the U.S. behind in the twilight of its past dominance during the Age of Sail. By 1905, of the 11,365 British ships engaged in foreign trade, less than twenty percent were vessels that operated under the power of sail. By contrast, of the United States' meager 1333 ships engaged in foreign trade, 73 percent were sailships. These disparities in both size and technological capacity of fleets produced an imbalance in the total amount of cargo under each nation's respective control. By 1905, Britain had control of seventeen-million tons of foreign trade, while the U.S. accounted for less than one-million tons, a number that the German, French, and Italian fleets all surpassed on their own.[7]

As maritime policy historians Andrew Gibson and Arthur Donovan describe it, these imbalances produced two corresponding "maritime scenarios" in the United States: first, the steady industrial and civilian decline of maritime power produced an anxious national desire to recapture lost American glory as an international maritime power; and second, as the U.S. became increasingly entangled in global imperial competition, the American government became newly determined to develop the diplomatic and military instruments necessary to protect American interests overseas.[8] Both of these scenarios depended on seapower. The impacts of Alfred Thayer Mahan's 1890 treatise on the subject were profound, infiltrating political economic thought and shaping U.S. foreign policy for decades following its publication. In *The Influence of Seapower upon History*, Mahan theorized that oceans represented a "great common," in which the balance of exchange, trade, and wealth between nations were all determined. Merchant shipping, protected by armed navies, was therefore essential for a nation to thrive economically.[9]

The Spanish-American War had exposed the U.S. merchant marine as a major point of vulnerability in U.S. foreign policy. The lack of U.S. citizen merchant seamen forced American shipping companies to employ non-citizens on ships acting as auxiliaries for naval operations during the War, relying particularly on Chinese seamen to work in the Pacific. Following the War, Congress convened a Merchant Marine Commission in 1903 to investigate the roots of the nation's weaknesses in global maritime shipping. The Commission found three principal flaws preventing the U.S. from maintaining a viable merchant fleet and stable maritime labor pool of U.S. citizen seamen. First, the high capital cost of American ships was preventing shipping companies from expanding their fleets without relying on foreign shipbuilding and foreign flag registry. Second, the high operating costs incurred by American ships, primarily due to the cost of labor relative to cheaper foreign competition, discouraged shipping companies from recruiting and employing American mariners. Third, American shipping companies were competitively disadvantaged by a lack of government subsidies that operators in Britain and European nations enjoyed.[10]

The 1903 Commission proposed solutions that represent what H. David Bess and Martin T. Farris call the three "pillars of maritime policy": subsidy, preference, and cabotage. Government subsidies were distributed to shipping companies in the form of mail carrier contracts. The 1904 Cargo Preference Act stipulated that all supplies moved by sea for the U.S. armed forces had to be carried by American vessels under U.S. registry, or in vessels owned by the U.S. government itself. Additionally, longstanding cabotage laws that restricted maritime trade along U.S. coastlines to U.S.-owned, U.S.-built, and U.S.-crewed vessels were extended to Alaska, Hawaii, Puerto Rico, and Guam.[11] Through its actions to bolster the U.S. merchant fleet and maritime labor pool, the federal government indicated its embrace of Mahan's theories regarding seapower and its willingness to respond to the symptoms of decline identified by the 1903 Merchant Marine Commission.

The impacts of government action would take time to manifest, however. President Roosevelt's Great White Fleet, launched in 1907 with the intention of demonstrating the regained glory and might of the U.S. Navy, was hampered throughout its tour of the Pacific by a lack of adequate provisions for bunkering coal, forcing the government to purchase and charter foreign tramp ships to keep the Fleet in motion. As maritime historian Samuel Lawrence summarizes, "this grand demonstration of

American power was attended by a motley array of colliers, tankers, and tenders bearing the flags of the world."[12]

The problems that the 1903 Merchant Marine Commission identified would linger up to the outbreak of the Great War in Europe, casting new urgency on the issue of American preparedness (or lack thereof) for engagement in international conflict on the high seas. Long before U.S. entry into the War, U.S. export shipping was crippled by persistent weaknesses in the nation's merchant fleet. War meant that the two largest merchant fleets, Britain and Germany, had been removed from global routing commerce, leaving a relatively tiny American fleet to attempt, and fail, to pick up the slack.[13] President Wilson's administration responded immediately in order to get cargo moving again, establishing a Bureau of War Risk Insurance to underwrite potential losses for American shipowners operating in hostile waters, liberalizing ship registry provisions established by the 1912 Panama Canal Act to allow for transfer of certain foreign vessels to the American registry, waiving certain stipulations requiring officers and crew to be U.S. citizens, and suspending cabotage laws for the duration of the war.[14]

With the sinking of *Luisitania* on May 7, 1915, President Wilson gained widespread public support for immediate military preparedness, which included direct government funding of shipbuilding through the Shipping Act of 1916 and the Emergency Shipbuilding Program. The 1915 Seamen's Act, which determined the future of government regulation over the U.S. maritime labor pool, was, in many ways, a predecessor to these emergency measures to bolster the U.S. merchant fleet.

Political Context

While labor historians such as Leon Fink hail the 1915 Seamen's Act as a signature Progressive achievement of its time, some maritime policy historians are less celebratory, questioning the Act's impact while attributing the dramatic changes in U.S. merchant shipping and maritime labor to the conditions of the command economy that World War I created. More recent scholarship, such as that of Justin Jackson, has emphasized the white supremacist and economic nationalist roots of early twentieth-century maritime labor reform, of which the 1915 Seamen's Act was the culmination. In reality, the politics behind the bill's development was a nuanced combination of all of these factors. According to Hyman Weintraub, the primary focus of Furuseth and the ISU in the wake of the passage of the White Act was to advocate for protectionist legislative measures meant to exclude Asian seamen from work on American vessels. The first incarnation of legislation containing provisions for the abolition of imprisonment of seamen who deserted in foreign ports was introduced in March 1904 by Rep. Edward J. Livernash of San Francisco. Livernash's bill also provided for the right of U.S. citizen merchant seamen to desert in foreign ports, and for foreign seamen to desert in American ports without fear of imprisonment, clauses that would become the most radical aspects of the 1915 Seamen's Act. This proposal was met with emphatic opposition from a minority of legislators who objected to the U.S. interfering in the regulation of commerce in foreign nations, as well as the specter of an influx of "the scum of all the foreign sailors." Indeed, when a later version of the bill eventually was passed in both the Senate and the House of Representatives in 1912, President Taft vetoed it in one of the final acts of his presidency on the grounds that it might create "friction with the commerce of foreign nations."[15]

The elections of 1910, swept by Progressive candidates, including the United Mine Workers' William B. Wilson, who joined with La Follette to reintroduce the bill, and the incoming presidency of a seemingly sympathetic Woodrow Wilson in 1912, gave the bill new momentum. This political climate, combined with the sinking of *Titanic*, lent rhetorical weight to the ISU and Furuseth's advocacy. As Weintraub describes it: "Safety was the new theme now used to drive home the need for the seamen's bill." Statements from survivors of the sinking and reports from subsequent investigations were introduced during committee hearings as evidence of the need for immediate reform.[16]

After more than a year of fits and starts, the bill was reintroduced and finally passed in February 1915. Senate stalwarts like Henry Cabot Lodge and Elihu Root maintained opposition to the bill's provisions granting seamen the near-universal right to desertion based on its potential impact for "unilaterally abrogating commercial treaties" that might lead to "serious international complications." President Wilson, as it turned out, shared these concerns. In correspondence with Furuseth, he expressed reservations about signing the bill: "What is troubling me at this moment is that it demands of the government what seems a truly impossible thing, namely the denunciation of some twenty-two commercial treaties." Furuseth responded by paying the President a personal visit during which he offered a final plea. Wilson came out of the meeting convinced, and eventually announced his support, albeit with a lingering reluctance: "I debated the matter of signing the bill very earnestly indeed, weighing the arguments on both sides with a good deal of anxiety, and finally determined to sign it because it seemed the only chance to get something like justice to a class of workmen who have been too much neglected by our laws."[17]

The political economy behind the Seamen's Act ostensibly focused on revising existing maritime labor law so as to bring the industry up to modern standards regarding freedom of contract, acceptable working conditions and accommodations on ships, and safety reforms for both passengers and crew in the wake of public outcry over the sinking of *Titanic* in 1912. The Act's provision granting seamen the right to quit work without facing imprisonment, whether in U.S. or foreign ports, had deep roots that manifested itself in the *Arago* Supreme Court case *Robertson v. Baldwin* in 1897. Regulations regarding hours worked while at sea and in port, as well as minimum standards established for provisions and sleeping quarters addressed complaints that merchant seamen had put forth for centuries. Finally, safety provisions did much to address public concern awakened by the blockbuster tragedy of *Titanic* and the subsequent new consciousness about the danger and extreme isolation of life at sea. The Act, however, went significantly further than simply modernizing an industry that had long represented an archaic and dangerous system of marginalized labor. Perhaps most innovative of all the Act's impacts was the fact that Congress approved the extension of its regulations beyond American ships and ports to apply to all foreign vessels as well. Legitimizing a merchant seaman's right to desertion enabled sailors to take advantage of higher wages and better working conditions in foreign ports.

Desertion had been transformed from an offense punished by imprisonment as late as the 1897 *Arago* seamen's case, to a tool used to reverse "race to the bottom" employment conditions and create a competitive incentive for higher wages and better conditions for merchant seamen on the free market. While internationalist in its scope, the protectionist roots of the Seamen's Act actually represented an extreme version of nationalist approaches to labor and commerce regulation.

The 1915 Seamen's Act was a complex piece of legislation that harnessed the rhetorical power of safety at sea and seamen's emancipation to achieve the true goal of its architects: equalization. Furuseth, La Follette, and the many merchant seamen they represented were able to successfully repackage rhetoric that had previously been used to control seamen as wards of the state and of charitable society into a powerful argument for radically protectionist maritime labor policies. These policies were motivated by xenophobia and racism but also intended to equalize wages between white American sailors and the foreign seamen with whom they competed and to ensure the self-preservation of a maritime unionism that was dependent on a membership of skilled, white, U.S. citizen seamen. The arguments of reformers consistently put shipowners on the defensive, forcing them to concede most of the bill's provisions regarding safety at sea, the abolition of flogging and the threat of imprisonment for desertion, and minimum standards for conditions on ships. Robert Dollar, of the Pacific-going Dollar Steamship Company, facing questioning in front of Congress, summed up the general feeling of the shipowners regarding their situation, and the inevitable momentum of reform that they found themselves swept up in: "I am not accustomed, Mr. Chairman," testified Dollar, "to this police court kind of investigation … I do not know that I ever undertook a thing that I hated as much, and that hurt my feelings as much, as to come here before you gentlemen today."[18]

White Supremacy

As both Fink and Jackson argue, practically all facets of the bill were directly or indirectly motivated by white supremacy and nativist protectionism that was characteristic of West Coast labor unionism, as well as Progressive Era labor politics in general. Jackson pushes further, arguing that the doctrine of "flexible capacity," which emphasizes the necessary role that an American citizen merchant marine takes on during times of war in providing support for military operations independent of other nations' maritime fleets and labor pools, was also essential to the bill. During and immediately after the Spanish-American War, labor unions and Progressive politicians projected their vision of white supremacy overseas, expanding the colonial footprint of the United States to the Caribbean and the Philippines as a supposed act of civilizing racial influence, for which the state would require a merchant marine capable of providing the auxiliary support necessary to sustain these imperial projects.[19]

The position that merchant seamen and their union representatives occupied by 1915 was determined, in large part, by the impacts of an industrializing maritime industry. The transition from sail to steam-powered vessels had radically disrupted traditional hierarchies of labor on ships and, by extension, changed the nature of the maritime workforce in terms of skill, ethnicity, and culture. Specifically, the absence of sails on a modern steamship, "with her short masts, little rigging, and almost no sails" meant that some aspects of traditional skilled labor were no longer necessary, replaced, as W. M. Brittain, Secretary of the American Steamship Association testified before the U.S. Senate Committee on Commerce, by "the most ordinary kind of unskilled labor that can be imagined, consisting, for the most part of washing decks, scrubbing paint, and polishing brass work" often done by "unskilled" non-white, non-U.S. citizen seamen.[20] Britain continued by claiming that the "center of gravity" of skilled labor on ships had shifted from the deck to the engine department, with most of the "heavy work" on deck operated by machinery controlled by the ship's engine.

Section 13 of the proposed bill was designed to counter these forces. Most notorious of that section's provisions, the requirements that seventy-five percent of a ship's crew be able "to understand any order given by the officers," explicitly intended to counter the wave of foreign labor being hired by shipping companies, especially on the West Coast, and specifically Chinese, Japanese, and "Lascar" seamen from the Indian subcontinent, Southeast Asia, or the Middle East. This provision was also designed to prevent unskilled laborers from filling jobs that were previously held by white American seamen. A second provision, requiring that sixty-five percent of a ship's crew be manned by sailors with a rating of no less than able seaman (a member of the deck department with a minimum required amount of experience), reinforced this attempt to restore skilled labor on steamships. Finally, a third provision requiring that a seaman have three years' experience before attaining the rating of able seaman further emphasized the desire to restore skilled, white, American labor.

More than any other facet of the bill, shipowners opposed these provisions. "In the old days of sailing ships," testified Robert Dollar, "this was necessary; but on the modern steamers such experience is altogether unnecessary ... the real object of it [Section 13] is to put the entire shipping of sailors by law in the hands of the sailors' union, who in time of a strike could effectually tie up the entire shipping ... in American ports."[21] Dollar, who frequently acted as spokesman for West Coast shipowners during Congressional committee hearings, repeatedly attempted to package the threat of unbalanced power in the hands of maritime unions with arguments that warned of the threat of foreign competition, extolling the principles of freedom of contract, and insisting that sailors were inherently irresponsible and therefore not to be trusted with their own wages in port.

Safety at Sea

In the weeks following the *Titanic* disaster, the United States Senate and the British Board of Trade both launched inquiries that investigated the cause of the incident and made recommendations for preventing similar incidents in the future.[22] The American inquiry held its initial hearing on April 19, while many of the surviving crew and some passengers were still in New York City. J. Bruce Ismay, managing director of the White Star Line, and Arthur Henry Rostron, captain of *Carpathia*, offered testimony. Guglielmo Marconi was also in attendance to provide consultation regarding the operation of the ship's wireless radios.[23] The inquiry lasted eighteen days, during which a series of officers, crewmembers, and passengers who had survived the sinking were questioned. A London commission carried out a similar inquiry beginning in May and lasting thirty-six days.[24] The American committee issued its report on May 28 while the British report followed on July 30. The inquiries resulted in an international conference held in London that produced recommendations for reforms to life-saving equipment and practices on merchant ships, presented for adoption to a consortium of nations, including the United States.

In March 1914, La Follette presented remarks prepared by Furuseth and V. A. Olander, also of the International Seamen's Union, before the Senate Committee on Foreign Relations. The remarks were titled "Welfare of American Seamen, A Memorial of the seamen of the United States praying for the disapproval by the Senate of the International Convention on Safety of Life at Sea, signed at London, January 20, 1914, and for the enactment by Congress of S. 136," referring to the bill introduced by La Follette and designed by Furuseth and his collaborators. Their main objection to the regulations proposed by the London conference, relating to the safety of life at sea, navigation, construction of ships, radiotelegraphy, life-saving appliances and fire protection, and safety certification ostensibly boiled down to a nationalist argument for maintaining independent control of such regulations. As Furuseth wrote and La Follette presented, "It appears to your petitioners that by the adoption of these articles the United States will surrender its power to regulate foreign vessels coming to its ports. We believe that as a result of such action foreign ships will continue to have the advantages over American ships which, in the past, have been one of the main factors in destroying the American mercantile marine in the foreign trade."[25]

Furuseth went further, claiming that the provisions for safety at sea put forward by the London Conference were simply not stringent enough to address the problem of lives lost at sea. Indeed, the bill favored by Furuseth and his allies set extensive and painstakingly specific requirements for new ships operating in U.S. ports. More than thirteen pages of the twenty-two-page bill in its final form were dedicated to safety at sea provisions, including section 14, which set standards for life-saving boats, including type, construction, strength, buoyancy, capacity, weight of persons, marking of lifeboats, equipment on lifeboats, stowage, handling, manning, embarkation, and several pages of text concerning regulation of davits. Additionally, the bill set standards for the use of qualified seamen as replacements for lost crewmembers, requirements for the keeping of continuous watches, and requirements for vessels thought to be unseaworthy to inspections from shipping agents.[26]

Rather than attempt to fight advocates of the bill on these numerous and detailed points, shipowners seemed resigned to accept these standards, knowing that resistance would require moving against the tide of public sympathy that *Titanic* had produced. Dollar, representing shipowners of the West Coast, declared that he in fact "cheerfully and willingly" agreed to all conditions reached at the London Conference regarding safety at sea, and offered only minor resistance to a few points of the bill's safety provisions while testifying in front of Congress.[27]

Furuseth, on the other hand, was being less than genuine in claiming that differences in safety at sea provisions were his only objections to the possibility of the U.S. adopting the London Conference resolutions. As with the rhetoric of white supremacy and flexible capacity, Furuseth and other allies of the bill repeatedly utilized the rhetoric and overwhelming public support for safety at sea provisions in order to mask more radical aspects of the bill: namely, emancipation and equalization.

Emancipation

As with the case of the *Arago* deserters, the issue of "emancipation" for merchant seamen loomed large in debates over the 1915 Seamen's Act. Whereas *Robertson v. Baldwin* had focused exclusively on the issue of imprisonment as punishment for desertion, emancipation in the 1915 Act was a complex of provisions that directly or indirectly impacted the range and extent of a seaman's mobility in ports, both domestic and foreign. Specifically, the bill prioritized the abolition of imprisonment for desertion in foreign ports, the abolition of flogging or corporal punishment on American ships, and the abolition of advances and partial pay to seamen, the latter being an attempt to disrupt systems of crimping.

Rhetorically, these provisions were packaged within the oratorical gamesmanship of Furuseth and La Follette, who insistently linked seamen's status under the law with the ideology of antislavery and free labor. "Abolish the slave laws," Furuseth wrote boldly in a pamphlet read before Congress by La Follette: "[l]et American freedom extend to the decks of the American ship. Let American soil become free soil for seamen as it is for all other men."[28] Such high rhetoric demanded the attention not just of Congress, but of the American public. In reality, the 1898 White Act had all but accomplished this very goal by abolishing imprisonment for desertion in American and nearby foreign ports. Furthermore, by 1915, the issue of abolishing imprisonment was not one that shipowners contested. In fact, Dollar testified that not only he but the entire body of the San Francisco Chamber of Commerce, and "the shipowners of the Pacific Coast" had instructed him to testify that they were "opposed to any further imprisonment of sailors on American ships, or on foreign ships either."[29] Dollar off-handedly mentioned that shipowners no longer took action on the letter of the law, even in foreign ports where imprisonment was still legal. The same went for flogging, which the proposed bill finally and explicitly abolished. "It is a dead letter," Dollar insisted, "as I have not heard of a man being flogged in the past fifty years. By all means abolish it." As for the provisions of the bill that called for minimum standards for rations, sleep quarters, and washing stations, Dollar testified that his ships already met union demands and more, producing before his Congressional audience a bill of fare that detailed the meal schedule from one of his ships as evidence.[30]

As with the issue of safety at sea, advocates of the bill put the public attention and sympathy generated by sensational antislavery rhetoric to use as a cover for more nuanced, and ultimately more radical, reforms. Section 16, which abolished imprisonment for desertion, was at the heart of these reforms. But Section 4, entitling seamen in every port that the ship loaded or delivered cargo to one-half of his wages earned, applicable to both American and foreign vessels "while in the harbors of the United States," and Section 11, making it illegal to pay advances to seamen who signed shipping articles, were essential to Furuseth's plan for "equalization": essentially, to allow the rate of wages in port to float in an open market so that ships seeking crews in low-wage foreign nations would be forced to raise their standards so as to compete with U.S.-flagged ships and attract seamen to sign shipping articles with American vessels.

Vigorously opposed by shipowners who anticipated that their crews would be enticed to desert in every port, Furuseth insisted that these provisions, too, were necessary for seamen to achieve full emancipation. "If a sailor can not get any money out of his vessel," he testified, "and can not pawn his body for a few dollars, then he is tied to the vessel." According to Furuseth, without such provisions as Sections 4 and 11 provided, a seaman's freedom under Section 16 would be a useless gesture: "if they are going to take as liquidated damages all the wages that are due to him ... and then place him in a position so that he can not get any credit ... if they can keep the man from getting some money the freedom will be barren right."[31]

Equalization

As Fink argues, perhaps the most innovative of all the Act's clauses was the fact that Congress approved the extension of its regulations beyond American ships and ports to apply to all foreign vessels and ports as well. The irony of the U.S. Congress taking on such an internationalist approach to industry regulation is that it was done with the objective of protecting the nationalist interests of American shipowners and shipping companies. In establishing such high marks for conditions on American ships, and requiring such relatively accommodating treatment of American seamen, Congress ran the risk of creating a "race to the bottom" in which shippers would enlist foreign-flagged vessels and employ foreign seamen to carry out their trade, in search of the most lax regulations and lowest rates in terms of wages, provisions, and working conditions that they would be required to follow by law.[32]

As Rep. Rufus Hardy (D-TX) summarized in Committee, "[t]he idea you [Furuseth] are presenting is, that by doing away with this involuntary servitude—arrest for desertion and presenting the foreign vessels which come here with cheap crews from holding them subject to arrest in our port for desertion—that you will equalize, or practically raise the wages of seamen the world over."[33] Legitimizing a merchant seaman's right to desertion enabled seamen to take advantage of higher wages and better working conditions in foreign ports. As the bill's proponents argued, in imprisoning merchant seamen who quit their vessels, the U.S. government was effectively aiding foreign shipowners in maintaining lower wage rates and standards on deck than those prevailing in American ports and on American ships. Eliminating a ban on desertion on a global scale would essentially create free market competitive conditions that would ultimately benefit American industry. American shipping companies would adopt the role as a leader in providing well-regulated wage rates and provisions that made for attractive jobs for merchant seamen by positing a single world market for maritime labor in the foreign trade and allowing maritime labor to "float" at market price like a common commodity.[34]

V. A. Olander, President of the Lake Seamen's Union, offered an anecdote involving seamen on the British-flagged *Carlo* in 1900 that exemplified the problem under the law prior to the 1915 Act:

> One evening as I was standing at the rail of my ship I saw two policemen come down with two men carrying their bags; saw those two men taken aboard of the *Carlo* ... I saw those men taken aft; saw the mate open their bags, take out a set of overalls and give them to the men; and saw the men go forward into the forecastle. They came up again and handed their shore clothes over to the mate, he taking the bag and clothes into his room and locking them up. I knew then, of course, what was going on. These men, finding that the prevailing wages in the country in which they were working were three times the wages that they were being held at, did not like to continue under such conditions and tried to quit. The law and the treaties governing these questions were brought into force, and they were brought back on board the ship.[35]

For Olander, Furuseth, and their allies, the laws preventing seamen from pursuing better wages were artificial distortions placed arbitrarily upon what should otherwise have been a free market created by competition between shipowners. "Imagine two ships," Furuseth implored his audience, "one flying the American flag, the other a foreign flag, moored at the same dock in New York. The crew of the American vessel has been hired in New York at American wages; that of the foreign ship at some low-wage in the Mediterranean. The two crews come into contact, each discovering the wages and conditions of the other. What is the natural result?

Unless prevented by force, the crew of the foreign vessel would either get the same wages as paid on the American vessel or they would quit."[36]

Once again, advocates of the bill were successfully able to turn bipartisan rhetoric, this time of free labor and the free market, against their opponents to argue for radical policy reforms that would restructure the very nature of maritime labor, making it more difficult for shipowners to turn the profits that they were accustomed to, and endowing merchant seamen and their union representatives with unprecedented negotiating power in the market of maritime commerce.

Conclusion

The 1915 Seamen's Act passed on March 4, 1915 in the exact form that it was introduced by Senator La Follette, nearly three years after the sinking of *Titanic* had captured the hearts and minds of the public and Congress alike. Shipowners had lost the contest in a decisive fashion. The impact of the Seamen's Act has been the subject of substantial debate among historians. Whereas Fink hails the Act as visionary in its prescient approach to confronting the downward pull of a globalizing economy, other historians attribute any gains claimed by Furuseth and the ISU in the wake of the bill's passage to the fleeting conditions of the command economy created by World War I. Gibson and Donovan point out that while union membership and wages were indeed exponentially higher at the war's end, these increases were the result of direct government intervention through the 1916 Shipping Act and the Emergency Shipbuilding Program. With the government replacing private industry as the major employer in the shipping industry during the war years, these gains proved unsustainable when the war ended and private companies returned to old practices. By 1921, wages had returned to the prevailing prewar rate, and the steep decline in government cargo sent the entire U.S. shipping industry spiraling into depression.[37] The U.S. citizen maritime labor pool that had been temporarily reenergized by the war found themselves unemployed "on the beach" or leaving the industry altogether for other work.

Given these statistics, it is difficult to contest the conclusion Joseph Goldberg reached regarding the Act's legacy: "The most that could be said for the Seamen's Act was that it had provided seamen with the same freedom to work or quit which was available to shore workers. In its effort to protect and entrench the seafaring crafts, and to equalize wages and working conditions nationally, and even internationally, it failed."[38] However, the right to quit that seamen had won with passage of the Seamen's Act was far more impactful than Goldberg's passing dismissal suggests. Seamen's mobility, having been subjected to mechanisms of containment by nineteenth-century maritime ministry reformers and officially denied by the U.S. Supreme Court in 1897, had been enshrined in law as a fundamental right.

The preservation of a seamen's right to mobility was only part of the complicated legacy of the 1915 Seamen's Act, however. As Fink and Jackson have argued, white supremacy was a consistent motivating factor that fueled the passage of the Act. In one of his speeches before Congress on the Seamen's Bill, Furuseth began his comments in a manner that made this clear in no uncertain terms. "I shall speak to you to-day," he said, warming up to his defense of the proposed bill, "if I am able to do so, as I never spoke before, because I think that this is the last struggle of the white man to maintain himself on the seas and the last chance of the United States to ever become a sea power."[39]

As Jackson documents, arguments for the preservation of a white, U.S. citizen-manned merchant marine were inextricably tied to national defense and the concept of flexible capacity. According to this line of reasoning, the decline of American seamen, caused in part by falling wages and conditions on ships produced by the hiring of foreign crews, not only impacted the livelihoods of white American seamen but also impaired the ability of the U.S. to defend itself and conduct military operations overseas. Furuseth equated the crisis of competition from foreign maritime labor with the crisis of a diminished flexible capacity that the U.S. merchant fleet was capable of providing: "[t]he Caucasian is leaving the sea," the champion of White merchant seamen pleaded with Congress, "the Oriental is filling the vacancy. Sea power is in the seamen; vessels are the seamen's working tools; tools become the property of nations or races who handle them."[40]

Furuseth and the ISU wholeheartedly embraced this narrative of a declining white, U.S. citizen merchant marine and rejected the TWF's more radical syndicalism, in part based on the threats that such intersectional industrial unionism posed to the stability of the ISU's skilled, white membership. Choosing instead to pursue practical gains through political means that were undergirded by potent ideologies of xenophobia and white supremacy, the ISU and its Progressive allies in Congress succeeded in winning overwhelming support for the 1915 Seamen's Act, which would theoretically sustain a steady pool of white, U.S. citizen, skilled merchant seamen while adding to the ISU's strength through increased membership and political clout. The central irony of this legislative achievement was that in solidifying and extending merchant seamen's right to mobility in port, the 1915 Seamen's Act unwittingly compounded legal problems and anxieties over the presence of non-white, non-U.S. citizen merchant seamen in U.S. ports. The "alien seamen problem," as it became known following the Act's passage, created crises for both civil society and the state that involved confrontations over seamen's morality, spirituality, and citizenship.

Asian seamen, specifically Chinese, were at the heart of these anxieties. Under the 1882 Exclusion Act, Chinese seamen were not explicitly codified as a category unto themselves. Therefore, they fell under special rules and entitlements as a de facto result of prevailing maritime law. Chinese seamen were entitled to the same privileges as any other nationality of alien seamen, specifically the right to shore leave, with the caveat that should a Chinese seaman desert while in port, the shipping company with which he had been employed would be fined. Subsequently, a "bond rule" developed in which masters of vessels were required to post $500 for each Chinese seaman afforded shore leave, not to exceed thirty days in the U.S. Additionally, a photograph and complete personal description were required to be attached to each bond posted.

This system inevitably resulted in shipowners denying shore leave to the Chinese seamen that they employed. As Furuseth testified, "it is financially a business interest for the shipowner to keep them [Chinese seamen], and he hires them because he can keep them," not only under continual and reliable contracts but at wage rates far lower than their white American competition. Thus, the white American seamen's mobility, in addition to the higher wage rates that he commanded, made competition with foreign labor untenable. The laws on the books following the 1882 Chinese Exclusion Act empowered ships' masters who employed Chinese labor with the protections of "not only his own watchman and his own personal interest... but Government officials; that is, the Immigration Service, in keeping his cheap crew on the vessel."[41]

Whereas the bond rule appears to have been standard practice in ports up to 1915, federal district courts in the wake of the 1882 Act's passage were quick to rule in favor of the right of Chinese seamen to shore leave, establishing that they did not qualify as "laborers" under the law, and were therefore entitled to the same mobility in port as any other nationality of non-citizen seamen.[42] In 1907, the Second Circuit Federal Court ruled that the clause of immigration laws requiring shipping companies to "take precautions to prevent the landing of aliens at time or place not designated" applied only to passengers and not seamen, and that shore leave did not constitute "landing." The Court concluded its ruling with the proclamation that "sailors should go ashore."[43] The 1915 Act's provisions abolishing imprisonment for desertion and entitling seamen to partial pay at every port provided a legal platform that simultaneously resolved long-standing confrontations between merchant seamen and the state over restrictions on mobility in port, and provided to non-citizen migrants an enticing means to circumvent increasingly exclusionary immigration laws passed by Congress. A new era of contested citizenship originating in U.S. sailortowns had begun.

Notes

1. Andrew Furuseth and V. A. Olander, International Seamen's Union, "Welfare of American Seamen: A Memorial of the Seamen of the United States Praying for the Disapproval by the Senate of the International Convention on Safety of Life at Sea, Signed at London, January 20, 1914, and for the Enactment by Congress of S. 136," presented by Mr. La Follette and referred to the Committee on Foreign Relations, March 20, Washington, D.C.: Government Printing Office, 1914, Records of the Seamen's Church Institute of New York and New Jersey, 3.
2. Democratic Party Platform, 1912.
3. Woodrow Wilson, "Acceptance Speech," New Jersey, 1912.
4. Democratic Party Platform, 1912.
5. Justin Jackson, "'The Right Kind of Men': Flexible Capacity, Chinese Exclusion, and the Imperial Origins of Maritime Labor Reform in the United States, 1898–1905," *Labor* 10, no. 4 (2013): 39–60.
6. Andrew Gibson and Arthur Donovan, *The Abandoned Ocean: A History of United States Maritime Policy*, (Columbia, SC: University of South Carolina Press, 2000), 86.
7. Ibid.
8. Gibson and Donovan, *The Abandoned Ocean*, 88–89.
9. Alfred Thayer Mahan, *The Influence of Seapower Upon History*, (Boston: Little, Brown, 1890).
10. H. David Bess and Martin T. Farris, *U.S. Maritime Policy: History and Prospects*, (New York: Praeger Publishers, 1981), 36.
11. Bess and Farris, *U.S. Maritime Policy*, 44.
12. Samuel Lawrence, as cited in Bess and Farris, *U.S. Maritime Policy*, 36.
13. Alex Roland and W. Jeffrey Bolster, *The Way of the Ship: America's Maritime History Re-envisioned, 1600–2000*, (Hoboken, NJ: John Wiley and Sons, Inc., 2008), 265–266.
14. Gibson and Donovan, *The Abandoned Ocean*, 104.

15. Hyman G. Weintraub, *Andrew Furuseth: Emancipator of the Seamen* (Berkeley: University of California Press, 1959), 115, and 120–121.
16. Ibid., 116 and 120.
17. Ibid., 131–132.
18. U.S. House of Representatives Committee on the Merchant Marine and Fisheries, "The Seamen's Bill," (Washington, D. C.: Government Printing Office, 1914), Part II, 43 and 48.
19. Leon Fink, *Sweatshops at Sea: Merchant Seamen in the First Globalized Industry, from 1812 to the Present* (Chapel Hill, NC: University of North Carolina Press, 2011), Chapter Four, and Justin Jackson, "The Right Kind of Men".
20. United States Senate Committee on Commerce, "Involuntary Servitude Imposed Upon Seamen," (Washington, D. C.: Government Printing Office), 1914, 414.
21. U.S. House of Representatives Committee on the Merchant Marine and Fisheries, "The Seamen's Bill," (Washington, D. C.: Government Printing Office, 1914), Part II, 33.
22. *Titanic* Inquiry Project, http://www.titanicinquiry.org, accessed November 2, 2023.
23. "The U.S. Senate Inquiry," *Titanic* Inquiry Project.
24. "British Wreck Commissioner's Inquiry," *Titanic* Inquiry Project.
25. Furuseth and Olander, "Welfare of American Seamen," 4.
26. U.S. Congress, "An Act to promote the welfare of American seamen in the merchant marine of the United States; to abolish arrest and imprisonment as a penalty for desertion and to secure the abrogation of treaty provisions in relation thereto; and to promote safety at sea," March 4, 1915.
27. U.S. House of Representatives Committee on the Merchant Marine and Fisheries, "The Seamen's Bill," (Washington, D. C.: Government Printing Office, 1914), Part II, 5.
28. Furuseth and Olander, "Welfare of American Seamen," 9.
29. United States Senate Committee on Commerce, "Involuntary Servitude Imposed Upon Seamen," 92.
30. U.S. House of Representatives Committee on the Merchant Marine and Fisheries, "The Seamen's Bill," Part II, 8.
31. Ibid., Part II, 221.
32. Fink, *Sweatshops at Sea*, 100–102.
33. U.S. House of Representatives Committee on the Merchant Marine and Fisheries, "The Seamen's Bill," Part II, 200.
34. Fink, *Sweatshops at Sea*, 102.
35. United States Senate Committee on Commerce, "Involuntary Servitude Imposed Upon Seamen," 470.
36. Furuseth and Olander, "Welfare of American Seamen," 8.

37. Gibson and Donovan, *The Abandoned Ocean*, 116–118.
38. Joseph P. Goldberg, *The Maritime Story: A Study in Labor-Management Relations* (Cambridge: Harvard University Press, 1958), 11–12.
39. U.S. House of Representatives Committee on the Merchant Marine and Fisheries, "The Seamen's Bill," Part II, 184.
40. Furuseth and Olander, "Welfare of American Seamen," 21.
41. U.S. House of Representatives Committee on the Merchant Marine and Fisheries, "The Seamen's Bill," 218.
42. *In re Ah Kee*, 22 F 519 (SD NY 1884); *U.S. v. Burke* 99 F. 895 (SD Ala. 1899); *U.S. v. Jamieson* 185 F. 165 (SD NY 1911).
43. *Taylor v. U.S.* (151 F.1 (2nd Cir. 1907)).

CHAPTER 5

Deserters, Stowaways, and Mala Fide Sailors: Merchant Seamen and the Shaping of U.S. Immigration Policy, 1917–1936

The 1915 Seamen's Act protected the right of foreign seamen to both shore leave and desertion, creating a central venue for illegal immigration by ensuring that foreign seamen, regardless of their citizenship status, would be able to come ashore without being subjected to full official inspection on deck or at official sites at points of entry. Instead, merchant seamen were within their rights to take leave of their ship, circumventing the official processes of immigration inspection altogether. Special protections afforded to foreign seamen, including a provision of the Immigration Act of 1917 that set the statute of limitations for deportations at three years for merchant seamen as opposed to a five-year statute for all other non-citizen residents, made merchant ships a possible mode of entry into the country for immigrants who lacked the resources to enter through more official channels. Following the passage of the Seamen's Act, incidents like that of the SS *Magnolia* in October of 1915, which involved the detention of eighty-six Chinese stowaways who were impersonating seamen in an attempt to get ashore, became increasingly common. In reports of the incident, officials suspected that an additional thirty to fifty Chinese individuals who were onboard *Magnolia* escaped detention and disappeared once on shore.[1]

A combination of increasingly restrictive immigration legislation, a sharp increase in wartime internments and deportations, and widespread turmoil and violence across much of Europe made the war years an

J. Thayer, *Citizenship, Subversion, and Surveillance in U.S. Ports*, Global Studies in Social and Cultural Maritime History,
https://doi.org/10.1007/978-3-031-45618-3_5

especially tumultuous time for foreign-born American residents and would-be immigrants. The Immigration Act of 1917 tightened restrictions on immigration into the U.S. by extending Chinese exclusion to much of the Asian continent, while the Espionage Act of 1917 and Sedition Act of 1918 established broad frameworks for the mass deportation of suspect non-citizens during wartime. More stringent rules for immigrants and would-be migrants made pathways for illegal entry through merchant ships and the impersonation of seamen much more attractive for immigrants of all ethnicities. Launching what would become known as the Palmer Raids beginning in January 1919, the U.S. government, led by Attorney General A. Mitchell Palmer, announced the mass internment and deportation of thousands of "enemies from within," including many German and Italian merchant seamen and officers. In June 1919, Palmer estimated that there were 4000 men confined in Army internment camps, approximately half of whom were merchant seamen.[2] Under such intense scrutiny, and up against the forces of federally mandated exclusion policies backed by public fear of subversion from within, those aspiring or desperate to emigrate to the U.S. from all nations devised elaborate plans for circumventing recently established restrictions on entry.

A news report from Washington D.C. in 1920 described a typical incident involving an "organized gang" thought to be running a smuggling ring via merchant vessels in Baltimore. On August 5, Capt. Larsen of the Danish steamship *Fredericksborg* reported that two of his crew, John Madsen and Magnus Olsen, who had been confined on board for unspecified reasons, literally jumped ship by leaping overboard into a harbor launch that had pulled alongside their vessel. With the men safely aboard, the launch sped off for shore. Whereas Olsen appears to have escaped, Madsen was not as fortunate. Upon his capture, Madsen testified that he and his co-conspirator had arranged their escape ahead of time in collaboration with a man in Baltimore to whom they paid six dollars each in exchange for their illicit passage. Another case, in which Capt. Firs of the Swedish steamship *Volkarth Tham* was fined $1000 for the escape of four of his crew, leading a newspaper to editorialize that "[s]o many of these aliens have escaped from their ships recently that it has become a source of considerable trouble and expense to the ships and has led to the conviction that there is collusion between alien seamen who desire to get into this country and men ashore."[3]

Whereas Chinese individuals had been excluded from emigration entirely since 1882, and all other South Asians had been effectively barred entry with passage of the Immigration Act of 1917, the Johnson-Reed Act of 1924 established quotas for all other immigrants based on a hierarchy of selective inclusion. In addition to boldfaced pseudo-scientific racism, increasingly restrictive immigration policies were also an attempt to counter competition from cheap foreign labor and the potential infiltration of radical politics from Southern and Eastern European nations. The pangs of a developing socialist economy under Stalin in the Soviet Union, the rise of fascist regimes in Italy, Germany, and Spain, and a cauldron of revolution and civil war sweeping across China combined to make immigration to the U.S., with its booming domestic economy and relatively stable political and social landscape, all the more attractive. Rather than embracing its role as a safe haven and source of economic opportunity for international asylum seekers, the U.S. turned inward through restrictive immigration legislation and enforcement at points of entry. Despite these mechanisms of exclusion and border control, would-be immigrants continued to successfully devise plans to enter the country illegally, either by negotiating encounters with inspectors and immigration officials themselves or by circumventing such encounters altogether via merchant ships and the impersonation of seamen. Under the 1924 Act, merchant seamen were subject to inspections on board their vessels, but only to check for infectious diseases and other mental or physical ailments that explicitly excluded immigrants from entry. In all other respects, the burden of proof in terms of identifying a foreign-born individual on a merchant ship as a bona fide seaman as opposed to a passenger, stowaway, or "mala fide" seaman, resided fully with an appointed ship's officer who was responsible by proxy for the accuracy of the ship's crew list and roster.[4] This arrangement opened the possibility for manipulation and bribery among bona fide merchant seamen and officers who were willing to collaborate in smuggling impostors or stowaways into the country for a fee. The entire process was further complicated by the fact that with the exception of major port cities like New York and Los Angeles, immigration inspectors at smaller ports along the East and West coasts complained of chronic underfunding that spread resources thin and made consistent, thorough inspections of merchant vessels impossible.[5] Even when immigration officials were present and able to reach merchant ships before they emptied their crews ashore, inspections and encounters were often inadequate and subject to the cooperation, or lack thereof, of those under inspection. In Norfolk, Virginia, for example, a Chinese crew who would have otherwise been barred from shore leave rushed the gangway, assaulted the immigration inspector assigned there, and made their way freely ashore.[6]

Given the porous state of inspections involving merchant vessels and seamen, it is hardly surprising that in 1924 alone, the U.S. Labor Secretary estimated that 38,000 non-citizen merchant seamen, or those posing as merchant seamen, had deserted their vessels in American ports.[7] While shipping company officials maintained that as much as seventy-five percent of these desertions involved men who were intent on reshipping out on different ships, as was their right under the 1915 Seamen's Act, immigration officials and congressmembers on the Committee on Immigration and Naturalization remained suspicious.[8] Indeed, committee hearings held by the U.S. House of Representatives Committee on Immigration and Naturalization during 1925 and 1926 were dedicated solely to the issue of "alien seamen," in which representatives from Congress, the U.S. Department of Labor, shipping companies, and maritime labor unions debated the viability of amendments to existing immigration regulations proposed with the intent of curbing the problem of illegal immigration within the maritime shipping industry.

These hearings left unresolved many questions about the legal status of merchant seamen under U.S. immigration law. Merchant ships and the impersonation of seamen remained a viable channel for entering the country while circumventing much of the official encounter with the state required of other non-seamen immigrants until 1931. In March of that year, the U.S. Supreme Court ruled on a case involving merchant seaman Demetrius Philippides, a Greek citizen who brought suit initially against Benjamin M. Day, Commissioner of Immigration for the Port of New York, alleging that his arrest some three years and three months after he deserted his vessel in New York constituted a violation of the protections afforded merchant seamen under the 1917 Immigration Act, which stipulated a three-year statute of limitations after which merchant seamen could not be prosecuted for illegal entry into the country. The Court ruled against Philippides, arguing that the language of the Johnson-Reed Act altered the terms of the Immigration Act of 1917 by incorporating merchant seamen under the category of "Quota Aliens" who were all subject to the same five-year statute of limitations, as opposed to the three-year statute specially provided to merchant seamen in earlier legislation.[9]

Philippides v. Day prompted a wave of immigration raids in the nation's port cities. A new era of exclusion, surveillance, and forcible deportation had begun, catalyzed in part by the deep economic slump and scourge of unemployment brought about by the Great Depression. In this new context, policies regarding the exclusion of foreigners that had previously been shaped by racial and ethnic prejudice as well as a backlash against political radicalism were now increasingly couched in economic terms.

Merchant ships and the impersonation of seamen stand out as an overlooked site of mobility for immigrants who lacked the means to successfully negotiate encounters with the state, or who otherwise chose to circumvent the process altogether. Indeed, historians who do focus on illegal entry tend to focus on geographic crossings from the Mexican or Canadian borders or on methods for manipulating the inspection process itself.[10] Merchant seamen provide a necessary addition to scholarship on immigration history in tracing both the legislative discourse and strategic approach of immigrants and cooperative agents within the commercial maritime industry who capitalized on protections afforded foreign merchant seamen under U.S. law.

Despite the lack of attention paid by historians, the issue of alien seamen dominated immigration law from 1917 to 1936, as well as the rhetoric of seamen's unions and maritime reformers. In fact, the very first paragraph of the Immigration Act of 1917 establishes definitions for three terms, and three terms only: "alien," "United States," and "seaman." In total, the words "seaman" or "seamen" appear 138 times, accounting for an astounding twenty-five pages of the ninety-five-page bill. At least four separate hearings of the Committee on Immigration and Naturalization were convened between the years 1925 and 1936 to specifically discuss the issue of "Deportation of Alien Seamen," with representatives from Congress, the U.S. Department of Labor, police departments, organized labor, and shipping companies on both coasts testifying as to how to address the flow of immigrants who were entering the country illegally via merchant ships. Additionally, pages upon pages of the International Seamen's Union's (ISU) publication *The Seamen's Journal* discuss the issue of "alien seamen," devising a complex stance on immigration policy that would simultaneously protect the interests of American seamen while preserving rights gained with the passage of the 1915 Seamen's Act.

It is of little surprise that merchant seamen would find themselves at the center of discourse surrounding the issue of migration and foreign labor. Merchant seamen themselves had long embodied transnational networks of transmission, whether it be of information, political ideology, or even disease.[11] Close analysis of the position of merchant ships and seamen within the complicated landscape of illegal immigration during the exclusion and quota eras provides a necessary addition to our understanding of how immigrants were able to negotiate the process of entering the U.S. under increasingly restrictive laws and processes.

1917–1924

Before the Immigration Act of 1924, merchant seamen who were not citizens of the United States were granted a range of mobility not afforded to foreigners of other classes and professions. Under the Immigration Act of 1907, aliens on merchant ships "who are to be found as seamen" were granted freedom to shore leave, protected under law, stipulating that they:

> shall not be examined by officers of the Immigration Service further than may be necessary to determine their status as seamen, and to ascertain that they are not insane, idiots, imbeciles, epileptics, or persons afflicted with tuberculosis or with a loathsome or dangerous contagious disease; head tax shall not be certified on their account; they shall not be prevented from landing temporarily in the United States, nor required to land at any designated time or place; neither shall any manifest of them be required, nor shall they necessarily be returned to the country whence they came by the vessels bringing them.[12]

This litany of protections is indicative of the paradoxical status of merchant seamen under U.S. law. The White Act of 1898 essentially overturned the Court's ruling in *Robertson v. Baldwin* and, under the 1907 law, legislators prioritized a seaman's right to shore leave over the threat that his mobility posed to nascent mechanisms of the enforced borders of citizenship. The 1915 Seamen's Act codified a seaman's right to shore leave by granting seamen the right to desertion in both domestic and foreign ports and outlawing the practice of arresting "runaway" seamen and returning them to their employers. Further, the law represented a decidedly nationalist solution to the downward pull on wages and working conditions created by competition with foreign ships and labor.[13] As a result, merchant seamen, both American and foreign-born, emerged from the victory of the 1915 Seamen's Act under an unprecedented umbrella of new rights and protections.

These strengthened protections for merchant seamen collided with the intensifying immigration restrictions and narrowing definition of American citizenship that developed during World War I. In addition to establishing a literacy test over President Wilson's veto, the Immigration Act of 1917 defined a long list of "undesirables" banned entirely from entering the country based on perceived mental or moral deficiencies, as well as those who were evaluated to be carrying certain contagious diseases. The law also expanded the Asiatic Barred Exclusion Zone beyond China to include the Middle East and much of Southeast Asia. In regard to merchant seamen, the 1917 law upheld much of the framework established by the 1907 act in exempting seamen from increasingly restrictive immigration regulations. Under the 1917 law, an alien seaman who intended "to reship on board any other vessel bound to any foreign port or place" was to be allowed to "land for the purpose of so reshipping."[14] Whereas the 1907 law required no inspection of a ship's manifest, the 1917 law placed the burden of responsibility for attesting to a seaman's bona fide status on an appointed ship's master or other officer who would be required to testify under oath as to the accuracy of the crew list, including "any alien member of the crew who has been treated or furnished with medicine during the voyage for any of the diseases or disabilities" specified in an earlier section of the law.[15] Further, the 1917 law stipulated that any alien seaman "who shall land in a port of the United States contrary to the provisions of this act shall be deemed to be unlawfully in the United States" and would be subject to detention and deportation within a statute of limitations of three years. For all other aliens found to be unlawfully in the country, the statute of limitations was five years.[16]

Whereas non-seamen aliens seeking to enter the country lawfully were subject to thorough examinations at official sites of entry, merchant seamen encountered relatively light inspections while on a ship that placed most of the burden of proof as to an individual's suitability for legal entry on the ship's master or appointed officer. Crew lists maintained by the presiding ship's officer provided sufficient proof of a seaman's personal legality, and he would be granted entry based on such documents alone. For many outside observers, this system seemed ripe for manipulation. An article published in the *Norwich Bulletin* in January 1921 lamented the porousness of this backdoor to the framework of exclusion that had been meticulously built during the war years to keep out undesirable aliens. Titled "Where Attention Is Needed," the article points out that "while close attention seems to be given to dealing with aliens who come here to make their homes, none too much if any attention is given to those alien seamen who desert on reaching these shores, or who in fact come here as seamen for the purpose of getting around the laws of this country." The writer then relates an account of a certain unnamed seaman who had entered the country via desertion, and who was later detained as a "bolshevist" who had confided to an acquaintance his possession of "two powerful bombs." As the writer describes, the seaman "had snapped his fingers at the immigration restrictions and was as there are reasons to believe, an individual who had come here for the purpose of creating trouble."[17] Norwich, Connecticut being a small port town situated at the base of the Thames River north of New London, the newspaper's readers would certainly be familiar with the comings and goings of maritime vessels and their crews. Such a lurid account, drawing on contemporary fears of radical violence and illustrating the apparent inability of the mechanisms of immigration restriction to keep out such undesirable aliens, likely proved compelling reading for residents concerned with the security of their nation's ports.

Similarly, an article from the *Dearborn Independent*, a paper owned by Henry Ford and mouthpiece for his River Rouge factory complex located in the town of Dearborn, Michigan, ran on July 2, 1921, drawing further attention to the inadequate inspection procedures in place for merchant vessels and seamen. The article points out that medical inspections performed on ships were carried out in a manner "not wholly conducive to efficiency," an obtuse way of stating more specific criticisms that describe the procedures as "hurried," lacking suitable equipment and resources, and devoid of the privacy necessary to carry out inspections adequately. Finally, the article concludes with the recommendation that "some legislation" be adopted that would provide "a penalty against steamship companies in cases where diseased alien seamen are discovered," similar to the penalties put in place by the 1917 law against employment of diseased non-seamen immigrants.[18] As with the *Norwich Bulletin* article, the unnamed Dearborn journalist saw a disparity between the treatment of aliens entering the country with the explicit intention of permanent residence and that of alien seamen who were granted the right to shore leave or desertion with the implied intention of re-shipping. But what lay behind this disparity? What was it about merchant vessels and seamen that required that they be allowed a fast-track to both legal and illegal entry? Why were merchant seamen granted a reprieve from most aspects of official encounters with the state that all other aliens were subject to when arriving at border inspection sites and ports of entry?

The most obvious answer is that maritime commerce had long represented an essential priority for the nation's industrial interests and for its lawmakers, who found common ground in the mandate to provide for a stable, well-regulated, and free-flowing maritime trade necessary for the United States to assert itself as a viable participant within international markets. By the early-twentieth century, American ports and consumer markets were dependent on an increasingly foreign-flagged merchant fleet, as well as rising numbers of non-citizen seamen, particularly from regions of "new" immigration in Southern and Eastern Europe and Chinese and other Asian labor markets. American maritime labor unions, seeking to protect jobs for American seamen, resisted these new sources of international labor, but U.S. lawmakers, backed by powerful shipping companies, passed immigration legislation that privileged mobility of merchant seamen regardless of citizenship status. Following the 1915 Seamen's Act, the upward pull on wages that a seaman's right to desertion created within American ports added economic incentive to maintain such mobility. Protecting foreign seamen's right to desertion encouraged them to weigh their options while in port before reshipping on a vessel with better pay and more favorable conditions. This model benefited American ships by creating a market in port in which all ships were incentivized to adhere to similar minimum wage rates and working conditions that were required by law of U.S.-flagged ships. The porousness of the Immigration Acts of 1907 and 1917 was therefore essential to maintaining labor competition and the viability of the American merchant marine as ingeniously devised in the 1915 Seamen's Act.[19]

Further, legislation related to the regulation of merchant seamen's labor and immigration restrictions was firmly couched in the theory of "flexible maritime capacity," which maintained that a viable, properly manned citizen merchant marine was essential to national security interests by providing an auxiliary to the Navy in times of war and imperial expansion. Flexible capacity derived from Alfred Thayer Mahan's *The Influence of Sea Power Upon History: 1660–1783*, published in 1890, and was endowed with greater urgency by imperial projects pursued during the Spanish-American War, and later, the global crisis of World War I. As Justin Jackson argues, flexible capacity drove legislative support for a subsidized, citizen-manned merchant marine through protective labor legislation such as the 1915 Seamen's Act.[20] The same politics emphasizing a citizen-manned American merchant marine in the interests of national security motivated immigration policy from 1917 to 1936, as well as the reactions of American merchant seamen's primary public representative, the ISU.

The ISU, intent on preventing foreign, and especially Chinese crews from taking American jobs and creating a downward pull on wages and working conditions, took a decidedly less tolerant position regarding the mobility and employability of foreign seamen in American ports and on American ships. Through the organ of its newsletter, *The Seamen's Journal*, the Union remained conspicuously silent on the details of legislation that would become the Immigration Act of 1917 during the war years, instead adopting a simplistic patriotism that focused on mariners' heroic contributions and sacrifices to the war and approving coverage of the detention and deportation of alien seamen hailing from the nations of the enemy. An article titled "No More Hyphens" from the early months of U.S. involvement in the war adopts the Wilsonian rhetoric of "one-hundred-percent" Americanism and the myth of democratic universalism: "[a]s a result of this war will be a wonderful amalgamation of races within America. The melting pot is boiling now," and, "[a]t this time we know only Old Americans and New Americans. The hyphen is gone. It changed to vapor in the melting pot."[21] But the inclusiveness of this vision was limited to either citizens by birth ("Old Americans"), or citizens by naturalization ("New Americans"). There was no room for non-citizen residents, aliens, or other foreigners seeking to carve out space within this imaginary new America that the winning of the war would produce.

The hiring of Chinese seamen on American vessels, a particularly common practice among Pacific steamship companies operating under federal mail-carrier subsidies, became a rallying cry for the ISU during and immediately after the war. The business practices of Robert Dollar, owner of the Dollar Steamship Co., generated a torrent of articles in *The Seamen's Journal*, especially during 1918. Dollar was known for manning his steamships with Chinese crews, picked up in the Far East or at California port cities like San Francisco, where the ISU was headquartered. The Union employed a nationalistic wartime rhetoric to criticize Dollar: "[i]t is becoming impossible to take him seriously … actuated solely by the desire to retain his cheap Oriental crews at a time when all America—the Government, the shipowners and the organized seamen are heartily co-operating to man our great new merchant fleet with loyal and patriotic Americans."[22] The ISU reveled in Dollar's failures and capitalized on the steamship line's misfortunes by emphasizing the danger of relying on foreign crews who, the ISU claimed, lacked the proper training and experience possessed by "white" American seamen. Reacting to an incident in which the SS *Stanley Dollar* lost three out of four boilers mid-voyage, leaving the vessel stranded in the middle of the Pacific Ocean, the ISU offered a nationalistic explanation as to the cause of the Dollar line's misfortunes: "[t]he vessel had been drifting for four days," and had "happened on her last trip after Captain Dollar had replaced an efficient white crew by his favorite Asian pets."[23]

The use of Chinese crews on American steamships was not limited to the Dollar Line. Articles in *The Seamen's Journal* identify other lines, many operating under government contracts to carry the nation's international mail, that made use of Chinese crews to man Pacific voyages. An article titled "More Imported Chinese" from May 15, 1918, references the China Mail Steamship Company, which "has followed the example of Captain Robert Dollar" in bringing to California a crew of approximately 150 Chinese for service on the American-flagged SS *Nanking*. Again, the ISU's grievances were carefully couched in patriotic wartime rhetoric: "[n]o self-respecting American youth will voluntarily embrace a calling in which he must compete with Asiatic coolie labor. For this reason, more than any other, the response to the appeal recently issued to young men in the West to take up a career in the merchant marine has not been up to expectations." The combination of a wartime boom in the construction of American ships and the increased demand for a citizen-manned American merchant marine created a climate in which the call for excluding foreign seamen could be put forth in a manner that made claims on national patriotism and enflamed fears of hypothetical weaknesses abroad. This was particularly true at a time when global war seemed to threaten the very foundations of American democracy. Within this context, the ISU could sincerely ask its readers whether Dollar should be allowed to continue his business practices without reprimand or consequences: "[s]hall he be permitted to go on? Will the American nation tolerate this sort of profiteering while every man, woman and child is making patriotic sacrifices to make the world safe for democracy?"[24]

Given the ISU's focus on the perceived threat of Chinese seamen, what little is written about immigration legislation in *The Seamen's Journal* is entirely sympathetic to federal initiatives to tighten restrictions. The union's alignment with federal policy makers is evident in its support for a newly created seaman's identification card, issued by the Immigration Service and ostensibly required in order to exclude those "[r]aces or Nationals which are especially subject to contagious diseases" and ensure that they "will not be brought to the United States in any considerable numbers." Rather than push back against the introduction of a sweeping new surveillance measure intended to restrict and control the mobility of merchant seamen in American ports, a right that had just been codified with the passage of the 1915 Seamen's Act, the ISU instead interpreted the new requirements as necessary to keep out undesirable aliens and protect the American merchant marine: "[o]fficers of the International Seamen's Union or its district unions should give all possible assistance to the department [of Immigration] by making it plain to all seamen concerned that this action under the Immigration Law is specifically for their own protection."[25]

Economic downturn following World War I further agitated tensions among the nation's native or naturalized citizens, and incoming immigrants and non-citizen residents. By the early 1920s, the intense glut of shipyard production had created a bubble that the return to normal domestic market conditions simply could not sustain. The increased demand for trained merchant seamen during the war dropped off precipitously with the signing of the Treaty of Versailles, and the nation's shipping magnates struggled to figure out where to direct their excess ships and seamen, whose production and employment had thrived at levels not seen since the heyday of antebellum American shipping. By September 1921, an estimated 15,000 non-citizen and 20,000 American seamen were idle and without work in New York City alone.[26] Turmoil overseas in the wake of the war made the city an attractive option for many foreign seamen, even if job prospects were poor to nonexistent. The Washington, D.C. *Evening Star* reported that thousands of alien seamen who were stranded in New York "because of the slack shipping business" were declining to take jobs on ships bound for Europe, "say[ing] they would rather be idle in New York than in their own ports".[27]

Backlash against such widespread economic dependency along the nation's waterfronts combined with long-established racial prejudice, particularly against Chinese seamen, culminated in the ethnic quotas of the Immigration Act of 1924. In September 1921, the Chairman of the shipping board, steeped in xenophobic nationalism and the mandates of flexible capacity, announced an initiative to "Americanize" all United States-flagged shipping lines.[28] Newspapers from Bisbee, Arizona, fresh off the scandalous deportation raids of striking workers, many of whom were immigrants, carried out by local vigilante justice groups during 1917, reported somewhat gleefully in 1921 that "the elimination of alien seamen is well under way" and hypothesized that the Chairman's "Americanization plan" would eliminate approximately twenty-five percent of all alien seamen from American port traffic.[29] The ISU, led by Andrew Furuseth, joined in this chorus of voices denouncing the continued presence of unnaturalized alien seamen who had descended on the nation's ports in the midst of a period of decline for maritime shipping. It is from this context of overwhelming nativist sentiment that Congress passed a new wave of restrictive immigration laws, beginning with the supposedly temporary Emergency Immigration Act of 1921 and the Johnson-Reed Act in 1924.

The Johnson-Reed Act, 1924–1925

The end of World War I left Europe in a state of economic and social chaos. Heavily subsidized mobilization during U.S. intervention in the war transitioned to a peacetime economy in which thriving industrial markets, especially those related to maritime commerce, returned to their pre-war levels, or worse, dipped into a prolonged economic slump, creating widespread unemployment and economic displacement. In Europe, the dissolution of both the Ottoman and the Austro-Hungarian Empires severed long-standing national ties and spurred mobility and migration of peoples on a massive scale. Additionally, the Russian Revolution of 1917 seemed to confirm American fears that subversive ideologies from Eastern Europe would now pose a legitimate threat to domestic stability and, ultimately, the democratic-capitalist system itself. Reacting to such fears, Rep. Albert Johnson (R-WA) sponsored a bill that proposed setting a temporary cap on immigration into the United States based on a three percent quota per foreign nation relative to all individuals living in the United States from each foreign country as of the 1890 census. This formula targeted individuals who participated in the "new immigration" of the 1890s onward, primarily from Eastern and Southern European countries that were viewed as being particularly active breeding grounds for subversive political ideologies. The bill, known as the Immigration Restriction (or the Emergency Immigration) Act of 1921, passed with virtually no opposition from Congress. Just one year after its passage, the Act reduced Immigration into the U.S. by more than half.

Rather than serving as a temporary solution to provisional post-war problems, the 1924 Johnson-Reed Act solidified the exclusionary components of the 1921 Act and heightened the restriction of its three percent quotas by limiting immigration to two percent of all individuals from foreign nations, relative still to the statistics of the 1890 census. This further limited immigration from Eastern and Southern Europe, as well as Africa, the Middle East, and other geographic regions that did not have a large presence in the U.S. as of 1890. Further, the Act maintained and strengthened the Barred Asiatic Zone established by the Immigration Act of 1917, prohibiting immigration entirely from the Middle East to much of Southeast Asia. This policy placated white supremacist fears of race-based contagious disease and moral degeneracy, as well as validating the virulent attacks against Chinese and "coolie" workers that had been promulgated by organized labor, including the ISU, for decades. The 1924 Act functioned by dividing all immigrants into two categories: "Quota Immigrants" and "Non-Quota Immigrants." Non-Quota Immigrants included minors, children or wives of resident citizens, individuals returning from a temporary visit abroad, individuals born in a country contiguous to the United States, ministers, professors, and bona fide students. Additionally, the classification of "immigrant" was not applied to "a bona fide alien seaman serving as such on a vessel arriving at a port of the United States and seeking to enter temporarily the United States solely in pursuit of his calling as a seaman." All other aliens entering the country were considered "Quota Immigrants" and thus subject to all the rules and specifications established by the 1924 Act.[30]

Regarding deportation, Section 14 of the 1924 Act stipulated that "[a]ny alien who at any time after entering the United States is found to have been at the time of entry not entitled under this Act to enter the United States, or to have remained therein for a longer time than permitted under this Act or regulations made thereunder, shall be taken into custody and deported in the same manner as provided for in sections 19 and 20 of the Immigration Act of 1917." Most significant about this provision as it applied to merchant seamen was that it made no special provisions for mala fide *alien* seamen, such as the three-year statute of limitations established by the 1917 Act. Alien seamen who sought pursuits outside of their calling or otherwise violated their bona fide status were therefore subject to the same restrictions and rules as applied to all other quota immigrants. This was a reality that took several years to fully develop into functional policy and which ultimately required the intervention of the Supreme Court in 1931 to define exactly what protections alien seamen could expect. In the interim, the reactions of the ISU reflect its continued support of the law based largely on the persistence of nativist sentiment within the Union, but also on an apparently less-than-comprehensive understanding of the changes regarding the regulation of merchant seamen's mobility in American ports. In an article published in the *Seamen's Journal* less than two months after passage of the Johnson-Reed bill, the journal's editors reflected on the "The New Immigration Law," claiming that "[s]o far as seamen are concerned the new United States Immigration law, effective July 1, 1924, does not very materially change their former status."[31] Despite this initial assertion, an article from November 1924 began by reminding readers that any "bona fide alien seaman serving as such on a vessel arriving at a port of the United States and seeking to enter as an immigrant shall be subject to all the immigration laws, rules and regulations applicable to immigrants."[32] Here the Union seems to have come to terms with the fact that the 1924 Act had eliminated special provisions for alien seamen provided for under the 1917 Act, a reality that would not be officially acknowledged for another seven years when the case of *Philipiddes v. Day* was brought before the Supreme Court. The same article announced requirements that all alien seamen must carry and present authenticated immigration visas and have their identities and status as bona fide seamen corroborated by their ship's crew list and through confirmation from the appointed ship's master. If a seaman engaged in pursuits outside of his calling, entered the coastwise trade (which was restricted to American citizen seamen only by the Jones Act of 1920), or remained longer than sixty days without re-shipping "he shall be deemed to have abandoned his status as a non-immigrant ... and shall be taken into custody and deported at any time thereafter."[33]

The Union's support for the increasingly restrictive regulation of alien seamen's mobility in American ports was consistent with what Justin Jackson calls a long-standing "laborite ideology of national sea power engendered by U.S. imperial expansion and the racist working-class Americanism of white maritime labor reformers."[34] American maritime reformers emphasized the proper training and character of white American seamen in contrast to seamen of non-white races and nationalities—particularly the Chinese—who were depicted as morally corrupt, engaged in the widespread smuggling of people and narcotics, and a threat to national security.[35] Accordingly, organized maritime labor emerged as one of the staunchest supporters of Asian exclusion and immigration restriction, fortifying its arguments in the nationalist rhetoric of flexible capacity in order to eliminate foreign wage competition. As the Union's argument went, if conditions and wages were not favorable enough to attract able young white American men to enter the maritime profession, then the country would be forced to rely on foreign labor and thereby weaken itself abroad, according to the theories regarding sea power put forward by Mahan.

In order to shape the domestic labor market to better accommodate its vision for an American citizen-dominated merchant fleet, the ISU adopted two primary lines of argument to strengthen restrictions put forward by the Johnson-Reed Act. First, the Union plied on racial fears of a "yellow peril" at sea by sensationalizing news reports of smuggling that involved Chinese seamen. Second, the Union called attention to loopholes that existing immigration legislation created. A series of articles followed in the wake of the Johnson-Reed Act's passage chronicling reports of smuggling "via the Oriental employees of American ships plying between Asia and American ports."[36] Raids throughout the "underworld" of San Francisco revealed large smuggling cartels trafficking in the opium, morphine, and heroin trades. Citing unnamed "oldtimers" in the San Francisco Customs Service as their source, the article claimed that many Chinese seamen on merchant ships whose names were listed on shipping articles as members of the crew were in reality engaged in so-called scientific smuggling, their claimed identities as merchant seamen merely serving as a means to desert their vessels in American ports with the smuggled goods:

> These men are uncanny in their ability to masquerade as ship employees when their real business is smuggling dope. As seamen, they are able to get by where they couldn't as ordinary passengers. Working aboard ship is not their business—many of them are wealthy and as a matter of fact don't need to work. But the temptation for big profits is more than some of them can withstand and so they go on as waiters, galley boys, etc., until by some slip-up or misadventure, they fall into the meshes of the law.[37]

The article goes on to describe a Chinese seaman who was caught in possession of more than $16,000 while in port. The seaman had been under surveillance by American authorities for nearly two years, and the amount of cash in his possession was sufficient to confirm his role as a smuggler in the city's drug trade.

Cases involving Chinese seamen continued to appear in the *Seamen's Journal* following the passage of the Johnson-Reed Act, ostensibly serving as proof that tighter restrictions were needed both in the overarching legislation regulating the entry of alien seamen and in the processes of inspection and detention at American ports. But there was a different side to this story, articulated in a remarkable editorial published without commentary by the ISU in the September 1925 issue of the *Seamen's Journal.* Sent to many press outlets by a "Chinese Seamen's Union," the editorial, titled "Declaration, Through the Labor Press of All Countries of the World. To The Labor Organizations, Public Bodies, Shipping Companies, Boards of Directors, Shareholders, Labor Movement Promoters and All Interested in Social Reconstruction," argued that "the condition of the Chinese workers is worse off than elsewhere in the world, not excluding the Chinese seamen." The editorial went on to describe the exploitative conditions under which Chinese seamen were recruited, operating through agents or contractors who had a monopoly on the maritime labor supply chain in China and who were free to "practice the most vicious forms of exploitation." After these agents had collected their "dues" for securing employment for clients, estimated at two to three dollars per every month's wages, or having had to purchase their jobs outright if a seaman wished to sail as a head steward, cook, or other relatively desirable position, and having paid fees for dormitories and the services of "public organizations," the Chinese seaman was left with very little. This situation, the editorial argued, left Chinese seamen with little recourse but to engage in "smuggling passengers and contraband" into the United States: "[t]hose unaware of the situation often blame the Chinese seamen for smuggling, whereas it is but the consequence of economic necessity." If Chinese seamen were afforded proper payment of their full wages, the editorial rationalized, and granted the same protections that "all interested in improving the conditions of workers" advocated for on behalf of white Americans, then smuggling would be eliminated, or reduced to a negligible presence. The editorial ended with a thinly veiled threat: "In making this declaration to the world, we expect a satisfactory settlement of the matter in question. If the situation should remain as it is, we should be obliged to resort to final measures, for which we should not be blamed."[38]

While the ISU willingly published the Chinese Seamen's Union provocative editorial, no other such content in its journal suggested any sympathy for the plight of Chinese seamen, whom the union saw as undercutting jobs in a climate of severe scarcity along the nation's waterfronts. The glut of federally subsidized shipping during the World War I had left a bloated postwar market in which idle ships and unemployed seamen clogged the nation's ports. In such a weak labor market, shipowners were free to seek out crews willing to work for the lowest wages, with little real recourse available to American seamen or their union representatives. Considering these economic realities, the appeal of Chinese seamen to their American brethren fell on deaf ears. Chinese seamen continued to be portrayed as degenerate smugglers and incompetent mariners whose presence in place of American seamen on American ships was a threat to national security. U.S. courts, when given the opportunity, consistently rejected the sentiments put forward in the Chinese Seamen's Union editorial. In a case involving two Chinese crewmembers of the SS *President Cleveland* accused of smuggling cocaine into Hawaii, one of the defendants, a man named Chang Po, pled for leniency by arguing that "he was the sole support of his seventy-four-year old mother and had a wife and four small children in the Orient," while the other defendant referred to his wife and two small children in his defense. Unimpressed by such appeals, the judge sentenced both men to three years imprisonment, citing Po's twelve-dollar per month contract as a sufficient rebuttal to the defendants' justification of economic hardship for smuggling narcotics onto American soil.[39]

Motivated by deep-seated anti-Chinese sentiment, and desperate to reclaim legal and economic agency amidst the shipping slump of the mid-1920s, the ISU staked out its position at its 1925 convention regarding the Johnson-Reed Act. The Union's enthusiasm for tighter restrictions and visa requirements imposed upon alien seamen stopped short of a full endorsement of the recent legislation. Arguing that the Johnson-Reed Act would "only accomplish the deportation of very few of the many that have entered illegally or violated their status," the convention delegates passed a resolution criticizing the bill for serving as "encouragement to some steamship companies to carry immigrants to the United States under the guise of seamen." Delegates also bemoaned the mobility granted to Chinese crews, who were allowed "additional facility for landing excluded aliens." Seeking to protect their bona fide "white" American seamen members, "who cheerfully obey the law of the land," the delegates filed protest against what they perceived as a perverse misuse of the 1915 Seamen's Act: "we protest against the seaman being used as a scapegoat and the Seamen's Act as an excuse for landing in the United States such persons who are specifically excluded … who under any circumstances are coming to this country with the purpose of remaining in violation of its law." The delegates concluded by passing a resolution in support of "the amendment to such deportation bill offered by the Honorable John E. Raker of California."[40]

The Raker Amendments, 1925–1930

The Raker Amendments, as they were commonly known, represented an attempt to strengthen the restrictive mechanisms of the Johnson-Reed Act by tightening control over alien merchant seamen. In addition to exclusionary provisions regarding Asian seamen and seamen with disease, Rep. John E. Raker (D-CA) proposed two additional requirements that proved to be particularly controversial. Amendment F required that all vessels entering American ports with crews that had been engaged or taken on at foreign ports should depart from the port carrying a crew of at least an equal number to that with which they entered. According to Raker's testimony, this amendment would address the reality of a "great desire for people to come to the U.S. illegally" via merchant ships: "[t]hey sign the crew list on the vessels either by paying a bonus to get on or by working, for, say, a dollar, and when they reach the U.S. they desert and get into the populace and into all kinds of business scattered all over the country."[41] Raker then accused an unspecified number of ships' masters of accepting "bonuses" and bribes from aliens desiring to get on ship by impersonating bona fide seamen. Since the Johnson-Reed Act left intact the clause from the 1917 Act placing the burden of proof as to a seaman's bona fide status on the ship's master or appointed officer, a well-placed bribe was all that was necessary for an individual to secure passage overseas and to be allowed ashore as a seaman as verified by the master or officer under pay. If vessels were required upon departure from American ports to take with them the same number of non-citizen crew with which they entered, Raker's logic argued, this back door to the supply chain of illegal immigration would be effectively cut off.

Raker's proposed Amendment G would have imposed even tougher restrictions on ships seeking to enter American ports with non-citizen crews. The amendment also stipulated that no vessel, unless in distress, should enter an American port with any non-citizen who would have been denied entry based on the restrictions established by the Johnson-Reed Act, except for vessels carrying crew members who were natives of the nation to which the ship was registered. For a country like China, which lacked any substantive national merchant marine, this clause would have effectively prohibited Chinese national seamen altogether from American ports. Raker's Amendment G returned to the outright ban on employing alien seamen on American vessels put forward by Rep. Edward J. Livernash (D-CA) and his allies in the SUP prior to the passage of the 1915 Seamen's Act.[42] Raker's testimony suggests that his investment in tightening control over the mobility of alien seamen derived from his belief that those foreigners who would engage in such underhanded tactics to come ashore illegally were among the "lowest, meanest class of people in the world." In questioning G. F. Ravenel, Assistant to the President of the International Mercantile Marine Co., Raker attempted to corner the shipowners' representative into admitting that the persistence of illegal desertions via merchant ships posed a threat to the racial character of the nation:

Raker:	I want to get this before you: You will admit that a lot of men sign up in foreign countries on foreign vessels, and possibly on American vessels who are not seamen, but who are farmers, lumber jacks, hotel men, and ordinary laborers, and sign up as seamen simply to come here and desert?
Ravenel:	Yes; but not so many as you are led to believe.
Raker:	What can we do to prevent that class of people from coming to the U.S. we ought to do?
Ravenel:	Yes.
Raker:	You will admit that they will not make good citizens?
Ravenel:	I think they will make good citizens, good farmers, and good laborers.
Raker:	The rough people who come over here as seamen?
Ravenel:	I do not know who you mean. If there are a lot of good farmers, mechanics, and laborers among them, they would make, I believe. It does not make any difference because this section is not going to stop it.[43]

Ravenel's evasion of direct answers to questions about desertion was typical of a stance taken by many with interests in industrial production and commerce who relied on cheap, foreign and immigrant labor in order to keep their business interests thriving. Contrary to Raker's depiction of corrupt ship masters and willing shipping companies complicit in the illegal trafficking of non-citizens via merchant vessels, Ravenel rejected the notion that any of the ships under his conglomerate were knowingly participating in channels of illegal immigration through desertion. Further, Ravenel claimed that placing responsibility for replacing men who desert in American ports on the shipping companies in order to fulfill the numerical quotas, as proposed in Raker's Amendment F, would set an impossibly high standard.[44] If such an amendment were to pass, Ravenel argued, maritime commerce would become so delayed and unwieldy that its economic inefficiency would be felt even by ordinary American citizens. Appealing to the Committee's responsibilities to American consumers and the federal mail system, Ravenel boldly pronounced that "[t]his is not going to be good for the commerce of the U.S., the welfare of the traveling public, or facilitate the transportation of American mails."[45] Further, Ravenel placed responsibility for the alleged porousness of merchant vessels in relation to immigration legislation on the 1915 Seamen's Act, claiming that desertions carried out by aliens attempting to enter the country illegally were permitted under the La Follette Act's protection of an individual seaman's right to break contract and desert his vessel.

Following Ravenel, Edwin H. Duff, an attorney representing the Pacific-American Steamship Association, read a written statement on behalf of his clients. Pacific steamship companies were particularly notorious among anti-Chinese labor advocates for employing non-American crews that were easily recruited while in foreign ports. Drawing attention to the fierce competition that American maritime commerce faced from foreign ships while operating in the Pacific, and the burden already endured in complying with U.S. maritime laws like the 1915 Seamen's Act, the letter argued that the new amendments would place undue hardship on American shipping interests in the Pacific. Clearly on the defensive in front of the Committee, the Steamship Association adopted a dubious line of racial theorizing in order to justify its hiring of Asian crews: "[o]ur American steamers trading out of the Pacific coast go through the Tropics where it is impracticable for white men to give efficient service. This has been demonstrated by years of experience in this trade in the Pacific. In fact great difficulty has been experienced in obtaining white crews of any kind satisfactory or unsatisfactory who will stick on the job."[46] According to this reasoning, Asian seamen were the only option for ships plying the trade in the sweltering heat of the tropical Pacific simply because white seamen refused to work there. Rather than an endorsement of the hardiness and competencies of Asian seamen, the Steamship Association's justification for their hiring practices fell within the same white supremacist framework that motivated organized maritime labor's vehement anti-Chinese rhetoric. Such hard, brutal work as took place on Pacific steamships was perceived to be simply beneath white seamen, and therefore the recruitment of Asian seamen was a necessary evil that the Raker amendments would eradicate, thereby destroying American shipping interests in the Pacific, wreaking havoc on commerce and the U.S. mail and weakening American sea power by making business for American ships in the Pacific untenable.

Ironically, the same white supremacist logic used by the Pacific Steamship Association to justify their employment of Asian seamen was also used by the ISU and its leader, Andrew Furuseth, to put forward an argument for a prohibition on the employment of Asian seamen on American vessels. Earlier testimony from Robert F. Hand, representing the American Steamship Owners' Association and Assistant Manager of the marine department of Standard Oil Co., got to the root of the disagreement between labor and management regarding the Raker amendments. Hand claimed that Amendment F would cause manning emergencies while in American ports, forcing shipping companies to "chase around to the boardinghouses and sign [seamen] up ... These deserters slip out at the last minute, and there may be one or five or six of them." While inconveniencing shipping management and possibly creating the widespread delays that Ravenel had warned about, this chaotic scenario would theoretically work in favor of merchant seamen in that last-minute replacements would command a higher wage rate. "Why should the ship be penalized by requiring it to pay his passage as well as being forced to engage a man at a very high rate of pay to take the deserter's place?" Hand asked the Committee. "The answer is, from the labor viewpoint, to require that ship to increase wages."[47] Hand's explanation for labor's support of the Raker amendments was essentially spot on. In placing ever-tightening restrictions on the employment of alien seamen on American vessels, requiring that mala fide alien seamen be rooted out and deported at the expense of the shipping companies, jobs would theoretically open up for bona fide "white" American seamen who would be hired at higher wage rates according to the mechanisms of market competition established by the 1915 Seamen's Act. The ISU and Furuseth's support for the Raker amendments amounted to a refinement of the 1915 Act, using immigration legislation as a fulcrum upon which to further edge out competition from foreign labor.

Furuseth's own testimony to the Committee offered a rebuttal to Ravenel and Duff by arguing that any notion that white seamen were inherently unfit for labor in tropical climates was nonsense; instead, he claimed racial mixing as the primary barrier to steamship companies' difficulties in recruiting white seamen: "They [shipping companies] tried for forty years to mix the ships' crews, but it has not been successful, except that they employ them in separate departments. They can mix them to the extent of having Chinese in the stewards' department and other nationals in the engineering or deck force. I am telling you the kind of men these sailors are."[48] By Furuseth's rationale, if Asian seamen were eliminated from crews on American vessels in the Pacific, then any difficulties in recruiting white seamen would vanish. Furuseth also argued that insufficient or weak restrictions on alien seamen's mobility in American ports had had a devastating impact on the coastwise and Great Lakes maritime labor market, where American seamen's jobs were protected under the Jones Act of 1920, which was signed into law with the intention of reserving inland and coastwise U.S. maritime labor for U.S. citizen mariners. According to Furuseth, the porousness of recent immigration legislation threatened to overturn gains made through the passage of the Jones Act and the 1915 Seamen's Act. The protection of a seaman's right to desertion for the purpose of reshipping had created an increase in American seamen in both the coastwise and ocean-going maritime trade, from seven percent in 1915 to fifty-one percent by 1920. Appearing before the Committee in 1925, Furuseth described a radically different landscape, facilitated by lax regulations for the mobility of non-citizen in American ports and widespread smuggling of mala fide seamen and stowaways. Regarding the smuggling of Chinese seamen, Furuseth testified, "I can say this to you, that the vessels coming across the Pacific bring more [seamen] than are needed under the rules of American law, and go out again and they leave them there."[49] Citing unspecified testimony, Furuseth alluded to recruiters who "come in spring" to port cities like New York "who go to these men [non-citizens], saying, 'We will take you upon the Lakes and give you a season's employment.'"[50] Furuseth claimed that a majority of men in the coastwise trade in 1925 "have no right in the country. They cannot pass the immigration law under any circumstances and they never did pass it ... When speaking of deporting men in the coastwise trade, there is not a single shipowner who wants you to do it, because it means that if you take the men out of the coastwise trade the shipowner will have to treat the men he gets in their places significantly better and he might have to pay more wages."[51]

Ultimately, debate over the Raker amendments boiled down to two conflicting views over the future of American maritime commerce: that of shipping companies and shipowners, who opposed increased restrictions because it impeded their ability to take advantage of cheaper wage rates and recruit Asian seamen, and that of organized maritime labor leaders, who were in favor of the amendments because they protected jobs and higher wage rates for white American seamen. Both sides put forward their arguments couched in the rhetoric of white supremacy and the national security imperatives of flexible capacity. According to shipowners, the labor required to operate a competitive American fleet required Asian seamen who were willing to do work that was beneath white seamen. Imposing restrictions on American ships' ability to recruit these willing laborers would devastate the American merchant fleet and impede its ability to serve as an effective auxiliary component of American sea power. On the other side of the debate, Furuseth and the ISU, who, along with its neighboring California Congressman Raker, had been the chief architects and proponents of the amendments, argued that increased restrictions on alien seamen and a near-ban on Asian seamen in American ports was necessary in order to maintain a viable pool of American citizen seamen. Allowing American ships to continue their dependency on what the Union perceived as a cheap, unreliable, and subversive Asian workforce would not only cut into jobs for white American seamen on both ocean-going and coastwise vessels but also pose a national security risk in creating a racially depleted American maritime workforce.

For a time, the shipping company argument won out, and the Raker amendments were scuttled in Committee. The amendments were again debated in January 1926, before being shelved for several years, eventually reemerging in 1930 as the King Bill, sponsored by Rep. William H. King (D-Utah). By then, the postwar shipping slump of the 1920s had been trumped by the global economic catastrophe set off by the market crash of 1929. With the scourge of unemployment impacting the daily lives of ordinary Americans, debate over alien seamen and foreign labor competition took on a new and enlarged resonance that touched on major themes that dominated national discourse throughout the 1930s.

Raids: 1930–1931

The U.S. entered the 1930s on the heels of a catastrophic market collapse, the depth and longevity of which were existentially uncertain. As economic production plummeted and unemployment rose, the perceived threat of foreign labor competition intensified. Within this context, the issue of alien seamen that had stalled in Committee by 1926 was resurrected in the form of the King Bill, a legislative measure sponsored by Senator William H. King (D-UT) containing language essentially identical to that articulated in F and G of the Raker amendments some four years prior. Once again, the Committee on Immigration and Naturalization, chaired by Sen. Albert Johnson, was summoned in February 1931 to discuss the issue of "Deportation of Alien Seamen." Just as in 1924 and 1925, the debates centered on two central propositions that would impose increased restrictions on shipping companies' ability to recruit and bring alien seamen into American ports: the requirement that all vessels entering American ports depart with the same number of crew with which they entered and a prohibition on manning ships with alien seamen who would otherwise be excluded from entry into the U.S. under the restrictions of the Johnson-Reed Act of 1924.

In 1930, King, suffering from an illness, had passed the bill over to Sen. La Follette, who raised it while in session, only to face a filibuster from Sen. Hiram Bingham (D-CT), apparently under the influence of shipowners opposed to further restrictions on their ability to recruit cheap labor, who "kept talking until 2 o'clock, so that automatically [the bill] went back into the same position that it was in when it was called up." The bill was subsequently pushed back to the next session, just as it had been delayed and shelved on and off since 1924.[52] Rep. Fiorello La Guardia (D-NY) went public with his dissatisfaction with Congress's refusal to take action regarding what he perceived as the scourge of alien seamen in American ports. In an interview published in the *Seamen's Journal*, La Guardia took Congress and President Hoover himself to task, declaring that responsibility for defeat of the King Bill "to stop the 'bootlegging' of aliens into this country disguised as seamen 'lies at the doorstep of the White House.'"[53] La Guardia noted that the bill had widespread support from organized labor (both the AFL and the ISU) and had enjoyed quick passage in the Senate before it was sidetracked in the House, allegedly owing to the fact that the "shipowners' lobby was able to reach someone in the State Department." After having passed unanimously in the Senate on April 14, 1930, the bill was held up by Sen. Bingham, upon which it was sent back to the House Committee on February 28, 1931. With Congress set to adjourn on March 4, the only way the bill could be brought back for an official vote was to "to induce Speaker [Nicholas] Longworth [R-OH] to permit the bill to be called up under suspension of the rules," a scenario that never materialized. Speaker Longworth justified his refusal to allow the bill to come up for a vote by alluding to his being "informed by the State Department that European nations protested against the bill," thereby complicating the geopolitical ramifications of its potential passage. As La Guardia summarized:

> The steamship interests again became active and moved against the bill from all sides … The bill having failed … American steamship companies will now crowd out American seamen with Chinese crews to the extent of the limit of the law, notwithstanding the fact that these American steamship companies are receiving millions of dollars of subsidies from the American government. Foreign steamship companies will continue to do business with undesirables endeavoring to enter the United States as seamen.[54]

Expressing the sentiment shared by many of his colleagues in the Senate and, no doubt the weary and economically desperate American public, La Guardia concluded that "[t]he whole thing is a sorry mess."

Where Congress failed to act, the nation's law enforcement agencies took up action in response to the growing chorus of public support for measures to eradicate the scourge of foreign labor competition. The decision of the U.S. Supreme Court in *Philippides v. Day* had effectively clarified what had been implicitly stated in the Johnson-Reed Act of 1924: namely, that merchant seamen were no longer considered a separate class distinct from Quota Immigrants and were therefore subject to the same rules and regulations that applied to all other aliens seeking admission to the U.S.[55] The case provided license for law enforcement agencies at both the federal and local levels to conduct sweeping raids along the nation's waterfronts, exceeding the boundaries of jurisdiction afforded agencies responsible for the detection and detainment of aliens subject to deportation.

Immediately following the Supreme Court's ruling in *Philipiddes v. Day*, the Labor Department, under the leadership of Secretary William Doak, issued a decree calling for local agencies to prepare for the deportation of up to 100,000 merchant seamen who were believed to have deserted in American ports and remained in the country illegally. A breathless *New York Times* headline blasted sensational claims about non-citizen seamen that were indicative of the nation's anxieties regarding foreign labor: "MOST NOW WORKING HERE: Labor Secretary Says They Are 'Depriving Citizens of Jobs' and Can and Will Be Expelled."[56] The Supreme Court ruling gave wide license for the mass deportation of non-citizen seamen "whenever found, without regard to the length of time they have been in the country." Indeed, the Labor Secretary seemed to have been waiting on such a decision in order to take action on an issue cutting severely into employment opportunities for bona fide American citizen seamen. As Doak explained, "Ever since the quota limit laws went into effect illegal entry in the guise of seamen has been a prolific source of immigration law violations," estimating that nearly 100,000 seamen had deserted ships in port in the U.S. since the passage of Johnson-Reed. "Most deserting seamen have taken employment in the United States, thereby depriving citizens and lawfully resident aliens of jobs, and Department of Labor officials are confident that it will now be possible to expel many who have evaded arrest for three years and believed they were safe from deportation."[57]

On the local level, Capt. Michael F. McDermott, head of the Bureau of Criminal Alien Investigation at the New York Police Department, coordinated with federal officials to conduct a spectacular raid in one of the nation's largest ports. The Seamen's Church Institute, in the heart of the City's lower Manhattan port district at 25 South Street, was the declared permanent residence of more than 5000 merchant seamen in 1931 who were out of work and forced to remain in New York City due to the lack of employment opportunities in a severely slumping shipping industry. Seamen who claimed 25 South Street as their home included men who paid nominal fees to rent out one of the 580 dormitory-style rooms within the building's 13 floors; they also included men who had taken out post-office boxes at the Institute's thriving postal office. This cluster of merchant seamen—many of them foreign, whether naturalized or residing in the country illegally—represented a prime target for immigration officials under orders to clean up the nation's waterfronts. "The majority of undesirable aliens in this city today represent 'ship-jumpers,'" Capt. McDermott told the press, "and the present hard times make them potential criminals of whom the city would be well rid."[58] Rather than rely on ad hoc tactics, such as picking up suspects on the technical charge of vagrancy, McDermott pivoted to more direct intervention: "I believe that a raid on the seamen's home will result in ridding the city of several hundred men of the undesirable type, who might turn to crime as a means of getting sufficient money for food and sleeping accommodations during the winter."[59]

The actual raid took place on the morning of February 3, 1931, with 102 men in total being detained and sent for processing at Ellis Island. A similar raid took place in Hoboken, New Jersey just days earlier on January 27, in which some 300 aliens were detained and interrogated, consisting principally of German seamen. Sixty-three men were sent to Ellis Island facing deportation charges. The raid itself took place in an almost identical fashion to that on Manhattan's Seamen's Church: "Inspector Kaba, with the aid of Hoboken police and his own staff visited the German Seamen's Mission, at 63 Hudson Street, about 8 p.m. The exits to the mission were guarded by the raiders for four hours, during which time about fifty aliens entered the mission but were unable to leave." A Hoboken reporter who entered the mission was detained for four hours until he established his identity."[60] Among those sent to Ellis Island were twelve cooks reported to have deserted from their vessels. Most of the detainees faced similar charges of illegally gaining entry into the U.S. via merchant vessels. The article concluded by stating that "[t]his is the largest group of aliens rounded up at one time at Hoboken in several years."[61] Similar raids occurred throughout the city during the early months of 1931, including at a ball held at the Finnish Workers' Education Association, in which 1000 men and women were detained without warrant.

It did not take long before backlash mounted against this proliferation of dragnet-style raids in which thousands of men and women were illegally detained under vague suspicion of having violated terms of immigration legislation which may or may not apply to them. The American Civil Liberties Union led complaints against these "alien drives," protesting the "high-handed and unlawful" tactics of immigration agents.[62] Eventually, members of congress took up opposition to the raids. Rep. Samuel Dickstein (D-NY) publicly questioned the constitutionality of such tactics: "I don't suppose," Dickstein mused, "that the 'alien squad's' warrantless dragnet raids in February on the Finnish ball in New York, with its illegal detention of one-hundred men and women while credentials were being overhauled; on the Seamen's Church Institute, where 4000 men were restrained of their liberty en masse by officials having no jurisdiction over them; later on the municipal lodging house. I don't suppose that these incidents here occurred to the labor secretary as mere lawless, anarchistic proceeding than those of any of the 'reds' he is trying to deport."[63] By April 1931, responding to public backlash, the Labor Department announced the end of all raids targeting alien seamen in the nation's port cities.[64]

Rep. Dickstein's comments cut to the heart of the economic and political conditions which fostered the use of such extraordinary tactics to root out those in violation of immigration law, many of them seamen, in the first place. The "alien raids" conducted by both local and federal law enforcement agencies in early 1931 were the manifestation of a complex of anxieties that dominated the psyche of mainstream American society during the early years of the Great Depression. The specter of totalitarianism in Europe cast a sinister light over the widespread unemployment that plagued the nation's urban centers, as many middle-class and elite Americans feared that the scourge of unemployed, transient men could transform into an army of political radicals intent on subversion from within.

Conclusion

Following the 1915 Seamen's Act, and increasingly under the restrictive policies of the Immigration Laws of 1917 and 1924, merchant ships and the impersonation of seamen were viable options for immigrants who lacked the means to successfully negotiate encounters with the state, or who otherwise chose to opt out of such encounters altogether. During the quota era of immigration restriction, alien seamen enflamed the anxious imaginations of middle-class and elite Americans, who feared the influx of a transient population of working-class men they characterized as politically subversive and racially and morally degenerate. These anxieties sprung from deep-seated ideologies of white supremacy and the lingering cult of Victorian-era morality. The containment and purge of these threatening workers from the nation's ports was carried out through the mechanisms of the Johnson-Reed Act, in addition to the mandates articulated in *Philipiddes v. Day* and zealous law enforcement agencies at both the federal and local levels. Only in overstepping their authority through the spectacle of indiscriminate dragnet raids did these enforcement agencies lose their credibility in the public eye and the raids temporarily ceased.

Notes

1. For discussion of the SS *Magnolia*, see: Mae Ngai, *The Lucky Ones: One Family and Extraordinary Invention of Chinese America* (New York: Houghton Mifflin Harcourt, 2010), Chapter Thirteen.
2. "U.S. To Send 2,500 Enemy Aliens Home," *New-York Tribune* (New York, NY), June 11, 1919, 6, and "May Ask New Law To Curb The I.W.W.," *Evening Star*. (Washington, D.C.), March 28, 1919, 1.
3. "Allege Gang Is Smuggling Aliens": *The Washington Times*. (Washington [D.C.]), August 6, 1920, 8.
4. U.S. Congress, Immigration Act of 1924.
5. U.S. House of Representatives, Committee on Immigration and Naturalization, "Deportation of Alien Seamen," January 26, 1925.
6. Ibid., 172.
7. Ibid., 113.
8. Ibid., 126–127.
9. U.S. Supreme Court, *Philippides v. Day*.
10. For recent examples, see: Dorothee Schneider, *Crossing Borders: Migration and Citizenship in the Twentieth-Century United States*, (Cambridge, MA: Harvard University Press, 2011), and Mae Ngai, *Impossible Subjects: Illegal Aliens and the Making of Modern America* (Princeton University Press,

2004), chapter two. Erika Lee, in *At America's Gates*, reconstructs the complicated and often ingenious networks of illegal entry designed and capitalized upon by Chinese immigrants who would otherwise be denied entry during the exclusion era. Focusing on the paid agents who assisted Chinese immigrants in preparing false identities and obtaining forged papers in order to pose as "paper sons" or members of exempt classes such as merchants and students, as well as corrupt American immigration agents, Lee's narrative succeeds in illuminating how transnational networks of negotiation empowered Chinese immigrants in their encounter with the American state at official sites of inspection along the nation's borders and ports of entry. While this history of Chinese immigrants' success in manipulating U.S. policies of exclusion at the site of their encounter with the state is essential research, it does not account for the alternative option that merchant ships and impersonation of seamen presented in circumventing an encounter with the state altogether. Erika Lee, *At America's Gates: The Exclusion Era, 1882–1943*, (Chapel Hill, NC: University of North Carolina Press, 2003), Chapter Six.

11. For examples, see Marcus Rediker, *Between the Devil and the Deep Blue Sea: Merchant Seamen, Pirates and the Anglo-American Maritime World, 1700–1750* (New York: Cambridge University Press, 1987), Introduction and Conclusion, and Bruce Nelson, *Workers on the Waterfront: Seamen, Longshoremen, and Unionism in the 1930s* (Urbana, IL: University of Illinois Press, 1990), Chapter One.
12. U.S. Congress, Immigration Act of 1907.
13. Leon Fink, *Sweatshops at Sea*, Chapter Four.
14. Immigration Act of 1917, Sec.33.
15. Ibid., Rule 10. Subd3. (f).
16. Ibid., Sec.34.
17. "Where Attention is Needed," *Norwich Bulletin*, (Norwich, CT), March 16, 1921, 4.
18. "Safeguarding the Public Health," *Dearborn Independent*, (Dearborn, MI), July 2, 1921, 2.
19. Leon Fink, *Sweatshops at Sea*, Chapter Four.
20. Justin Jackson, "'The Right Kind of Men': Flexible Capacity, Chinese Exclusion, and the Imperial Origins of Maritime Labor Reform in the United States, 1898–1905," *Labor* 10, no. 4 (2013): 39–42.
21. International Seamen's Union, *The Seamen's Journal*, "No More Hyphens."
22. International Seamen's Union, *The Seamen's Journal*, "Captain Dollar's Humor," September 4, 1918.
23. International Seamen's Union, *The Seamen's Journal*, "Mr. Dollar's Chinese Crews."
24. International Seamen's Union, *The Seamen's Journal*, "Mr. Dollar Again," April 24, 1918.

25. International Seamen's Union, *The Seamen's Journal*, "Seamen's Identification," July 10, 1918.
26. "City Spurned by 20,000 Idle, Many Spurn Jobs," *New-York Tribune*, September 3, 1921, 1 and 5.
27. "New York's 'Unemployed,'" *Evening Star*, (Washington, D.C.), September 4, 1921, 2.
28. "200 Alien Seamen Dropped from Washington's Crew," *Evening World* (New York), September 30, 1921, 28.
29. "All American Ships Are Being Operated Now by U.S. Crews," *Bisbee Daily Review* (Bisbee, AZ), September 30, 1921, 5.
30. Immigration Act of 1924.
31. International Seamen's Union, "The New Immigration Law," *Seamen's Journal*, July 1924.
32. International Seamen's Union, "Immigrant Seamen Must Have Visa," *Seamen's Journal*, November 1924.
33. "Immigrant Seamen Must Have Visa," *Seamen's Journal.*
34. Jackson, "'The Right Kind of Men,'" 60.
35. Ibid., 47.
36. International Seamen's Union, "Professional Smugglers," *Seamen's Journal*, March 1925.
37. Ibid.
38. International Seamen's Union, "Appeal of Chinese Seamen," *Seamen's Journal*, September 1925.
39. International Seamen's Union, "Professional Smugglers."
40. International Seamen's Union, "Seamen and the Immigration Law," *Seamen's Journal*, February 1925.
41. U.S. House of Representatives, "Deportation of Alien Seamen," 109.
42. See Jackon, "'The Right Kind of Men,'" 50–51, 57 and 59. This "seamen's clause" had a long lineage dating back to a bill introduced by Representative William Astor Chanler (D-NY) in early 1900, which sought to plug a hole in an 1898 subsidy bill requiring that all ships receiving subsidies from the federal government, primarily in the form of mail-carrier contracts, must hire U.S. citizens for at least twenty-five percent of their crews. Chanler, taking up the Union line in criticizing the subsidies bill for allowing exemptions to the rule if the mandated number of American citizens "could not be reasonably obtained," proposed a requirement that any alien seaman hired in a foreign port for whom federal law prohibited entry into the U.S. be deported at the shipowners' expense upon entry. While the Chanler bill never left committee, its legacy was picked up by Rep. Edward J. Livernash (D-CA) and his allies in the Sailor's Union of the Pacific and Furuseth, who between 1901 and 1904 advocated for a bill that would have excluded Chinese seamen from American ships altogether. The crux of Livernash's bill depended on an interpretation of American

ships as U.S. territory for the purposes of immigration law. Under this interpretation, the restrictions embedded in the Chinese Exclusion Laws would apply on the high seas just as they would on land. Like the Chanler bill, Livernash's proposals never passed in Congress, but they were revived in the form of language requirements and manning standards that did pass in the 1915 Seamen's Act. These skill and language regulations effectively imposed a ban on hiring alien seamen over a certain percentage without explicitly establishing race or nationality-based quotas as proposed by both Chanler and Livernash.

43. U.S. House of Representatives, "Deportation of Alien Seamen," 116.
44. Ibid., 110.
45. Ibid., 112.
46. Ibid., 131.
47. Ibid., 134.
48. Ibid., 147.
49. Ibid., 156.
50. Ibid., 151.
51. Ibid., 148.
52. International Seamen's Union, "Furuseth's Legislative Report," *Seamen's Journal*, August 1930.
53. International Seamen's Union, "Defeat of the King Bill," *Seamen's Journal*, April 1931.
54. Ibid.
55. U.S. Supreme Court, *Philipiddes v. Day*.
56. "Prepare to Deport 100,000 Seamen," *New York Times*, March 25, 1931.
57. Ibid.
58. "Seamen's Home Raid Planned in Drive on Aliens," unknown. Seamen's Church Institute of New York Scrapbook 1930–1932, Records of the Seamen's Church Institute of New York and New Jersey.
59. Ibid.
60. "63 Aliens Held for Deportation in Hoboken Raid," *Herald Tribune* (New York), January 27, 1931. Seamen's Church Institute of New York Scrapbook 1930–1932, Records of the Seamen's Church Institute of New York and New Jersey.
61. Ibid.
62. "Complaint Answered on U.S. Alien Drive," *New York American*, March 30, 1931. Seamen's Church Institute of New York Scrapbook 1930–1932, Records of the Seamen's Church Institute of New York and New Jersey.
63. Ibid.
64. "Raids Are Stopped," *Oklahoma City Banker*, April 10, 1931. Seamen's Church Institute of New York Scrapbook 1930–1932, Records of the Seamen's Church Institute of New York and New Jersey.

CHAPTER 6

The "Million-Dollar Home for Sailors," Industrial Maritime Unionism, and Sailors' Agency in New York City's Sailortown, 1930–1932

On the morning of February 3, 1931, agents from Immigration Inspector John Kaba's "flying squad" descended on the thirteen-story headquarters of the Seamen's Church Institute (SCI) at 25 South Street in New York City. Locking the doors behind them to prevent anyone from leaving, the inspection team spent the next seven hours interrogating more than 4000 merchant seamen who had congregated inside the building on that particular morning. Operating on intelligence gathered by undercover agents and cooperative administrators at the Institute, the inspectors set to work rooting out seamen whom they suspected of having entered the country illegally via merchant ships. Those who were able to respond satisfactorily to inspectors' questions regarding legal residency were allowed to leave. Those suspected of illegal residency "were brought out in dejected groups, under guard, to be taken to Ellis Island." By the end of the day, 102 seamen had been detained and three arrested for possession of forged birth certificates.[1]

Little more than two months after the raid on SCI, the Department of Labor issued orders for immigration officers to prepare for the deportation of 100,000 merchant seamen who were suspected of residing in the country illegally.[2] Ironically, the very Institute that had been founded to

J. Thayer, *Citizenship, Subversion, and Surveillance in U.S. Ports*, Global Studies in Social and Cultural Maritime History,
https://doi.org/10.1007/978-3-031-45618-3_6

infiltrate, convert, and control merchant seamen based on their inherent transience and foreignness had itself become a target of U.S. immigration forces. The full weight of the nation's immigration law would be weaponized, particularly against seamen during this era of the war for control of sailortown. Contestants in this war included shipping companies and shipowners invested in maintaining economic advantage over foreign competitors; maritime union leaders dependent on a white, U.S. citizen seamen membership; the U.S. government, adamant in its resolve to protect national security interests through the strength of American seapower and a self-sustaining U.S. merchant fleet; and merchant seamen themselves, who created methods and mechanisms to navigate and subvert immigration law and political persecution in order to retain mobility under increased surveillance, regulation, and control.

25 South Street

From its origins, SCI's headquarters at 25 South Street was a heavily trafficked site for merchant seamen in port. Figure 6.1 represents data for boarders and passers-through who were documented by census takers from 1915 to 1940. The data reveals a significant population of non--U.S. citizen seamen present at SCI.

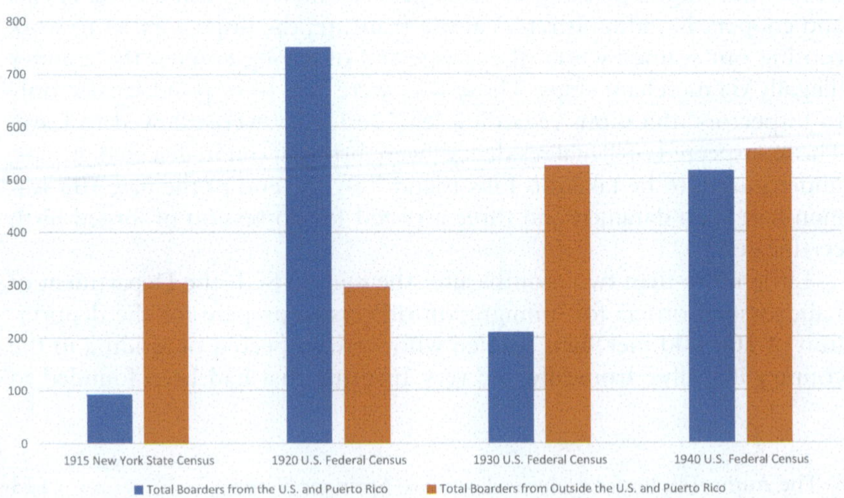

Fig. 6.1 Total boarders at 25 South Street—U.S. and Puerto Rico

Figure 6.2 shows the number of total boarders from seven of the most common nationalities outside of the U.S. recorded in the state and federal censuses. The nationalities documented formed a block of northwestern Europe and the British Isles, representing a significant proportion of SCI's clientele. Seamen from these nations were, not incidentally, also provided special accommodations such as seamen's clubs individually catered to their respective home nations.

Figure 6.3, in contrast, represents boarders from nations in Eastern and Southern Europe. Russia, Spain, and Finland are all relatively well represented in the census data, but not to the extent of most of the Northwestern European nations of Fig. 6.2. Seamen from Eastern and Southern European nations rarely appear in SCI's propaganda imagery, which often featured white, Nordic seamen as subjects. Nor do their numbers suggest that these Eastern and Southern European seamen were attracted to or welcomed by the Institute.

Finally, Fig. 6.4 represents the total number of boarders from Latin America and the Caribbean. While their numbers do not suggest a significant presence at 25 South Street for seamen of any of the nations plotted, they do provide a glimpse at the spectrum of multiculturalism housed under the Institute's roof. While SCI accommodated and serviced a

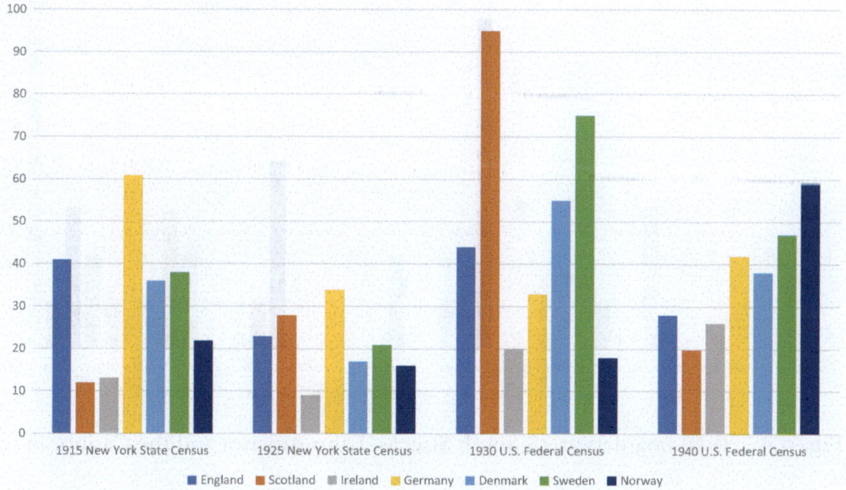

Fig. 6.2 Total boarders at 25 South Street—Northwestern Europe

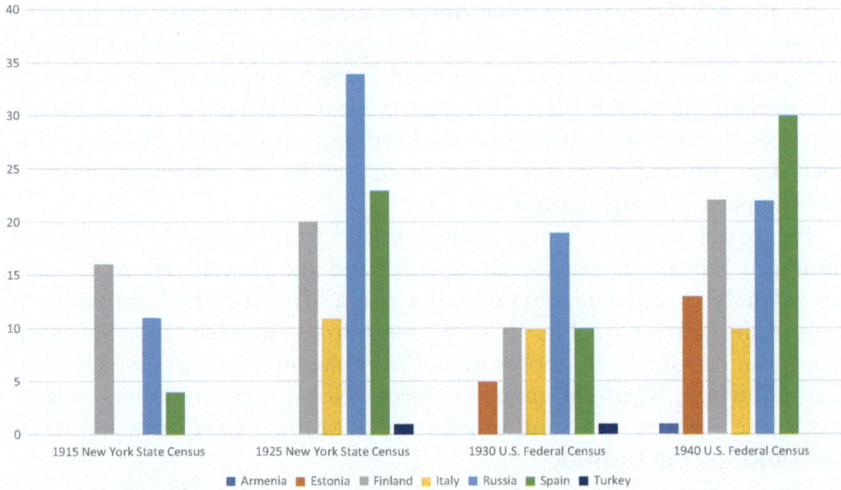

Fig. 6.3 Total boarders at 25 South Street—Eastern and Southern Europe

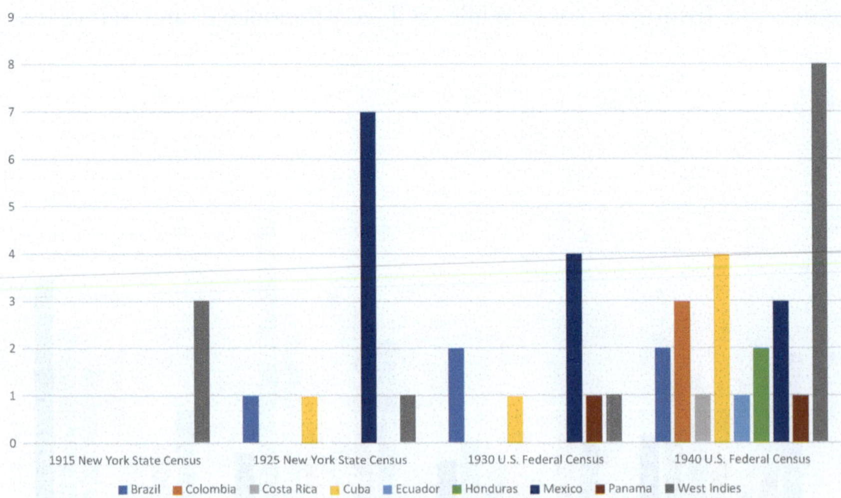

Fig. 6.4 Total boarders at 25 South Street—Latin America and the Caribbean

clientele that was relatively diverse and multicultural, certain nations, ethnicities, and races remained on the margins of what was already a marginal space for workers along the city's waterfront. Black seamen, recorded in the census as "N" or "Neg" for their race, appear a total of nine times in all of the four censuses consulted. Filipino ("Fil") and Mexican ("Mex") seamen also account for a total of nine entries. Perhaps most glaring of all is the total absence of Chinese seamen, who were a common nationality to be found working on merchant ships in U.S. ports, and a frequent target of American labor unions and sympathetic legislators. South Indian, or "lascar" seamen, are also nowhere to be found in the data. In fact, with the exception of the 18 black, Filipino, and Mexican seamen, all of the other 3240 seamen who appear as boarders in the census data between 1915 and 1940 are recorded as "White."

In consulting census data, one must account for the subjectivities, eccentricities, and prejudices of the individuals responsible for recording data on the people whom they encountered. It is simply untrue, for example, that 99.4 percent of all boarders at 25 South Street between 1915 and 1940 were white. Seamen from nations in the West Indies, Asia, and the Middle East are all represented in the data, and they appear in SCI's photographic archives, albeit rarely, and in far less flattering framing than the Nordic sons of Neptune who were chosen as subjects for the Institute's promotional images. All of these men were apparently recorded as white, perhaps because the census takers lacked an adequate vocabulary of race and ethnicity to describe such individuals accurately, or perhaps because of larger structural limitations of the census as a system and the parameters of how it was administered during the first half of the twentieth century. Even accounting for census takers' errors, the majority of SCI's boarders were white, from northwestern European nations, and found themselves "at home" at 25 South Street through services that catered explicitly to certain nations. Other seamen from nations less commonly found at the Institute's headquarters found themselves less explicitly welcome, and possibly excluded in a more absolute manner that has eluded the archival record (see Fig. 6.5).

The racial makeup of boarders at 25 South Street aligned with that of the membership of the International Seamen's Union (ISU), and the racial agenda promoted by its leader, Andrew Furuseth, leading up to the passage of the 1915 Seamen's Act. Furuseth and the Union championed regulation of the U.S. merchant fleet that provided protections for white, skilled seamen through language and skill requirements for crews. Reacting

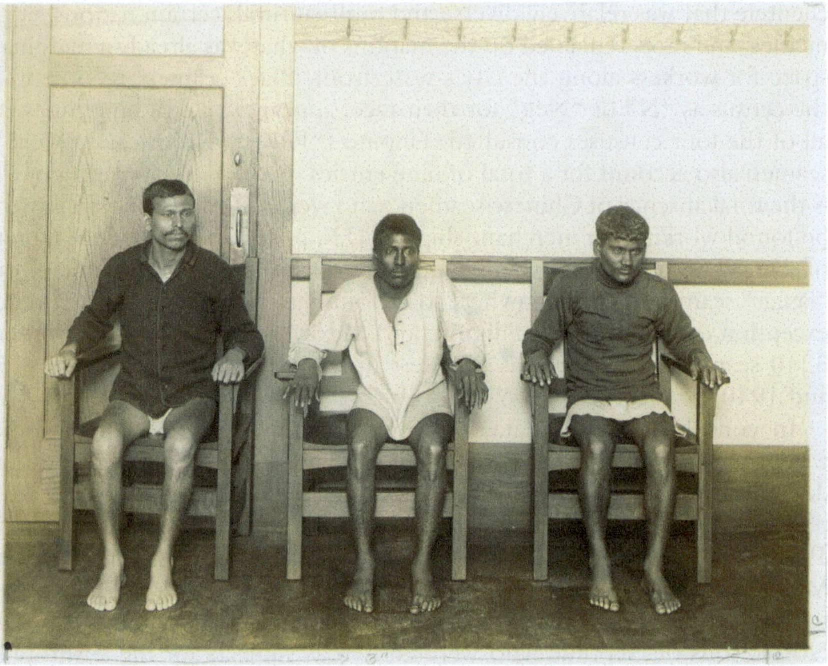

Fig. 6.5 A rare photograph of non-white seamen waiting for service in SCI's Medical Clinic. While there is no evidence that seamen were excluded explicitly based on their race, the census records suggest that 25 South Street was predominantly a space for white American and Northwestern European seamen. Seamen's Church Institute Digital Archives

primarily to the impact of industrialization on the value of skilled labor, and the threat of cheaper sources of labor in Asian ports, Furuseth and the ISU lamented the "drift from the sea on the part of the Caucasian" and predicted that without protections, the sea would become "the domain of the Oriental."[3]

Industrial Maritime Unionism

SCI's accommodation for white, skilled seamen, combined with legislative protections, worked to bolster a model of craft unionism that Furuseth and the ISU fought to maintain against critiques and attempts to build industrial forms of maritime labor organization. Industrial unionism, which sought to cultivate solidarity across all waterfront transport crafts and ethnicities, was most potent among non-white, "unskilled" seamen, as with the Spanish firemen who assumed leadership roles in the Transport Workers' Federation strike of 1912. As Furuseth wrote, the way to address the challenge of industrial maritime unionism was to pursue legislative protections similar to the 1915 Seamen's Act: "[t]he seamen have prayed, watched and waited until a large number of them … are so void of hope that they are now joining the I.W.W. [Industrial Workers of the World] to try, in their desperation, to get by direct action, what they have lost all faith in being able to get from Congress and the President."[4]

The 1920s was a decade of crisis for the American shipping industry. Increased competition from foreign-flagged merchant ships as well as expanding rail systems meant less American shipping commerce and fewer jobs for seamen. Unemployed seamen crowded the slips of lower Manhattan like never before, packing SCI's dormitory rooms to capacity on a nightly basis. Seamen "on the beach" organized during this time to form formidable political labor groups. According to Paul Chapman, the climate of a consistent, unified seamen's presence in lower Manhattan lent new energies to the organization of industrial maritime unionism: "in contrast to workers in factories, schools, or offices, many of whom are together every day at the workplace, seafarers are rarely together in one place. Rather, they are scattered around the globe in small, isolated groups."[5] Unemployment brought seamen together in New York during the 1920s. SCI, pushed to the brink by the increase in demands from their clientele, became the target of the disappointment and anger of these newly organized industrial maritime workers.

Considering the ISU's interrelated campaign to protect jobs for skilled, white seamen and their fight against industrial unionism, the racial makeup of SCI's clientele confirms the role of the Institute as a steady adjunct to the craft unionist cause and puts SCI direct conflict with the city's industrial maritime unions. During the 1920s and 1930s, dozens of industrial maritime unions formed in lower Manhattan, demanding that local organizations and federal policy makers take action in order to alleviate the effects of a prolonged shipping slump that was compounded by the stock market crash of 1929. Groups such as the Waterfront Section of the Communist Party, the Waterfront Unemployed Council, the Seamen's Unemployed Council, the Marine Transport Workers Industrial Union, and the National Industrial Union of Marine Transport Workers all established headquarters and held meetings in lower Manhattan, often just a few blocks from 25 South Street. In 1926, the Communist Party of the United States of America opened a branch of the International Seamen's Club down the street from SCI and offered a library, reading room, and an inexpensive lunch counter for all waterfront workers. In addition to directly competing with SCI, the International Seamen's Club openly sought to cultivate solidarity across crafts along the waterfront and encouraged seamen to agitate for an industrial approach to waging class struggle that would challenge the relatively conservative ISU.[6]

Rev. Archibald R. R. Mansfield, referring to his early years as SCI's Superintendent, describes the relationship between the waterfront unions and SCI as decidedly unfriendly, even before the post-World War I economic climate gave momentum to industrial labor movements of the 1920s and 1930s: "[a]ll we ever tried to do was to help the seaman get and keep the status of a self-respecting human being, and one might suppose the unions would like that. I do not know why they were down on us, but they were. Perhaps they wanted a monopoly of the sailor's welfare, or perhaps they had not taken the trouble to find out what we were actually aiming at."[7] Historian Bruce Nelson elaborates on the nature of SCI's relationship to antagonistic rank-and-file seamen:

> Many of them [seamen] regarded them [Seamen's Church Institute administrators] with contempt and distrust. They nicknamed it [25 South Street] the Dog House and the Shipowners' Institute. Perhaps it was the air of paternalism, or the security guards who were sometimes overzealous in enforcing the house rules, or the fact that many a destitute seaman couldn't pay the storage fee on his baggage and had his personal belongings auctioned off to someone else. There were frequent charges that much of the charitable money intended for the seamen went instead for the 'fat salaries' of SCI officials or for religious literature.[8]

Regardless of the specific reasons for the industrial maritime unions' hostility towards SCI, the severe economic conditions of the 1920s and 1930s only exacerbated relations between the Institute and its clientele. Economic relief in the form of guaranteed work, full crews on ships, no wage cuts, and financial payments for those out of work was at the heart of the conflict between industrial maritime unionists and SCI. As Nelson points out, merchant seamen's transiency made them ineligible for official sources of government relief that were available to other American citizens, so that many seamen were driven to "beg at the sacred portals of the Missions and holy rollers that [were] springing up on the skidroad and doing a thriving depression business," as the *Marine Worker's Voice* described it.[9] Whereas members of the Marine Workers Industrial Union in Baltimore had temporary success in taking over relief operations from the Seamen's Y.M.C.A. in 1934, control over the distribution of relief remained a volatile point of contention between merchant seamen in New York and charitable operations like SCI throughout the 1930s.[10]

This conflict climaxed when the Marine Workers Industrial Union (MWIU), which had formed in 1930 with the mission of "building a viable revolutionary industrial union on the waterfront," provoked a series of incidents that led to violence when MWIU members stormed the lobby of 25 South Street, inciting a melee in which several shots were fired. In July 1932, thousands participated in a rally led by the MWIU in front of SCI headquarters. The Union also held a public "mock trial" of SCI administrators based on accusations that the Institute had mishandled relief funds and in protest of the thirty-five-cent fee for a bed.[11]

In addition to public rallies and mock trials, labor groups expressed their dissatisfaction through the distribution of handbills, pamphlets, and other ephemeral printed material. A handbill issued by the Seamens Unemployed Council is indicative of the material produced by waterfront labor groups during this time. Next to a sketch of a worker raising his right arm with an open palm, the title "Seamen Unite; Close Your Ranks; and Fight!; Unemployed Seamen Organize" is laid out on the top half of the page in basic hand-scrawled penmanship. Slanted, off-centered type provides the details of the handbill in two paragraphs:

> Fellow Seamen: None of the fake charity outfits are doing anything for us ... They are only using us for a bait to catch suckers, who believe they are helping the unemployed seamen, but in reality they are putting fat on the hips of Mother Ropeyarn [SCI's Janet Lord Roper] and the rest of her gang of <u>PARASITES</u>. We don't want ten cent dog stews either, we want square meals when we demand relief from the bosses. They must be forced to give us free beds, free meals and free clothing; also free medical aid. Don't let us tolerate any discrimination in the distribution of relief on account of race or nationality.[12] (see Fig. 6.6)

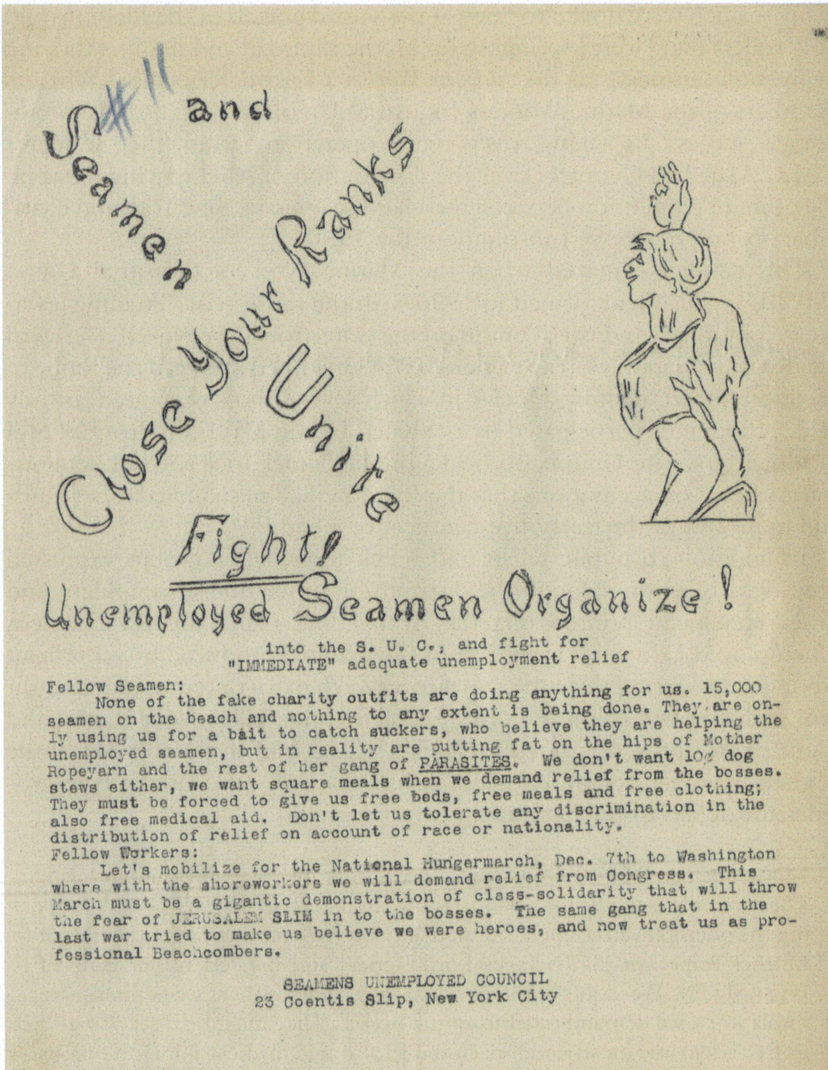

into the S. U. C., and fight for
"IMMEDIATE" adequate unemployment relief

Fellow Seamen:

None of the fake charity outfits are doing anything for us. 15,000 seamen on the beach and nothing to any extent is being done. They are only using us for a bait to catch suckers, who believe they are helping the unemployed seamen, but in reality are putting fat on the hips of Mother Ropeyarn and the rest of her gang of PARASITES. We don't want 10¢ dog stews either, we want square meals when we demand relief from the bosses. They must be forced to give us free beds, free meals and free clothing; also free medical aid. Don't let us tolerate any discrimination in the distribution of relief on account of race or nationality.

Fellow Workers:

Let's mobilize for the National Hungermarch, Dec. 7th to Washington where with the shoreworkers we will demand relief from Congress. This March must be a gigantic demonstration of class-solidarity that will throw the fear of JERUSALEM SLIM in to the bosses. The same gang that in the last war tried to make us believe we were heroes, and now treat us as professional Beachcombers.

SEAMENS UNEMPLOYED COUNCIL
23 Coentis Slip, New York City

Fig. 6.6 Seamen's Unemployed Council handbill [1931?]. Seamen's Church Institute Digital Archives

The second paragraph urges seamen to attend a national hunger march in Washington, D.C., most likely one that took place on December 7, 1931. The form and content of the mimeographed handbill suggests that it was likely distributed at the street level to seamen, hoping to recruit them in their fight against SCI. The Seamen's Unemployed Council had its headquarters at Coenties Slip at this time, meaning they were operating in close proximity with SCI and probably interacting with many of the seamen who had either stayed at 25 South Street or (better for the Council) had been turned away by SCI.

In addition to handbills, industrial maritime unions produced more sophisticated newsletters that openly mocked and attacked the sense of conservative authority SCI worked so hard to project through the production and distribution of its printed material and photographic propaganda. An internal SCI memorandum titled, "A Statement on Communistic Attacks on the Institute" refers to "the Communistic Sheet, the *Daily Worker* ... the *Marine Workers Voice*, and the so-called *Institute-Log*, a mimeographed sheet issued daily and distributed throughout the district and within the Institute Building."[13] It can be argued that this "invasion" of 25 South Street's print culture necessarily existed alongside, or even preceded, physical invasions to SCI's headquarters, such as the violence that took place in 1932. Indeed, the survey of industrial maritime unions' print production in the "Communistic Attacks" memoranda is followed by a description of the waterfront labor groups' physical infiltration of 25 South Street:

> Not satisfied with this propaganda they have made attempts to hold meetings in the Institute and by personal contacts to influence the Institute guests. There are constant efforts being made to prevail upon the men to boycott the Institute to the extent of even attacking on the Street men known to be loyal to the Institute. Although there was a lull after we established the ten-cent meals and during the winter when the extensive relief program was in effect recently the attacks have become more serious, culminating in brutal assaults by the Communists made simultaneously from within and outside of the Institute, when the Institute guards were seriously injured.[14]

In response to such tactics, SCI administrators launched a campaign of undercover infiltration of the meetings of waterfront labor groups such as the Marine Worker's Unemployed Council. In a letter, SCI Attorney George Gray Zabriske recommends that "[i]f any of your men go to the meeting tomorrow night or any other such meetings, it would be well if possible to have someone take notes of what is said for purposes of evidence." Included with his letter was a list of offenses that SCI could pursue in prosecuting offenders, including disorderly conduct for offensive language and behavior, congregating, loitering, and collecting a crowd. Perhaps most significant was Chapter 22, Article 2, Section 15 of the Code of Ordinances regarding handbills, cards, and circulars, which prohibited (with the exception of the postal service) the distribution of printed material upon "any street of public place, or in a front yard or court yard, or on any stoop, or in the vestibule or any hall of any building, or in a letterbox therein."[15] Armed with such legal advice and with the cooperation of lower Manhattan's police, SCI engaged in a battle with industrial maritime labor groups in which both sides attempted to infiltrate and delegitimize the other: SCI through institutional publications and secret memoranda reporting on waterfront meetings, and the unions through scathingly critical handbills, pamphlets, placards, and telegraphs.

SCI staff members took Zabriske's advice and sat in on industrial maritime union meetings, reporting back to SCI's administration through memoranda and meeting minutes. In a report filed on December 18, 1930, SCI agent J. J. Kelly documented a meeting held by the Marine Workers Solidarity League. Kelly described a "Mr. Sizemore" who spoke of an incident in which he "came into the Institute with several of his men" and began to hand out circulars produced by the Solidarity League. Sizemore was immediately seized by police and brought to Kelly's office, where Kelly told him that "he would not allow anyone to give out circulars of any description and would have his men stop those who attempted to do so. He also said that if we were looking for trouble his men would be ready at anytime, with a force of sixty men, to enforce the law."[16] Such a swift reaction from Kelly is a testament to the subversive power of the unions' printed material. The distribution of circulars and handbills had been employed against the Institute as a means of recruiting seamen to the side of the labor groups in opposition to SCI. The incident that Sizemore describes is one in which a perceived-radical has infiltrated the institutional sphere of 25 South Street both physically, and perhaps more significantly, through the distribution of the printed material that he carried. Such a violation was threatening enough for Kelly to summon the threat of a violent reaction to Sizemore's act of protest.

Within this context, a final coda on "Mother" Janet Roper comes at a time when unemployed and striking seamen took up SCI as a target at which to direct their overflowing anger, acting on an interpretation of the

Institute and its administrators as beneficiaries of an exploitative system not altogether different from that of the crimps whom Mansfield and his army of reformers claimed to be waging war against. The animosity between industrial maritime unions and SCI was so pervasive during this time that even the biographer Finn, in his sympathetic portrayal of Roper and the Institute, was forced to address it in his manuscript.[17]

According to Finn's narrative, Roper was sympathetic to the unionists' cause, conceding that "there is no doubt that radicals improve conditions on ships," and even paying union dues for penniless seamen out of her own personal account, a violation of house rules for which she was supposedly nearly fired. Finn also claims that Roper purchased every issue of *The Dog House News*, a handbill published by the Waterfront Unemployed Council that was a satirical version of SCI's *The Lookout*. The *Dog House News* pilloried SCI staff and administrators, including Roper, whom the newsletter depicted as having gotten rich off the seamen's plight (See Fig. 6.7).

While Finn depicts Roper as responding to the union's mocking with good-natured tolerance, he leaves out an incident in which a group of seamen physically attacked an aged Roper inside 25 South Street, leading to a full investigation and a crisis of management within the Institute. In a letter dated October 21, 1932, from SCI administrator J. M. Wainwright to Secretary of Labor William Doak, Wainwright describes the attack:

> The Seamen's Church Institute of New York, of which I am one of the managers, contains, as you are undoubtedly aware, probably the greatest seamen's benevolent institution in any of our ports. Recently, the Institute and its employees have been subject to really dangerous attack by the communistic element which congregates on the water front near the Association's building.[18]

Wainwright goes on to identify Leo Solomi, "alias Nick Salami," and Henry Endlekoff as the perpetrators of the assault, and he claims that the former had been identified as a "Russian alien." The purpose of the letter was for Wainwright to express his disappointment with a recent Congressional hearing wherein it was ruled that such an individual could not be deported because "he came from Soviet Russia" and the United States did not at that time have diplomatic relations with the Russians: "[t]he fact being, therefore, that this alien, bent upon subversive activities, is again at large and absolutely free to continue his seditious activity."[19]

Fig. 6.7 Waterfront Unemployed Council, *Dog House News*, 1932. Seamen's Church Institute Digital Archives

Zabriske, in a separate letter, describes a "couple of hand bills," "one of which advertises a meeting to be held tomorrow night at the corner of White Hall and South Streets," immediately down the block from 25 South Street, "to 'try Mother Roper and the grafting officials of Seamen's Church Institute.'"[20] Zabriske then goes on for several pages detailing a litany of laws "under which these Communists can be dealt with," suggesting that "if you can get satisfactory cooperation from the police to break up the proposed meeting and arrest the leaders and prosecute them vigorously, that would be desirable." Realizing that this approach might be untenable on short notice, Zabriske suggests an alternative "counterattack":

> Among the papers Dr. Mansfield sent me was a letter signed by Leslie H. Jones, in which the writer showed his indignation about the attack on Mrs. Roper and undertook to do everything he could to avenge it. I notice under date of July 13th you reported that the speaker who particularly attacked Mrs. Roper was subsequently well beaten up. It may be that this was the work of Leslie H. Jones, but whoever did it, there is evidently a good body of men in the Institute who would be only too glad to take a hand in such a proceeding. I should think that it might be well if a hint were judiciously dropped here and there tomorrow to the effect that this trial of Mother Roper was to take place at eight o'clock at Whitehall and South Streets, and that some of her friends in the Institute might find it interesting to attend in a body. If enough of them should go and thoroughly beat up the participants in the meeting it might have a salutary effect for some time. Of course some of them might get arrested by mistake along with the "Reds." If your relations with the nearby police are satisfactory it ought to be possible to prevent their being held.[21]

The Institute did indeed launch a counterattack to the pockets of unrest and resistance to SCI's presence and mission in New York's sailortown, enlisting the services of a private detective to infiltrate subversive meetings like the one Zabriske describes. The detective would have his hands full during the remainder of the 1930s, as industrial leftist maritime labor organizations splintered off from one another and established a network of headquarters and subversive publications along the waterfront streets surrounding 25 South Street. This era of discontent, in which seamen organized and advocated for relief in the face of a devastating shipping slump, unprecedented unemployment, and insufficient public services, produced an undercurrent of subversive resistance to SCI's mission that manifested itself in a series of incidents that culminated with the physical attack on Mother Roper.

Conclusion

Having embedded itself within the heart of sailortown during the nineteenth century, consolidated its services under the leadership of Mansfield and the roof of 25 South Street by 1912, and reached out beyond the confines of sailortown to shape the personal and familial lives of seamen through Roper's regime of domesticity, SCI clearly posed a serious threat to the autonomy of the seamen it served, as well as the character of sailortown itself (see Fig. 6.8).

Fig. 6.8 Mother Roper captured in an idealized pose waving *bon voyage* to her many "sons" at sea from atop the Institute's roof. Seamen's Church Institute Digital Archives

What characteristics of sailortown were so vital to the identities and culture of merchant seamen in New York that they were to be defended at all costs against the reformers who sought to eradicate them, even to the extent of physically attacking an aged woman? In other words, what was at stake in these confrontations between SCI and the commercial, leisure, and labor spheres of sailortown that had by the 1930s coalesced into a last stand waged by industrial maritime labor unions that surrounded 25 South Street? The answer, in part, is that seamen fought back to regain control over their own livelihood, their leisure, their ability to make decisions about their familial connections, how they spent their money, the freedom to define their own systems of morality, and even spirituality. In short, what was at stake for seamen was control over all of the gendered negotiations that were contested between seamen and the shoreside reformers of the Seamen's Church Institute.

As the maritime industry weathered the postwar shipping slump of the 1920s and the nation suffered through the Great Depression, these confrontations intensified and were projected onto the state, inciting legal battles that asked fundamental questions about the status of merchant seamen under U.S. labor and immigration law and the U.S. Constitution itself. As immigration law became increasingly restrictive and exclusionary, SCI became a target not just of industrial maritime labor unions but also of the state itself, which set its sights on the "million-dollar home for sailors" as the Institute once had on sailortown's boardinghouses. Despite their best efforts, the city's merchant seamen largely retained the inherent transience and foreignness that made them such a persistent threat to the parameters of social, cultural, and economic propriety, and their uncertain status as workers on the margins of immigration law.

Notes

1. "105 Aliens Seized at Seamen's Home," *New York Times*, February 4, 1931, 3.
2. "Prepare to Deport 100,000 Seamen," *New York TImes*, March 25, 1931, 5.
3. Andrew Furuseth, "The Decay of Seamanship in Europe and America," Records of the Seamen's Church Institute of New York and New Jersey.
4. Ibid.
5. Paul K. Chapman, *Trouble on Board: The Plight of International Seafarers* (Ithaca, NY: ILR Press, 1992), 79.

6. Bruce Nelson, *Workers on the Waterfront: Seamen, Longshoremen, and Unionism in the 1930s*, (Chicago, IL: University of Illinois Press, 1990), 76.
7. Alfred J. Nock, *Mansfield Biography*, unpublished manuscript, Records of the Seamen's Church Institute of New York Jersey, 374.
8. Nelson, *Workers on the Waterfront*, 18.
9. Ibid., 81.
10. Ibid., 96–100.
11. Ibid., 34–35.
12. Seamens Unemployed Council, "Seamen Unite; Close Your Ranks; and Fight!; Unemployed Seamen Organize," Records of the Seamen's Church Institute of New York and New Jersey.
13. Seamen's Church Institute, "A Statement on Communistic Attacks at the Institute," Records of the Seamen's Church Institute of New York and New Jersey.
14. Ibid.
15. Letter from George Gray Zabriske to Mr. Trench, July 16, 1932, Records of the Seamen's Church Institute of New York and New Jersey.
16. Letter from J.J. Kelly to Mr. Westerman, April 5, 1930, Records of the Seamen's Church Institute of New York and New Jersey.
17. Jonathan Finn, *Janet Roper: Mother to 50,000 Seamen*, unpublished manuscript, Records of the Seamen's Church Institute of New York and New Jersey, 361.
18. Letter from J. M. Wainwright to William Doak, October 21, 1932, Records of the Seamen's Church Institute of New York and New Jersey.
19. Ibid.
20. Letter from G. G. Zabriske to Mr. Trench, July 16, 1932.
21. Ibid.

Conclusion: Currents, Past and Future

The market crash of 1929 compounded the economic slump that the U.S. maritime industry had been experiencing since the end of World War I. Similar to other industrial workers, merchant seamen experienced a prolonged period of economic, social, and cultural shock during the Great Depression that profoundly transformed their daily lives. Merchant seamen, cast adrift by a severe lack of employment that augmented their inherent transience, found their traditional survival strategies undermined and turned to the federal government and its philanthropic auxiliaries for relief. Additionally, growing numbers of seamen "on the beach" and out of work embraced increasingly radical industrial unionism that thrived along the nation's waterfront as a means of negotiating their relationship with the state and its auxiliaries.

Congress passed the Merchant Marine Act of 1936 with the purpose of developing and maintaining a U.S. merchant marine that would be virtually self-sustaining and free from dependency on foreign fleets and labor. Theories of "flexible capacity" through the maintenance of a professionalized U.S. citizen merchant marine had bested both the interests of shipping companies that depended on cheap labor to remain competitive and radical maritime unionists seeking to maintain fluidity and mobility along the nation's waterfronts. The 1936 Act formed the U.S. Maritime Commission, established federal subsidies for the construction and operation of American ships, and founded the U.S. Merchant Marine

J. Thayer, *Citizenship, Subversion, and Surveillance in U.S. Ports*, Global Studies in Social and Cultural Maritime History, https://doi.org/10.1007/978-3-031-45618-3

Corps. These actions were accompanied by the enlistment of charitable organizations such as the Seamen's Church Institute of New York, which operated as auxiliaries of the state in accepting federal funding to provide relief, training, and housing for merchant seamen. Simultaneously, the rise of the Communist Party-affiliated Marine Workers Industrial Union and its many affiliates, and the founding of the CIO-affiliated National Maritime Union in May of 1937 opened the door to union membership for industrial maritime workers who had previously been excluded on the basis of race, nationality, and occupational status.

As preparedness for war heightened, the federal government built upon the interventionist regulatory framework it had initiated with the Merchant Marine Act of 1936, calling upon tens of thousands of young men to train and sail as professional merchant mariners. Federal funding added to the New York State Merchant Marine Academy at Fort Schuyler (now SUNY Maritime College) with the creation of the Sheepshead Bay Maritime Training Station (1942), the United States Merchant Marine Academy at Kings Point (1943), and a training station for radio operators at Hoffman Island in New York Harbor. Similar expansion occurred simultaneously along the West Coast and the Gulf of Mexico. When the U.S. eventually entered the war, the federal government called upon these reserve labor pools to transport cargo to allied fronts, dispatching civilian merchant mariners to dangerous combat zones in staggering numbers. In total 8300 civilian mariners were killed at sea during World War II, with some 12,000 wounded, 1100 of whom died from their wounds. 663 were taken prisoner, sixty-six of whom died in prison camps. By the end of the war, one in twenty-six merchant mariners had suffered casualties. The merchant marine had a higher casualty rate during the war than any branch of the armed forces, including the Army, Navy, and Marine Corps. And yet, the federal government excluded merchant mariners from G.I. Bill benefits, granting them nominal veteran status only in 1988, some thirty years after their service.

During the War, the merchant marine provided the crucial link between "factories for democracy" back home and war fronts overseas. As Alex Roland, Jeffrey Bolster, and Alexander Keyssar describe, the merchant marine "carried the sinews of war"[1] following Pearl Harbor, delivering fifteen-million tons of cargo to the United Kingdom and continental Europe, thirteen-million tons to the Pacific, eight-million tons to the Mediterranean, and five-million tons to the Soviet Union by the end of 1944, all to support Allied operations. U.S. merchant ships also carried

7,129,906 army personnel and 141,537 civilians during wartime, ultimately returning 4,060,883 soldiers and 169,626 civilians to the United States at the war's end.[2]

American merchant mariners experienced the impacts of the war long before Pearl Harbor, however. Partially in response to growing overseas threats to U.S. national security, the 1936 Merchant Marine Act resolved a debate over control and administration of the U.S. merchant fleet that had been ongoing in Congress for decades. The primary question at hand focused on the extent to which the federal government should be involved in subsidizing and regulating the merchant marine, with proposals for full nationalization and even militarization on the table at various times leading up to 1936. Legislation passed that year took up the agenda that President Roosevelt laid out in his March 1935 "Subsidy Message," in which he called for a federally subsidized merchant fleet and a stable pool of American mariners for the purposes of commercial independence and military self-defense. The 1936 Act established the U.S. Maritime Commission and made it responsible for the planning and management of an elaborate subsidy system intended to ensure a viable American merchant marine.[3]

Meanwhile, Congress passed Neutrality Acts in 1935, 1936, 1937, and 1939 that were designed to curtail American involvement in foreign wars by preventing U.S. merchant ships from delivering goods to belligerent nations and in war zones. Again, attempting to respond to an increasingly urgent need for preparedness, President Roosevelt urged the repeal of the Acts as early as September 1939, eventually navigating a transition first to a cash-and-carry policy, and finally to the Lend-Lease Act, which passed in March 1941. U.S. ships were thereafter allowed to transport war cargo to any country whose interests and defenses aligned with those of the United States.[4]

The revision and ultimate repeal of the Neutrality Acts made for deadly conditions at sea for American ships carrying cargo for Allied nations. On March 21, 1941, the SS*Robin Moor*, carrying war cargo to the British, became the first American merchant ship sunk by a German submarine in World War II. German U-boats sank an additional three American merchant ships before the U.S. entered the war. U.S. intelligence services worked carefully to control the spread of information about these acts of aggression, and the American public remained largely unaware of the fact that German submarines were torpedoing American ships and killing civilian mariners.[5] By the time the realities of German aggression became undeniable, U.S. officials changed course and openly advocated for a more proactive approach to protecting American interests on the high seas. Taking the lead on this new policy, President Roosevelt responded to a German attack on an American destroyer in a fireside chat in which he described the threat of German "rattlesnakes of the Atlantic" to American shipping in lurid detail.[6]

Recruitment and Training

Having rallied public support, President Roosevelt established the War Shipping Administration (WSA) by executive order on February 7, 1942, appointing Admiral Emory S. Land as Chief Administrator with powers to "organize the operation, purchase, charter, insurance, repair, maintenance, and requisition of vessels" in the U.S. merchant fleet.[7] Working closely with the WSA and the U.S. Coast Guard, the Maritime Commission launched a massive labor recruitment program that established more than two hundred maritime training stations across the nation, including a system of maritime academies that altogether produced 262,474 qualified seamen and 31,986 officers by the end of the war.[8] Negotiations with the National Maritime Union, Sailors' Union of the Pacific, and the Seafarers International Union resulted in an agreement to assist the government with labor recruitment and cease all strikes during wartime in exchange for war risk compensation and insurance that made merchant mariners among the highest paid participants in the combat zones of the war.[9]

Federal intervention in the maritime shipping industry did not stop with recruiting and training mariners. The negotiation and subsidization of lucrative contracts with American shipyards led to an unprecedented period of intense shipbuilding and record levels of production on all fronts: labor, capital, raw materials, and technology. As Daniel Levine and Sara Ann Platt have argued, "[t]he record of the Maritime Commission can be summed up in a single sentence: 'during the Second World War, the United States built far more merchant ships than anyone thought possible.'"[10] The U.S. Maritime Commission's wartime shipbuilding program, lasting from 1939 to 1945, producing a total of 5601 vessels, including 2648 "Liberty" ships for emergency cargo. Other vessel types included long-range cargo ships, passenger ships, tankers, and "Victory" ships, built according to VC2 design beginning in April 1943 to replace slower, more vulnerable vessels in the fleet.[11,12]

Losses and Casualties

This unprecedented output of ships and labor cast the wide net of American shipping across the wartime seas, putting civilian vessels and lives in immediate danger in the process. Once the U.S. entered the war, German U-boats and submarines intensified their campaign against American shipping. Operation Drumbeat (*Paukenschlag*) targeted ships up and down the East Coast, wreaking havoc and sinking American ships within sight of land. During the first six-and-a-half months of U.S. entry in the war, German U-boats sank 360 Allied merchant ships carrying a total of 2,250,000 gross tons of cargo.[13] American ships were especially vulnerable due to a lingering clause of the Neutrality Acts that outlawed the arming of merchant ships and a baffling reluctance by the federal government and the U.S. Navy to resurrect convoying to protect merchant vessels, a strategy that had been used effectively during World War I.[14] It was not until the spring of 1942 that the Navy "rediscovered" convoying, but the damage was already well underway: one-half of all losses or damages to American ships during World War II occurred before the end of 1942.[15]

At sixteen years old, an orphan from the Lower East Side of Manhattan named Gabriel (Gabe) Frank heard a radio advertisement calling on young men to join the merchant marine. He gathered what few possessions he had and set out for the Sheepshead Bay Maritime Service Training Station in Brooklyn a few months after his seventeenth birthday. Gabe's description of the militarized nature of his training makes it clear that these young men, while civilians, were voluntarily joining the war effort on the lethal high seas:

> I joined up. Had five cents car fare to Sheepshead Bay. I got there penniless, and I went to boot camp … We had to do boot camp: marching, drills, obstacle course. We had to jump naked into a pool, climb over a ladder, drop in the water under a lifeboat in case we were attacked. We had machine guns, aircraft practice with machine guns, simulated guns. We were training for wartime, of course.[16]

Miles MacMahon trained as a radio operator on Hoffman Island after being turned away by the U.S. Navy due to his imperfect eyesight. Miles remembered riding the ferry in New York Harbor and navigating the anti-submarine nets that were laid to protect the city's coastline from enemy submarines:

> Hoffman Island was at one end of the submarine net for New York Harbor, which stretched from Coney Island to Hoffman Island. On the western side of Hoffman Island it was too shallow for submarines to sneak in, so there was no net there between the island and South Beach. But between Coney Island and Hoffman Island there was this large floating chain made of heavy wood blocks that floated and metal chains that chained them together. And when ships left, little boats would come out and open the gate in the middle. And the ships would leave, and the boats would close the gates, especially for the night... They were always waiting outside New York Harbor—U-Boats were. Many a ship was at sea for forty minutes before it was torpedoed. Right outside the Harbor they were leaving.[17]

Such immediate dangers so close to home only increased as merchant ships ventured further out to sea. The most lethal front of the war at sea took place along the dreaded Murmansk Run, from the Atlantic coast of the U.S. to Scotland and over to the Russian port city of Archangel where allied ships were sent to deliver supplies to sustain the Russian fight against the Nazis. The run to Murmansk was a brutal voyage through Arctic waters infested with enemy submarines. Despite sailing in convoys with armed escorts, many ships were sunk and many mariners killed. Convoy PQ17, which made the run in July 1942, consisted of thirty-five merchant ships, three rescue vessels, five destroyers, three British corvettes, three minesweepers, four anti-submarine trawlers, two anti-aircraft ships, and two submarines. Despite such protection, only eleven merchant ships reached port safely in Russia. Twenty-four ships were sunk and 153 mariners killed.[18]

Richard "Dick" Weir described the fear and agonizing uncertainty of taking a ship with an unknown destination, with Murmansk always in the back of young mariners' minds:

> I got on another Liberty, an American Export Lines Liberty, and as soon as I got aboard that ship, I checked in with the Chief Mate, or, before that, I found out which room I would have, went and opened the door, threw in my sea bag, and one of the fellas, the crewmen, was reading in his bunk. So I said, 'Where is this ship going?', and he said 'We don't know but we just came from Russia.' And I looked out at the outer bulkhead, the outer wall of the ship, and it was totally insulated. It had insulation on it. And I saw right away: insulated Liberty ship, only used for the Russian run. So I had to stop and make a very, very careful and quick decision: shall I take that ship, and go north? Or shall I find some excuse—maybe I hated the Captain, or the ship, or something. Then I decided, I prayed about it, and I decided, 'Lord, this is now my turn to face the North.' So I said alright, I went up

> and told the Mate 'Here I am.' And he said 'OK, you're on the twelve-to-four. So take your gear and settle in.' I did. And that was a very, very miserable experience. Not because of the ship, or because of the crew, or because of the officers. But because of the run.[19]

The realities of life at sea in convoy en route to Murmansk were full of constant trepidation. Luck of the draw, including what position a ship was assigned in the convoy's formation, could determine whether the men on board lived or died. If a ship was hit, there was no stopping or turning back for survivors. The convoy sailed on, leaving whatever wreckage, human and otherwise, behind in its wake. Dick learned from first-hand experience how precarious the lives of his convoy-mates were while in the thick of front-line combat:

> As we came over loaded, we were at the tail end of the line, and we were also at the corner. So that was what we called "coffin corner" of the convoy. And we were sailing along, and I was on the watch in the bow at night, at about one or two AM, and all of a sudden I saw little red lights shining in the water around us. And then I realized that each of those red lights represented one man who had turned on the little red light on his life jacket. These were seamen from the ship that had been sunk ahead of us. We had never heard anything. Because the ship was loaded, the torpedo when it blew up was very muffled, and it sank the ship, the lead ship in that line. The ship went straight ahead and down. And we came up the line after it, and there were some men still floating around in the water. We hoped they had been--they were rescued. But we didn't know what happened to them after that. That was the most terrifying experience, because it showed you that things were not always as they seemed to be.[20]

After the War

By the end of the war, the U.S. merchant marine had suffered tremendous losses to vessels, cargo, and men. American merchant ships supplied war material and cargo to every front of the war; carried troops and armed forces personnel to battle and back home again once the war was over; supported the invasions of Africa in 1942, Italy in 1943, France in 1944; and kept open supply routes to defeat the Nazis in Europe and Japan in the Pacific.[21] Towards the end of the war, Dwight D. Eisenhower, then Supreme Commander of Allied Forces, offered a reflection on the strategic importance of the merchant marine:

> Every man in this Allied command is quick to express his admiration for the loyalty, courage, and fortitude of the officers and men of the Merchant Marine. We count upon their efficiency and their utter devotion to duty as we do our own; they have never failed us yet and in all the struggles yet to come we know that they will never be deterred by any danger, hardship, or privation. When final victory is ours there is no organization that will share its credit more deservedly than the Merchant Marine.[22]

Despite such sacrifices and experiences of wartime trauma along the front lines of combat at sea as described by Gabe Frank, Miles MacMahon, Dick Weir, and countless others, American merchant mariners who sailed during World War II were excluded from the Servicemen's Readjustment Act of 1944, better known as the G.I. Bill. Upon signing the G.I. Bill on June 22, 1944, President Franklin D. Roosevelt, a life-long advocate for the significance of the merchant marine to national security and American economic prowess, declared, "I trust Congress will soon provide similar opportunities to members of the Merchant Marine who have risked their lives time and time again during war for the welfare of their country."[23]

Neither the 78th Congress, which passed the G.I. Bill, nor the 79th Congress, in power upon the death of President Roosevelt, nor any of the Congresses since have heeded Roosevelt's mandate to pass legislation that would recognize and provide just compensation to merchant mariners who sailed during World War II. On November 11, 1988, after a protracted lobbying effort led by the American Merchant Marine Veterans Association (AMMV), the Civilian Military Service Review Board, authorized to determine whether civilian or contractual groups should be considered "active duty" for the purposes of laws administered by the U.S. Department of Veterans Affairs (VA), granted veteran status to merchant mariners who sailed in hazardous waters before August 15, 1945 (V-J Day). This status entitles them to VA hospital services and the right to a veteran's burial. In 1998, the 105th Congress wrote this recognition into proposed legislation. The description on the website Merchant Marine at War, an organization that has served as a grassroots research repository for many years, makes clear the general dissatisfaction with the provisional nature of these mariners' status:

> These Bills [introduced by the 105th Congress in 1998] were to give mariners the right to call themselves 'Veterans of WWII' and would allow them to request as even dollar flag for their coffin and gravestone marker. In October of 1998, these Bills were incorporated into HR4110 and the words

> honorable 'discharge' was changed to 'certificate' by someone on the House Veterans Affairs Committee headed by Congressman Bob Stump. As a result mariners would receive the same thing they received after WWII—a certificate of honorable service, but apparently not recognition as veterans.[24]

Every year since 2008, a bill has been introduced in Congress that would provide compensatory payments to World War II veteran merchant mariners who were denied even these provisional benefits between 1945 and 1988. Recent versions have included annual proposals of an Honoring Our World War II Merchant Mariners bill that would establish a Merchant Mariner Equity Compensation Fund from which the Secretary of Veterans Affairs would make a single payment of $25,000 to mariners who "served as a crewmember of a vessel that was operated in U.S. waters by the War Shipping Administration or the Office of Defense Transportation and under contract to, or the property of, the United States." Re-introduction of the original version of the bill by Rep. Janice Hahn (D-CA) in 2015 mobilized the AMMV, who sent representatives from chapters nationwide, aided by canes and walkers, on a "Storm the Hill" campaign to the halls of Congress for marathon meetings with Representatives in June 2016.[25] Despite these actions, the bill was immediately referred to the Subcommittee on Disability Assistance and Memorial Affairs, where it was eventually scuttled.[26] Most recently, HR39: Honoring Our WWII Merchant Mariners Act of 2023 was introduced on January 9, 2023, in the House by Rep. Al Green (D-TX), calling for similar just compensation measures as in Rep. Hahn's bill. The bill remains stuck in the House Veterans' Affairs Subcommittee on Disability Assistance and Memorial Affairs as of the writing of this book.[27]

Conclusion

Veteran merchant mariners of World War II encapsulate so many historical truths about merchant seamen that this book has attempted to address. What are they, who sailed in combat zones and suffered the highest casualty rate of World War II, entitled to as citizens of the U.S.? If not the G.I. Bill, then what?

Shoreside people, communities, and institutions have never known what to do with these salty, cosmopolitan, transient, and sometimes radical individuals who temporarily invaded their much-coveted urban shorelines. Merchant seamen have always challenged the conceptions of propriety, economic stability, and by extension, U.S. citizenship itself. U.S. citizenship, in turn, has been expanded, constricted, and fundamentally transformed over time in response to the challenges that merchant seamen have persistently confronted civil society and the government with since the founding of the nation. Agents of maritime ministry countered the invasion of merchant seamen in New York City's sailortown with tactics of cooptation, conversion, control, and eradication that would be replicated in various forms by those with governmental and capitalist power. In *Robertson v. Baldwin*, the Supreme Court pushed the *Arago* deserters to the margins of the U.S. Constitution and citizenship itself. The resolution of their case, and the awakening of sentiment that it induced within the sphere of public opinion, gave belated shape to the parameters of contract labor in the wake of the Thirteenth Amendment and set fundamental precedent as the nation entered the twentieth century. Whereas the Transport Workers Federation gained traction following *Titanic* towards industrial unionism and intersectional solidarity among the waterfront working class, the International Seamen's Union remained fixated on practical gains through political means that eventually resulted in the passage of the landmark 1915 Seamen's Act. The Act's core objectives of seamen's emancipation, wage equalization, and safety at sea represented a revolutionary reconfiguration of the rights that seamen were entitled to expect protection of from local and federal governments. During the quota era of immigration restriction, "alien seamen" enflamed the anxious imaginations of middle-class and elite Americans who feared the influx of a transient population of working-class men they characterized as politically subversive and racially and morally degenerate. The determination of the parameters of citizenship during the first half of the twentieth century was directly shaped by the specter of "alien seamen" that was held in the minds of politicians and the general public.

This narrative could be extended past World War II into the era of containerization and foreign-flag registry, which initiated current issues involving port security, postwar maritime industry regulation, the perceived threat following the attacks of September 11, 2001 of non-citizen merchant seafarers working on massive cargo or container ships as potential national security risks, and the counter-proliferation of restricted shore leave and mobility in ports through increasingly draconian visa requirements and proposals for biometric identification systems. Merchant seamen persist in pushing boundaries, both geographic and imagined, and continue to challenge the nation's evolving conceptions of citizenship.

Notes

1. Alex Roland, W. Jeffrey Bolster, and Alexander Keyssar, *The Way of the Ship: America's Maritime History Reenvisoned, 1600–2000* (Hoboken, NJ: John Wiley and Sons, Inc.: 2008), 313.
2. Ibid., 307.
3. *Message from the President of the United* States, House Document 118, 73d Cong., as cited in H. David Bess and Martin T. Farris, *U.S. Maritime Policy: History and Prospects* (New York: Praeger Publishers, 1981), 57.
4. Daniel Levine and Sara Ann Platt, "The Contribution of U.S. Shipbuilding and the Merchant Marine to the Second World War," in Robert A. Kilmarx, ed., *America's Maritime Legacy: A History of the U.S. Merchant Marine and Shipbuilding Since Colonial Times* (Boulder, CO: Westview Press, 1979), 201.
5. Roland, Bolster, and Keyssar, *The Way of the Ship*, 305.
6. Franklin Delano Roosevelt, "Rattlesnakes of the Atlantic" (1941), as cited in Joshua M. Smith and the National Maritime Historical Society, eds., *Voyages: The Age of Engines: Documents in American Maritime History Volume II, 1865–Present* (Gainesville: University Press of Florida, 2009), 240–248.
7. Levine and Platt, "The Contribution of U.S. Shipbuilding and the Merchant Marine to the Second World War," 205.
8. Roland, Bolster, and Keyssar, *The Way of the Ship*, 308–309.
9. Levine and Platt, "The Contribution of U.S. Shipbuilding and the Merchant Marine to the Second World War," 195; Roland, Bolster, and Keyssar, *The Way of the Ship*, 309.
10. Ibid., 181.
11. Fischer, *Statistical Summary*, 17, 163, as cited in Roland, Bolster, and Keyssar, *The Way of the Ship*, 310.
12. See also: Frederick C. Lane, *Ships for Victory: A History of Shipbuilding under the U.S. Maritime Commission in World War II* (Baltimore, MD: Johns Hopkins University Press, 2001 (1951)).
13. Roland, Bolster, and Keyssar, *The Way of the Ship*, 303.
14. Andrew Gibson and Arthur Donovan, *The Abandoned Ocean: A History of U.S. Maritime Policy* (Columbia, SC: University of South Carolina Press, 2001), Chapter 8, "The Merchant Marine in World War II, 1939–1945"; and Levine and Platt, "The Contribution of U.S. Shipbuilding and the Merchant Marine to the Second World War," 198.
15. Roland, Bolster, and Keyssar, *The Way of the Ship*, 303.
16. Seamen's Church Institute of New York and New Jersey, "Frank, Gabe–Clip 1," *American Merchant Marine Veterans Oral History Project*, https://seamenschurch-archives.org/items/show/237, accessed

November 2, 2023; Seamen's Church Institute of New York and New Jersey, "Frank, Gabe–Clip 2," *American Merchant Marine Veterans Oral History Project*, https://seamenschurch-archives.org/items/show/238, accessed November 2, 2023.

17. Seamen's Church Institute of New York and New Jersey, "McMahon, Miles–Clip 6," *American Merchant Marine Veterans Oral History Project*, https://seamenschurch-archives.org/collections/show/36, accessed November 2, 2023.
18. Roland, Bolster, and Keyssar, 313–314.
19. Seamen's Church Institute of New York and New Jersey, "Weir, Dick–Clip 13," *American Merchant Marine Veterans Oral History Project*, https://seamenschurch-archives.org/items/show/216, accessed November 2, 2023.
20. Seamen's Church Institute of New York and New Jersey, "Weir, Dick–Clip 5," *American Merchant Marine Veterans Oral History Project*, https://seamenschurch-archives.org/items/show/208, accessed November 2, 2023.
21. Roland, Bolster, and Keyssar, *The Way of the Ship*, 307.
22. Atlas Video, Inc. (video), *War Stories: The Merchant Marine*, as cited in Brian Herbert, *The Forgotten Heroes: The Heroic Story of the United States Merchant Marine* (New York: Forge, 2004), 106.
23. American Merchant Marine at War, "Merchant Seamen's War Service Act," from http://www.usmm.org/seamanrights.html, accessed November 2, 2023.
24. American Merchant Marine at War, "Mariners' Struggle for Veteran Status," from www.usmm.org/strugglevetstatus.html, accessed November 2, 2023.
25. *Maritime Executive*, "WWII Merchant Marine Veterans 'Storm the Hill,'" June 23, 2015, from http://www.maritime-executive.com/article/wwii-merchant-marine-veterans-storm-the-hill, accessed November 2, 2023.
26. Congress.gov, "H.R. 563—Honoring Our WWII Merchant Mariners Act of 2015," from https://www.congress.gov/bill/114th-congress/house-bill/563, accessed November 2, 2023.
27. Congress.gov, "H.R. 39—Honoring Our WWII Merchant Mariners Act of 2023," from https://www.govtrack.us/congress/bills/118/hr39, accessed November 2, 2023.

References

Archival Collections

Library of Congress, *Chronicling America: Historical Newspapers.*
Library of Congress, Congressional Record.
National Archives, Records of the Supreme Court of the United States.
Records of the American Seamen's Friend Society.
Records of the International Seamen's Union.
Records of the International Transport Workers' Federation.
Records of the Seamen's Church Institute of New York and New Jersey.
Records of Trinity Church Wall Street.
Southampton Archives, Civic Centre, Civic Centre Road, Southampton, UK.
Titanic Inquiry Project.

Newspapers

Bisbee Daily Review (Bisbee, AZ).
Broad Ax (Salt Lake City, UT).
Cook County Herald (Grand Marais, MN).
Dearborn Independent (MI).
Evening Mail (New York, NY).
Evening Star (Washington, D.C.).
Evening World (New York, NY).

J. Thayer, *Citizenship, Subversion, and Surveillance in U.S. Ports*, Global Studies in Social and Cultural Maritime History,
https://doi.org/10.1007/978-3-031-45618-3

Hampshire Advertiser (Southampton, U.K.).
Hampshire Independent (Southampton, U.K.).
Herald (Los Angeles, CA).
New York Herald.
New York Times.
New York Tribune (New York, NY).
Norwich Bulletin (CT).
Oklahoma City Banker (OK).
Omaha Daily Bee (NE).
Record-Union (Sacramento, CA).
San Francisco Call.
Southern Daily Echo (Southampton, U.K.).
Sun (New York, NY).
Washington Times (Washington D.C.).
Wichita Daily Eagle (KS).
World (New York, NY).

Court Cases

Allgeyer v. Louisiana, 165 U.S. 578 (1897).
Lochner v. New York, 198 U.S. 45 (1905).
Harden v. Gordon United States Circuit Court for the District of Maine 480 (No. 6047), 2000 AMC 893 (1823).
In re Ah Kee, 22 F 519 (SD NY 1884).
H.R. 563—Honoring Our WWII Merchant Mariners Act of 2015.
H.R. 39—Honoring Our WWII Merchant Mariners Act of 2023.
Philippides v. Day, 283 U.S. 48 (1931).
Robertson v. Baldwin, 165 U.S. 275 (1897).
U.S. v. Burke 99 F. 895 (SD Ala. 1899).
U.S. v. Jamieson 185 F. 165 (SD NY 1911).

Legislation

The Maguire Act of February 28, 1895.
U.S. Congress, Immigration Act of 1907.
U.S. Congress, Immigration Act of 1917.
U.S. Congress, Immigration Act of 1924.

Congressional Records

U.S. House of Representatives, Committee on Immigration and Naturalization, "Deportation of Alien Seamen," January 26, 1925.

U.S. House of Representatives Committee on the Merchant Marine and Fisheries, "The Seamen's Bill," (Washington, D. C.: Government Printing Office), 1914.

U.S. Senate Committee on Commerce, "Involuntary Servitude Imposed Upon Seamen," (Washington, D. C.: Government Printing Office), 1914.

Manuscripts and Publications

Beaven, Brad; Bell, Karl; James, Robert, eds. *Port Towns and Urban Cultures: International Histories of the Waterfront, c. 1700–2000.* London: Palgrave Macmillan, 2016.

Beavan, Brad. *Leisure, Citizenship and Working-Class Men in Britain, 1850–1945.* London: Oxford University Press, 2009.

Bess, H. David and Farris, Martin T. *U.S. Maritime Policy: History and Prospects.* New York: Praeger Publishers, 1981.

Downing, Karen; Thayer, Johnathan; Begiato, Joanne, eds. *Negotiating Masculinities and Modernity in the Maritime World, 1815–1940.* London: Palgrave Macmillan, 2021.

Fingard, Judith. *Jack in Port: Sailortowns of Eastern Canada.* University of Toronto Press, 1982.

Fink, Leon. *Sweatshops at Sea: Merchant Seamen in the First Globalized Industry, from 1812 to the Present.* Chapel Hill, NC: University of North Carolina Press, 2011.

Fink, Leon. "From Autonomy to Abundance: Changing Beliefs about the Free Labor System in Nineteenth-Century America." in Stanley L. Engerman, ed. *Terms of Labor: Slavery, Serfdom, and Free Labor.* Palo Alto, CA: Stanford University Press, 1999.

Foner, Eric. *Reconstruction: America's Unfinished Revolution, 1863–1877.* New York: Harper & Row, 1988.

Gibson, Andrew and Donovan, Arthur. *The Abandoned Ocean: A History of United States Maritime Policy.* Columbia, SC: University of South Carolina Press, 2000.

Gilje, Paul. *Liberty on the Waterfront: American Maritime Culture in the Age of Revolution.* Philadelphia. PA: University of Pennsylvania Press, 2007.

Goldberg, Joseph P. *The Maritime Story: A Study in Labor-Management Relations.* Cambridge: Harvard University Press, 1958.

Gunn, Thomas Butler. *The Physiology of New York Boarding-Houses.* New York: Mason Brothers, 1857.

Gutoff, J. M. "Fugitive Slaves and Ship-Jumping Sailors: The Enforcement and Survival of Coerced Labor." *Journal of Labor and Employment Law* 9, no. 1 (2006): 87–116.

Jackson, Justin. "'The Right Kind of Men': Flexible Capacity, Chinese Exclusion, and the Imperial Origins of Maritime Labor Reform in the United States, 1898–1905." *Labor* 10, no. 4 (2013): 39–60.

Kverndal, Roald. *Seamen's Missions: Their Origins and Early Growth.* Pasadena, CA: William Carey Library, 1986.

Land, Isaac. "Tidal Waves: The New Coastal History." *The Journal of Social History* 40, no. 3 (2007): 731–743.

Land, Isaac. *The Coastal History Blog.* https://porttowns.port.ac.uk/coastal-history-blog/, accessed February 10, 2023.

Lane, Frederick C. *Ships for Victory: A History of Shipbuilding under the U.S. Maritime Commission in World War II.* Baltimore, MD: Johns Hopkins University Press, 2001 (1951).

Lee, Erika. *At America's Gates: The Exclusion Era, 1882–1943.* Chapel Hill, NC: University of North Carolina Press, 2003.

Levine, Daniel and Platt, Sara Ann. "The Contribution of U.S. Shipbuilding and the Merchant Marine to the Second World War." in Robert A. Kilmarx, ed. *America's Maritime Legacy: A History of the U.S. Merchant Marine and Shipbuilding Since Colonial Times.* Boulder, CO: Westview Press, 1979.

Mahan, Alfred Thayer. *The Influence of Seapower Upon History.* Boston: Little, Brown, 1890.

McCarthy, Kathleen D. *American Creed: Philanthropy and the Rise of Civil Society, 1700–1865.* Chicago: University of Chicago Press, 2003.

Milne, Graeme. *Sailortowns: People, Power, and Place on the Nineteenth Century Waterfront.* London: Palgrave Macmillan, 2016.

Montgomery, David. *Workers' Control in America: Studies in the History of Work, Technology, and Labor Struggles.* New York: Cambridge University Press, 1979.

Morris, Richard B. "Labor Controls in Maryland in the Nineteenth Century." *The Journal of Southern History* 14, no. 3 (1948).

Nelson, Bruce. *Workers on the Waterfront: Seamen, Longshoremen, and Unionism in the 1930s.* Chicago, IL: University of Illinois Press, 1990.

Ngai, Mae. *Impossible Subjects: Illegal Aliens and the Making of Modern America.* Princeton University Press, 2004.

Perl-Rosenthal, Nathan. *Citizen Sailors: Becoming American in the Age of Revolution.* Cambridge, MA: Harvard University Press, 2015.

Rafferty, Matthew Taylor. *The Republic Afloat: Law, Honor, and Citizenship in Maritime America.* University of Chicago Press, 2013.

Rediker, Marcus. *Between the Devil and the Deep Blue Sea: Merchant Seamen, Pirates and the Anglo-American Maritime World, 1700–1750.* New York: Cambridge University Press, 1987.

Rediker, Marcus and Linebaugh, Peter. *The Many-Headed Hydra: Sailors, Slaves, Commoners, and the Hidden History of the Revolutionary Atlantic.* Boston: Beacon Press, 2000.

Richardson, Heather Cox. *The Death of Reconstruction: Race, Labor, and Politics in the Post-Civil War North, 1865–1901.* Cambridge: Harvard University Press, 2001.

Roland, Alex and Bolster, W. Jeffrey. *The Way of the Ship: America's Maritime History Re-envisioned, 1600–2000.* Hoboken, NJ: John Wiley and Sons, Inc., 2008.

Schneider, Dorothee. *Crossing Borders: Migration and Citizenship in the Twentieth-Century United States.* Cambridge, MA: Harvard University Press, 2011.

Shoemaker, Nancy. *Native American Whalemen and the World: Indigenous Encounters and the Contingency of Race.* Chapel Hill: University of North Carolina Press, 2015.

Smith, Joshua M. and the National Maritime Historical Society, eds. *Voyages: The Age of Engines: Documents in American Maritime History Volume II, 1865-Present.* Gainesville: University Press of Florida, 2009.

Soifer, Aviam. "The Paradox of Paternalism and Laissez-Faire Constitutionalism: United States Supreme Court, 1888–1921." *Law and History Review* 5, no. 1 (Spring 1987), 249–279.

Steinfeld, Robert J. *Coercion, Contract, and Free Labor in the Nineteenth Century.* New York: Cambridge University Press, 2001.

Weintraub, Andrew. *Andrew Furuseth: Emancipator of the Seamen.* Berkeley: University of California Press, 1958.

Worthington, David, ed. *The New Coastal History: Cultural and Environmental Perspectives from Scotland and Beyond.* London: Palgrave Macmillan, 2021.

Index[1]

[1] Note: Page numbers followed by 'n' refer to notes.

J. Thayer, *Citizenship, Subversion, and Surveillance in U.S. Ports*, Global Studies in Social and Cultural Maritime History,
https://doi.org/10.1007/978-3-031-45618-3

W

X

SPRINGER NATURE

GPSR Compliance

The European Union's (EU) General Product Safety Regulation (GPSR) is a set of rules that requires consumer products to be safe and our obligations to ensure this.

If you have any concerns about our products, you can contact us on ProductSafety@springernature.com

In case Publisher is established outside the EU, the EU authorized representative is:

Springer Nature Customer Service Center GmbH
Europaplatz 3
69115 Heidelberg, Germany

The manufacturer's authorised representative in the EU is Springer Nature Customer Service Centre GmbH, Europaplatz 3, 69115 Heidelberg, Germany. If you have any concerns regarding our products, please contact ProductSafety@springernature.com

Printed and bound by CPI Group (UK) Ltd, Croydon, CR0 4YY
01/10/2026
02226183-0001